NEW CEN
COMM

CW01475615

Gene

RONALD E. CLEMENTS   MATTHEW BLACK
(Old Testament)   (New Testament)

Daniel

THE NEW CENTURY BIBLE COMMENTARIES

Other titles are in preparation

NEW CENTURY BIBLE
COMMENTARY

DANIEL

Based on the New Revised Standard Version

PAUL L. REDDITT

Copyright © 1999 Sheffield Academic Press

Published by
Sheffield Academic Press Ltd
Mansion House
19 Kingfield Road
Sheffield S11 9AS
England

Typeset by Sheffield Academic Press
and
Printed on acid-free paper in Great Britain
by Cromwell Press
Trowbridge, Wiltshire

British Library Cataloguing in Publication Data

A catalogue record for this book is available
from the British Library

ISBN 1-84127-009-1

CONTENTS

PREFACE

As the end of the millennium approaches, people are becoming more and more fascinated with the possible end of the world, and many turn to apocalyptic literature for help in coping with what they think might happen. There is nothing new in that approach. Klaus Koch (1997) has shown that Jews and Christians alike have searched Daniel for centuries to find insights into what the future holds. In doing so, readers have created and/or honed their own self-image and even their national image in dialogue with the book. Even so, that sort of reading is uncritical, and offers the critical reader no help with the question of whether the end of the world is near.

To be sure, the book anticipated 'the end', but did so in terms of a situation long since past. The failure of the end to materialize as expected has never affected the book's import, however, for it is much more about timeless things, such as the nature of God, the ultimate victory of God over evil, and the importance of fidelity to God despite all opposition.

In fact, Daniel is less a book about the future than about the past and present. The book casts a look back from the Maccabean period to the centuries and empires that preceded it and gave a new reading for its own day. In doing so it not only reformulated traditions it borrowed from the Gentile world (e.g. the idea of four successive world empires), it even recast biblical traditions (e.g. Jeremiah's prediction of a 70-year domination of the Babylonian Empire into 70 weeks of world domination by world empires). Later chapters also recast images from earlier chapters, for example, the view in Daniel 2 that a given empire—the Babylonian—could be golden. As the second half of the book continued the reflections of a community, it came to say that no human empire was golden, no human institutions deserved ultimate allegiance. Such insights are its real legacy to the twentieth century.

I am particularly grateful to Professor Ronald Clements for inviting me to undertake this study and to the Sheffield Academic Press for assuming the responsibility of publishing the last volumes in this series.

Gratitude is due as well to the Pew Charitable Trusts for a stipend from their Summer Research Program for College Faculty for the summer of 1997, which allowed me to write without the usual responsibilities of teaching.

I also wish to thank my colleague Dr Robert Kruschwitz, chair of the Department of Philosophy at Georgetown College, for helping me conceptualize some of the abiding insights of the book of Daniel. Our collaborative work appeared under the title 'Nebuchadnezzar as the Head of Gold: Politics and History in the Theology of the Book of Daniel' in *Perspectives in Religious Studies* 25 (1998), pp. 1-17. I would like to thank its editorial board and that of the *Catholic Biblical Quarterly*, who have acted as my sounding boards as I have developed my thinking over the last several years and who have accepted for publication articles growing out of this work.

May I add to the list of those who helped me Dr Samuel E. Balentine, who read a draft of my work on Daniel 9, and my pastor Dr Greg Earwood, who read the book of Daniel with me in Hebrew and Aramaic, offering support along the way. My indebtedness to other scholars who have written on Daniel will be made apparent by references within the body of this commentary.

Paul L. Redditt
August 1998

ABBREVIATIONS

BIBLICAL

OLD TESTAMENT (OT)

Gen.	Ruth	Ezra	Song	Joel	Zeph.
Exod.	1 Sam.	Neh.	Isa.	Amos	Hag.
Lev.	2 Sam.	Est.	Jer.	Obad.	Zech.
Num.	1 Kgs	Job	Lam.	Jon.	Mal.
Deut.	2 Kgs	Ps(s).	Ezek.	Mic.	
Josh.	1 Chron.	Prov.	Dan.	Nah.	
Judg.	2 Chron.	Eccl.	Hos.	Hab.	

APOCRYPHA (Apoc.)

1 Esd.	Jdt.	Sir.	Song 3 Childr.	1 Macc.
2 Esd.	Add. Est.	Bar.	Bel	2 Macc.
Tob.	Wis.	Ep. Jer.	Pr. Man.	

PSEUDEPIGRAPHA (Pseud.)

1 En.	*Ethiopic Enoch*	*4 Macc.*	*4 Maccabees*
2 Bar.	*2 (Syriac) Baruch [= Apocalypse of Baruch]*	*Sib. Or.*	*Sibylline Oracles*

NEW TESTAMENT (NT)

Mt.	Rom.	Phil.	2 Tim.	Jas	2 Jn
Mk	1 Cor.	Col.	Tit.	1 Pet.	3 Jn
Lk.	2 Cor.	1 Thess.	Phlm.	2 Pet.	Jude
Jn	Gal.	2 Thess.	Heb.	1 Jn	Rev.
Acts	Eph.	1 Tim.			

DEAD SEA SCROLLS (DSS)

1QDan[a]	First copy of Daniel from Qumran Cave 1
1QpHab	*Pesher on Habakkuk* from Qumran Cave 1
1QM	*Milhamah* (*War Scroll*) from Qumran Cave I
11QtgJob	*Targum of Job* from Qumran Cave 11
11QMelch	*Melchizedek* text from Qumran Cave 11

JOSEPHUS

Ant.   *The Antiquities of the Jews*

GENERAL

AB	Anchor Bible
ANET	James B. Pritchard (ed.), *Ancient Near Eastern Texts Relating to the Old Testament* (Princeton: Princeton University Press, 1950)
AOAT	Alter Orient und Altes Testament
AUSS	*Andrews University Seminary Studies*
BA	*Biblical Archaeologist*
BARev	*Biblical Archaeology Review*
BDB	Francis Brown, S.R. Driver and Charles A. Briggs, *A Hebrew and English Lexicon of the Old Testament* (Oxford: Clarendon Press, 1907)
BETL	Bibliotheca ephemeridum theologicarum lovaniensium
BHS	*Biblia hebraica stuttgartensia*
Bib	*Biblica*
BibRes	*Bible Research*
BKAT	Biblischer Kommentar: Altes Testament
BN	*Biblische Notizen*
BO	*Bibliotheca orientalis*
BB	*Bible Review*
BSac	*Bibliotheca Sacra*
BZ	*Biblische Zeitschrift*
CBC	Cambridge Bible Commentary
CBQ	*Catholic Biblical Quarterly*
CEV	Contemporary English Version
CTQ	*Concordia Theological Quarterly*
ETL	*Ephemerides theologicae lovanienses*
FOTL	The Forms of the Old Testament Literature
GKC	*Gesenius' Hebrew Grammar* (ed. E. Kautzsch; revised and trans. A.E. Cowley; Oxford: Clarendon Press, 1910)
HAR	*Hebrew Annual Review*
HAT	Handbuch zum Alten Testament
HBT	*Horizons in Biblical Theology*
HDR	Harvard Dissertations in Religion
HSM	Harvard Semitic Monographs
IB	*Interpreter's Bible*
ICC	International Critical Commentary
IDB	George Arthur Buttrick (ed.), *The Interpreter's Dictionary of the Bible* (4 vols.; Nashville: Abingdon Press, 1962)
Int	*Interpretation*

ISBE	Geoffrey Bromiley (ed.), *The International Standard Bible Encyclopedia* (4 vols. Grand Rapids: Eerdmans, rev. edn, 1979–88)
JBL	*Journal of Biblical Literature*
JETS	*Journal of the Evangelical Theological Society*
JNES	*Journal of Near Eastern Studies*
JQR	*Jewish Quarterly Review*
JSJ	*Journal for the Study of Judaism in the Persian, Hellenistic, and Roman Period*
JSOT	*Journal for the Study of the Old Testament*
JSOTSup	*Journal for the Study of the Old Testament*, Supplement Series
JTS	*Journal of Theological Studies*
KB	Ludwig Koehler and Walter Baumgartner (eds.), *Lexicon in Veteris Testamenti libros* (Leiden: E.J. Brill, 1953)
NAB	*New American Bible*
NIB	*The New Interpreter's Bible*
NIV	New International Version
NJB	*New Jerusalem Bible*
NRSV	New Revised Standard Version
OTS	*Oudtestamentische Studiën*
OTG	Old Testament Guides
OTL	Old Testament Library
PRSt	*Perspectives in Religious Studies*
REB	Revised English Bible
RSV	Revised Standard Version
ScrB	*Scripture Bulletin*
ST	*Studia theologica*
TLZ	*Theologische Literaturzeitung*
TOTC	Tyndale Old Testament Commentaries
TZ	*Theologische Zeitschrift*
VT	*Vetus Testamentum*
WBC	World Biblical Commentary
WO	*Die Welt des Orients*
ZAW	*Zeitschrift für die alttestamentliche Wissenschaft*

BIBLIOGRAPHY

Alexander, J.B.
1950   'Critical Note: New Light on the Fiery Furnace', *JBL* 69: 375-76.
Albright, W.F.
1921   'The Date and Personality of the Chronicler', *JBL* 40: 112.
Alfrink, B.J.
1959   'L'idée de résurrection d'après Dan. 12.1-2', *Bib* 40: 355-71.
Alon, A.
1967   *The Natural History of the Land of the Bible* (London: Hamlyn; New York: Doubleday).
Anderson, Robert A.
1984   *Signs and Wonders: A Commentary on the Book of Daniel* (International Theological Commentary; Grand Rapids: Eerdmans).
Armerding, Carl
1964   'Asleep in the Dust (Daniel 12.1-3)', *BSac* 121: 153-58.
Avalos, Hector I.
1991   'The Comedic Function of the Enumerations of the Officials and Instruments in Daniel 3', *CBQ* 53: 580-88.
Bader, Winfried
1994   'Reale und gedachte Welt: Die Modalitäten in Daniel 8', in Winfried Bader (ed), *'Und die Wahrheit wurde hinweggefegt': Daniel 8 linguistisch interpretiert* (Basel: A. Francke): 39-58.
Baldwin, Joyce G.
1978   *Daniel: An Introduction and Commentary* (TOTC; Leicester: Inter-Varsity Press).
Bampfylde, Gillian
1983   'The Prince of the Host in the Book of Daniel and the Dead Sea Scrolls', *JSJ* 14.2: 29-34.
Bauer, Dieter
1994   'Daniel 8: eine "Leitwortuntersuchung" ', in Bader (ed.) 1994: 73-86.
1996   *Das Buch Daniel* (Neuer Stuttgarter Commentar Altes Testament, 22; Stuttgart: Katholisches Bibelwerk).
Beasley-Murray, G.R.
1983   'The Interpretation of Daniel 7', *CBQ* 45: 44-58.
Begg, C.T.
1993   'Daniel and Josephus: Tracing Connections', in van der Woude (ed.) 1993: 539-46.
Bentzen, Aage
1952   *Daniel* (HAT, 19; Tübingen: J.C.B. Mohr).

Bergman, Ben Zion
1968   'Han'el in Daniel 2.25 and 6.19', JNES 27: 69-70.

Black, Matthew
1975   'Die Apotheose Israels: eine neue Interpretation des danielische
            "Menschensohns"', in Rudolph Pesch, Rudolf Schnackenburg and Odilo
            Kaiser (eds.), Jesus und der Menschensohn (Freiburg: Herder): 92-99.

Bogaert, P.-M.
1986   'La chronologie dans la dernière vision de Daniel (DN 10,4 et 12,11-12)',
            in A. Caquot, M. Hadas-Lebel and J. Riaud (eds.), Hellenica et Judaica
            homage à Valentin Nikiprowetzky (Leuven: Peeters): 207-11.

Bright, John
1981   A History of Israel (Philadelphia: Westminster Press, 3rd edn).

Broshi, M.
1976   'Estimating the Population of Ancient Jerusalem', BAREV 4.2:12-13.

Bucher-Gillmayr, Susanne
1994   'Gedankenverlauf und Textgliederung in Daniel 8', in Bader (ed.) 1994:
            59-72.

Buschhaus, Martin
1987   'Anunnakkū und Igigū im Buch Daniel', BibN 36: 17-21.
1987   'Traumpsychologisch—parapsychologische Bemerkungen zu drei Über-
            setzungsschwierigkeiten im Buch Daniel', BibN 38–39: 26-29.

Caragounis, C.C.
1987   'The Interpretation of the Ten Horns of Daniel 7', ETL 63: 106-13.
1989   'Greek Culture and Jewish Piety: The Clash and the Fourth Beast of
            Daniel 7', ETL 65: 280-308.
1993   'History and Supra-History: Daniel and the Four Empires', in van der
            Woude (ed.) 1993: 387-98.

Casey, P.M.
1976   'Porphyry and the Origin of the Book of Daniel', JTS 27: 15-33.

Cohen, S.J.D.
1990   'Religion, Ethnicity, and "Hellenism" in the Emergence of Jewish
            Identity in Maccabean Palestine', in Per Bilde (ed.), Religion and Reli-
            gious Practice in the Seleucid Kingdom (Studies in Hellenistic Civiliza-
            tion; Aarhus: Århus University Press): 204-23.

Collins, John J.
1975a   'The Court-Tales in Daniel and the Development of Apocalyptic', JBL
            94: 218-34.
1975b   'The Mythology of the Holy War in Daniel and the Qumran War Scroll:
            A Point of Transition in Jewish Apocalyptic', VT 25: 596-612.
1977   The Apocalyptic Vision of the Book of Daniel (HSM, 16; Missoula, MT:
            Scholars Press).
1979   'Introduction: Towards the Morphology of a Genre', in idem (ed.), Apo-
            calypse: The Morphology of a Genre (Semeia, 14; Missoula, MT: Schol-
            ars Press): 1-20.
1981a   'Apocalyptic Genre and Mythic Allusions in Daniel', JSOT 21: 83-100.
1981b   Daniel, First Maccabees, Second Maccabees (OTM, 16; Wilmington,
            DE: Michael Glazier).

1984   *Daniel, with an Introduction to Apocalyptic Literature* (FOTL, 20; Grand
            Rapids: Eerdmans).
1985   'Daniel and His Social World', *Int* 39: 131-43.
1990   'The Meaning of "the End" in the Book of Daniel', in H. Attridge (ed.),
            Of Scribes and Scrolls (Lanham, MD: University Press of America): 91-
            98.
1993a   *Daniel* (Hermeneia; Minneapolis: Fortress Press).
1993b   'Stirring up the Great Sea: The Religion-Historical Background of Daniel
            7', in van der Woude (ed.) 1993: 121-36.
1993c   'Wisdom, Apocalypticism, and Generic Compatibility', in Leo G. Perdue,
            Bernard Scott and William Wiseman (eds.), *In Search of Wisdom: Essays
            in Memory of John G. Gammie* (Louisville, KY: Westminster: John Knox
            Press): 165-85.
1996   'Prayer of Nabonidus', in J.C. VanderKam (ed.), *Qumran Cave 4.XVII:
            Parabiblical Texts, Part 3* (DJD, 22; Oxford: Oxford University Press):
            83-93.
1997   'The Expectation of the End in the Dead Sea Scrolls', in C.A. Evans and
            P.W. Flint (eds.), *Eschatology, Messianism, and the Dead Sea Scrolls*
            (Studies in the Dead Sea Scrolls and Related Literature; Grand Rapids:
            Eerdmans): 74-90.
Cook, Edward M.
1989   '"In the Plain of the Wall" (Dan 3.1)', *JBL* 108: 115-16.
Cook, Stephen L.
1994   *Prophecy and Apocalypticism: The Post-exilic Setting* (Minneapolis: Fort-
            ress Press).
Coppens, J.
1964   'Le fils d'homme Daniélique, vizir céleste?', *ETL* 40: 72-80.
1968   'Les origines du symbole du fils d'homme en Dan., VII', *ETL* 44 (1968):
            497-502.
1969a   'Un nouvel essai d'interpréter Dan., VII', *ETL* 45 (1969): 122-25.
1969b   'La vision Daniélique du fils d'homme', *VT* 19: 171-82.
1978   'Le chapitre VII de Daniel: Lecture et commentaire', *ETL* 54: 301-22.
1980   'Le Livre de Daniel et ses problèmes', *ETL* 56: 1-9.
Coxon, P.W.
1976   'Daniel iii.17: A Linguistic and Theological Problem', *VT* 26: 400-409.
1986   'The Great Tree of Daniel 4', in J.D. Martin and P.R. Davies (eds.), *A
            Word in Season: Essays in Honour of William McKane* (JSOTSup, 42;
            Sheffield: JSOT Press): 91-111.
1993   'Another Look at Nebuchadnezzar's Madness', in van der Woude (ed.)
            1993: 211-22.
Cross, F.M., Jr
1961a   *The Ancient Library of Qumran* (Anchor Books; Garden City, NY:
            Doubleday).
1961b   'The Development of the Jewish Scripts', in G.E. Wright (ed.), *The Bible
            and the Ancient Near East: Essays in Honor of William Foxwell Albright*
            (AB; Garden City, NY: Doubleday): 170-244.

Dangl, Oskar
    1994   'Ich-Konstanz und Welt-Kohärenz. Zum Verhältnis von Transzendental-philosophie und Exegese', in Bauer (ed.) 1994: 111-22.

Davies, P.R.
    1970   'Daniel Chapter Two', *JTS* 27: 392-401.
    1980   'Eschatology in the Book of Daniel', *JSOT* 17: 33-53.
    1985   *Daniel* (OTG; Sheffield: JSOT Press).
    1989   'The Social World of the Apocalyptic Writers', in R.E. Clements *et al.* (eds.), *The World of Ancient Israel* (Cambridge: Cambridge University Press): 251-71.
    1991   'Daniel in the Lion's Den', in Loveday Alexander (ed.), *Images of Empire* (JSOTSup, 122; Sheffield: Sheffield Academic Press): 160-78.
    1993   'Reading Daniel Sociologically', in van der Woude 1993: 345-61.

Deissler, Alfons
    1975   'Der "Menschensohn" und "das Volk der Heigen des Höchsten" in Dan 7', in Rudolph Pesch, Rudolf Schnackenburg and Odilo Kaiser (eds.), *Jesus und der Menschensohn* (Freiburg: Herder): 81-91.

Delcor, M.
    1968   'Les sources du chapitre 7 de Daniel', *VT* 18: 290-312.
    1993   'L'histoire selon le livre de Daniel, notament au chapitre XI', in van der Woude (ed.) 1993: 365-86.

Dequeker, L.
    1973   'The "Saints of the Most High" in Qumran and Daniel', in C.J. Lebuschagne (ed.), *Syntax and Meaning: Studies in Hebrew Syntax and Biblical Exegesis* (OTS, 18; Leiden: E.J. Brill): 108-87.
    1993   'King Darius and the Prophecy of Seventy Weeks', in van der Woude (ed.) 1993: 187-210.

Dimant, D.
    1993   'The Seventy Weeks Chronology (Dan 9, 24-27) in the Light of New Qumranic Texts', in van der Woude (ed.) 1993: 57-76.

Doukhan, Jacques
    1979   'The Seventy Weeks of Dan 9: An Exegetical Study', *AUSS* 17.1: 1-22.

Dressler, Harold H.P.
    1979   'The Identification of the Ugaritic DNIL with the Daniel of Ezekiel', *VT* 29: 152-61.

Eissfeldt, Otto
    1951   'Die Menetekel-Inschrift und ihre Deutung', *ZAW* 63: 105-14.
    1960   'Daniels und seiner drei Gefährten Laufbahn im babylonischen, medi-schen und persischen Dienst', *ZAW* 72: 134-48.

Emerton, J.A.
    1960   'The Participles in Daniel 512', *ZAW* 72: 262-63.

Ferch, Arthur J.
    1980   'Daniel 7 and Ugarit: A Reconsideration', *JBL* 99: 75-86.

Fewell, Danna Nolan
    1988   *Circle of Sovereignty: A Story of Stories in Daniel 1–6* (JSOTSup, 72; Sheffield: JSOT Press).

Flint, P.W.
    1997   'The Daniel Tradition at Qumran', in C.A. Evans and P.W. Flint (eds.), *Eschatology, Messianism, and the Dead Sea Scrolls* (Studies in the Dead Sea Scrolls and Related Literature; Grand Rapids: Eerdmans): 41-60.

Flusser, David
    1972   'The Four Empires in the Fourth Sibyl and in the Book of Daniel', in M.J. Kister (ed.), *Israel Oriental Studies* (Tel Aviv: Tel Aviv University): 148-75.

Fohrer, G.
    1960   'Die Struktur des alttestamentlichen Eschatologie', *TLZ* 85: 410-11.

Frieden, Ken
    1990   'Dream Interpreters in Exile: Joseph, Daniel, and Sigmund (Solomon)', in V.L. Tollers and John Meier (eds.), *Bucknell Review 33: The Bible as Text* (Lewisburg: Bucknell University Press): 193-203.

Fröhlich, Ida
    1993   'Daniel 2 and Deutero-Isaiah', in van der Woude (ed.) 1993: 266-70.

Funk, R.W.
    1962   'Furnace', *IDB*, II: 330.

Gammie, John G.
    1976   'The Classification, Stages of Growth, and Changing Intentions in the Book of Daniel', *JBL* 95: 191-204.
    1981   'On the Intention and Sources of Daniel 1-6', *VT* 31: 282-92.
    1985   'A Journey Through Danielic Spaces: The Book of Daniel in the Theology and Piety of the Christian Community', *Int* 39: 144-56.

Gese, Hartmut
    1983   'Das Geschichtsbild des Danielbuches und Ägypten', in Hellmut Brunner and Manfred Görg (eds.), *Fontes atque pontes: eine Festgabe für Hellmut Brunner* (Ägypten und altes Testament, 5; Wiesbaden: Otto Harrasowitz): 139-54.
    1991   'Die dreieinhalb Jahre des Danielbuches', in D.R. Daniels, Uwe Glessmar and Martin Rösel (eds.), *Ernten was man säet: Festschrift für Klaus Koch zu seinem 65. Geburtstag* (Neukirchen–Vluyn: Neukirchener Verlag): 399-421.

Ginsberg, H.L.
    1948   *Studies in Daniel* (Texts and Studies of the Jewish Theological Seminary of America, 14; New York: Jewish Theological Seminary of America).
    1954   'The Composition of the Book of Daniel', *VT* 4: 246-75.

Goldingay, John
    1988   ' "Holy Ones on High" in Daniel 7:8', *JBL* 107 :495-97.
    1989   *Daniel* (WBC, 30; Dallas, TX: Word Books).

Goldstein, J.A.
    1977   *1 Maccabees* (AB. 41; Garden City, NY: Doubleday).

Good, Edwin M.
    1984   'Apocalyptic as Comedy: The Book of Daniel', in J. Cheryl Exum (ed.), *Tragedy and Comedy in the Bible* (Semeia, 32; Decatur, GA: Scholars Press): 41-70.

Goudoever, J. van
 1993 'The Indications in Daniel that Reflect the Usage of the Ancient Theoretical So-Called Zadokite Calendar', in van der Woude (ed.) 1993: 533-38.

Grabbe, L.L.
 1987 ' "The End of the Desolations of Jerusalem": From Jeremiah's 70 Years to Daniel's 70 Weeks of Years', in Craig A. Evans and William F. Stinespring (eds.), *Early Jewish and Christian Exegesis: Studies in Memory of William Hugh Brownlee* (Atlanta: Scholars Press): 67-72.

 1988 'Another Look at the *Gestalt* of "Darius the Mede" ', *CBQ* 50: 198-213.

Grelot, Pierre
 1979 'L'orchestre de Daniel 3.5, 7, 10, 15', *VT* 29: 23-38.

 1985 'L'écriture sur le mur (Daniel 5)', in A. Caquot, S. Légasse and M. Tardieu (eds.), *Mélanges bibliques et orientaux en l'honneur de M. Mathias Delcor* (AOAT, 215; Neukirchen–Vluyn: Neukirchener Verlag): 199-207.

Gunkel, Hermann
 1895 *Schöpfung und Chaos in Urzeit und Endzeit: Eine religionsgeschictliche Untersuchung über Gen 1 und Ap Joh 12* (Gottingen: Vandenhoek & Ruprecht).

Gurney, R.J.M.
 1977 'The Kingdoms of Daniel 2 and 7', *Themolies* 2: 39-45.

Haag, E.
 1993 'Der Menschensohn und die Heiligen (des) Höchsten: Eine literar-, form und traditionsgeschichtliche Studie zu Daniel 7', in van der Woude (ed.) 1993: 137-56.

Harnickell, Bernhard
 1994 'Der historische Hintergrund des Danielbuches', in Bader (ed.): 123-47.

Hammer, Raymond
 1976 *The Book of Daniel* (CBC; Cambridge: Cambridge University Press).

Hanson, Paul
 1975 *The Dawn of Apocalyptic* (Philadelphia: Fortress Press).

Hartman, Louis F., and Alexander A. Di Lella
 1978 *The Book of Daniel* (AB, 23; New York: Doubleday).

Hasel, Gerhard F.
 1975 'The Identity of "The Saints of the Most High" in Daniel 7', *Bib* 56: 173-92.

 1979 'The Four World Empires of Daniel 2 against its Near Eastern Environment', *JSOT* 12: 17-30.

 1981a 'The Book of Daniel: Evidences Relating to Persons and Chronology', *AUSS* 19.1: 37-49.

 1981b 'The Book of Daniel and Matters of Language: Evidences Relating to Names, Words, and the Aramaic Language', *AUSS* 19.3: 211-25.

Heaton, E.W.
 1956 *The Book of Daniel* (Torch Bible Commentary; London: SCM Press).

Hengel, Martin
 1974 *Judaism and Hellenism: Studies in their Encounters in Palestine during the Early Hellenistic Period* (2 vols.; Philadelphia: Fortress Press).

Henten, J.W. van
    1993   'Antiochus IV as a Typhonic Figure in Daniel 7', in van der Woude (ed.)
            1993: 223-43.
Humphreys, W. Lee
    1973   'A Life-style for Diaspora: A Study of the Tales of Esther and Daniel',
            JBL 92: 211-23.
Hutter-Graz, Manfred
    1984   ' "Halte diese Worte geheim!"—Eine Notiz zu einem apokalyptischen
            Brauch', *BN* 25: 14-13.
Hyldahl, Niels
    1990   'The Maccabean Rebellion and the Question of "Hellenization" ', in Per
            Hilde (ed.), *Religion and Religious Practice in the Seleucid Kingdom*
            (Studies in Hellenistic Civilization; Aarhus: Århus University Press):
            188-203.
Jeffery, Arthur
    1956   'The Book of Daniel: Introduction and Exegesis' (IB, 6; Nashville:
            Abingdon Press).
Jepsen, A.
    1961   'Bemerkungen zum Danielbuch', *VT* 11: 386-91.
Jones, Bruce William
    1968   'The Prayer in Daniel 9', *VT* 18: 488-93.
Judisch, D.M.L.
    1989   'The Saints of the Most High', *CTQ* 53: 96-103.
Junker, Hubert
    1932   *Untersuchungen über literarische und exegetische Probleme des Buches
            Daniel* (Bonn: Hanstein).
Kaltenmark, Max
    1969   *Lao Tzu and Taoism* (Stanford: Stanford University Press).
Keil, Volkmar
    1985   'Onias III: Märtyrer oder Tempelgründer?', *ZAW* 97: 221-33.
Kennedy, Gerald
    1956   'The Book of Daniel Exposition', *IB* 6: 347-48.
Koch, Klaus
    1980   *Das Buch Daniel* (Darmstadt: Wissenschaftliche Buchgesellschaft).
    1983   'Dareios, der Meder', in Carol L. Meyers and M. O'Conner (eds.), *The
            Word of the Lord Shall Go Forth: Essays in Honor of David Noel Fried-
            man in Celebration of His Sixtieth Birthday* (American Schools of Orien-
            tal Research Special Volume 1; Winona Lake, IN: Eisenbrauns): 287-99.
    1985   'Is Daniel Also Among the Prophets?' *Int* 39: 117-30.
    1986   *Daniel* (BKAT, 22.1 and 2; Neukirchen–Vluyn: Neukirchener Verlag,
            1994).
    1993   'Gottes Herrschaft über das Reich des Menschen. Daniel 4 im Licht neuer
            Funde', in van der Woude (ed.) 1993: 77-120.
    1997   *Europa, Rom und der Kaiser vor dem Hintergrund von zwei Jahr-
            tausenden Rezeption des Buches Daniel* (Göttingen: Vandenhoeck &
            Ruprecht).

Kutsher, E.Y.
    1947   'Biblical Aramaic—Eastern or Western', in *World Congress of Jewish
                Studies, Summer 1947 (1; Jerusalem: Magnes Press, 1952): 123-27.
Kvanvig, Helge S.
    1978   'Struktur und Geschichte in Dan. 7,1-14', *ST* 32: 95-117.
    1981   'An Akkadian Vision as Background for Dan 7?', *ST* 35: 85-89.
    1989   'The Relevance of the Biblical Visions of the End of Time', *HBT* 11: 35-
                58.
Labonté, G.G.
    1993   'Genèse 41 et Daniel 2: question d'origine', in van der Woude (ed.) 1993:
                271-84.
Lacocque, André
    1979   *The Book of Daniel* (Atlanta: John Knox Press).
    1981   'Apocalyptic Symbolism: A Ricoeurian Hermeneutical Approach', *BR*
                26: 6-15.
    1988   *Daniel in his Time* (Studies on Personalities of the Old Testament;
                Columbia, SC: University of South Carolina Press).
    1993   'The Socio-Spiritual Formative Milieu of the Daniel Apocalypse', in van
                der Woude (ed.) 1993: 315-44.
Lambert, W.G.
    1960   *Babylonian Wisdom Literature* (Oxford: Oxford University Press).
    1978   *The Background of Jewish Apocalyptic: The Ethel M. Wood Lecture
                delivered before the University of London on 22 February 1977* (London:
                University of London).
Langer, Gerhard
    1994   'Die Isotypie der Macht', in Bader (ed.) 1994: 87-102.
Larkin, Katerina J.A.
    1994   *The Eschatology of Second Zechariah: A Study of the Formation of a
                Mantological Wisdom Anthology* (Kampen: Kok).
Lasine, Stuart
    1987   'Solomon, Daniel, and the Detective Story: The Social Functions of a
                Literary Genre', *HAR* 11: 247-66.
Lebram, J.C.H.
    1975   'König Antiochus im Buch Daniel', *VT* 25: 737-72.
    1982   'Zwei Danielprobleme', *BO* 39 (1982): 511-17.
Louis-Fletcher, C.H.T.
    1997   'The High Priest as Divine Mediator in the Hebrew Bible: Daniel 7.13 as
                a Test Case', *Society of Biblical Literature Seminar Papers, 1997*
                (Atlanta, GA: Scholars Press): 161-93.
Mason, Rex A.
    1988   'The Treatment of Earlier Biblical Themes in the Book of Daniel', *PRSt*
                15.4: 81-100.
Mastin, B.A.
    1988   'The Reading of 1QDan[a] at Daniel 2.4', *VT* 38: 341-46.
    1992   'The Meaning of *hala* at Daniel 4.27', *VT* 42: 234-47.
Meadowcroft, T.J.
    1995   *Aramaic Daniel and Greek Daniel: A Literary Comparison* (JSOTSup,
                198; Sheffield: Sheffield Academic Press).

Mercer, Mark K.
      1989   'Daniel 1.1 and Jehoiakim's Three Years of Servitude', *AUSS* 27.3: 179-
                92.
Michel, Diethelm
      1993   'Weisheit und Apokalyptik', in van der Woude (ed.) 1993: 413-34.
Millard, Alan
      1985   'Daniel and Belshazzar in History', *BARev* 11 (May/June): 73-78.
Miller, James E.
      1991   'The Redaction of Daniel', *JSOT* 52: 115-24.
Miller, Stephen R.
      1994   *Daniel* (New American Commentary, 18; Nashville: Broadman &
                Holman).
Montgomery, James A.
      1927   *The Book of Daniel* (ICC; Edinburgh: T. & T. Clark).
Morgenstern, Julian
      1961   'The "Son of Man" of Daniel 7.13f.', *JBL* 80: 65-77.
Morvan, Michael le
      1996   'Qumran: The Community', *ScrB* 26: 20-33.
Mosca, Paul G.
      1986   'Ugarit and Daniel 7: A Missing Link', *Bib* 67: 496-517.
Muilenburg, James
      1960   'The Son of Man in Daniel and the Ethiopic Apocalypse of Enoch', *JBL*
                79: 197-209.
Müller, H.P.
      1972   *Congress Volume, 1971* (VTSup, 12; Leiden: E.J. Brill): 268-91.
      1977   'Die weisheitliche Lehrerzahlung in Alten Tesament', *WO* 9: 77-98.
Müller, Karlheinz
      1975   'Der Menschensohn im Danielzyklus', in Rudolph Pesch, Rudolf
                Schnackenburg and Odilo Kaiser (eds.), *Jesus und der Menschensohn*
                (Basel: Herder): 37-80.
Nicol, George G.
      1979   'Isaiah's Vision and the Visions of Daniel', *VT* 29: 501-505.
Niditch, Susan, and Robert Doran
      1977   'The Success Story of the Wise Courtier: A Formal Approach', *JBL* 96:
                179-93.
Noth, Martin
      1984   'The Understanding of History in Old Testament Apocalyptic', in *The
                Laws of the Pentateuch and Other Studies* (London: SCM Press): 194-
                214.
O'Leary, Stephen D.
      1994   *Arguing the Apocalypse: A Theory of Millennial Rhetoric* (Oxford: Oxford
                University Press).
Oppenheim, A.L.
      1956   *The Interpretation of Dreams in the Ancient Near East* (Philadelphia:
                American Philosophical Society).
Osten-Sacken, P. von der
      1969   *Die Apokalyptik in ihrem Verhältnis zu Prophetie und Weisheit* (Theo-
                logishe Exitenz Heute, 157; Munich: Chr. Kaiser Verlag).

Otzen, Benedikt
1990   'Crisis and Religious Reaction: Jewish Apocalypticism', in Per Bilde
        (ed.), *Religion and Religious Practice in the Seleucid Kingdom* (Studies
        in Hellenistic Civilization; Aarhus: Århus University Press): 224-36.
Owens, J.J.
1971   *Daniel* (The Broadman Bible Commentary, 6; Nashville: Broadman).
Ozanne, C.G.
1965   'Three Textual Problems in Daniel', *JTS* 16: 445-48.
Paul, Shalom
1983   'Dan 3.29—A Case Study of "Neglected" Blasphemy', *JNES* 42: 291-94.
1984   'Dan 6.8: An Aramaic Reflex of Assyrian Legal Terminology', *Bib* 65:
        106-10.
Payne, J. Barton
1978   'The Goal of Daniel's Seventy Weeks', *JETS* 21: 97-115.
Péter-Contesse, R., and John Ellington
1993   *A Handbook on The Book of Daniel* (United Bible Society Handbook
        Series; New York: United Bible Societies).
Plöger, Otto
1968   *Theocracy and Eschatology* (Richmond, VA: John Knox Press).
Polak, F.H.
1993   'The Daniel Tales in their Aramaic Literary Milieu', in van der Woude
        (ed.) 1993: 249-65.
Porteous, Norman W.
1965   *Daniel* (OTL; Philadelphia: Westminster Press).
Poythress, V.S.
1976   'The Holy Ones of the Most High in Daniel 7', *VT* 26: 208-13.
Raabe, Paul R.
1985   'Daniel 7: Its Structure and Role in the Book', *HAR* 9: 267-75.
Rabinowitz, Jacob J.
1955   'A Legal Formula in the Susa Tablets, in an Egyptian Document of the
        Twelfth Dynasty, in the Aramaic Papyri, and in the Book of Daniel', *Bib*
        36: 74-77.
Rad, G. von
1965   *Old Testament Theology* (2 vols.; New York: Harper & Row, 1962,
        1965).
Rappaport, U.
1992   'Apocalyptic Vision and Preservation of Historical Memory', *JSJ* 23.2:
        217-26.
Redditt, P.L.
1983   'The Concept of *Nomos* in Fourth Maccabees', *CBQ* 45: 249-70.
1998a   'Daniel 11 and the Socio-historical Setting of the Book of Daniel', *CBQ*
        60: 463-74.
1998b   'Calculating the "Times": Daniel 12.5-13', PRSt 25.4: 373-39.
forthcoming 'Daniel 9: Its Structure and Meaning', *CBQ*.
Redditt, P.L., and Robert R. Kruschwitz
1997   'Nebuchadnezzar as the Head of Gold: Politics and History in the Theo-
        logy of the Book of Daniel', *PRSt* 24: 339-416.

Reicke, Bo
1960   'Official and Pietistic Elements of Jewish Apocalypticism', *JBL* 79: 137-
         50.
Reid, Stephen Breck
1989   *Enoch and Daniel: A Form Critical and Sociological Study of Historical
         Apocalypses* (Berkeley, CA: Bibal).
Rhodes, Arnold B.
1961   'The Kingdoms of Men and the Kingdom of God', *Int* 15: 411-30.
Richter, H.-F.
1993   'Daniel 4,7-14: Beobachtungen und Erwägungen', van der Woude (ed.)
         1993: 244-48.
Rieger, Reinhold
1994   '*We en mebin* (Dan 8.27): Die unverstandene Deutung oder das Trilemma
         des Verstehens', in Bader (ed.) 1994: 103-10.
Rimbach, James A.
1978   'Bears or Bees? Sefire I A 31 and Daniel 7', *JBL* 97: 565-66.
Ringgren, Helmer, and Åke V. Ström
1969   *Religions of Mankind* (Philadelphia: Fortress Press).
Rowley, H.H.
1948   'The Voice of God in Apocalyptic: Eternal Values in the Biblical Apoca-
         lypse', *Int* 2: 403-18.
1952   'The Unity of the Book of Daniel', in *idem*, *The Servant of the Lord and
         Other Essays in the Old Testament* (Oxford: Basil Blackwell, 2nd rev.
         edn): 249-80.
1955   'The Composition of the Book of Daniel: Some Comments on Professor
         Ginsberg's Article', *VT* 5: 272-76.
1961   'The Meaning of Daniel for Today: A Study of Leading Themes', *Int* 15:
         387-97.
1963   *The Relevance of Apocalyptic* (rev. edn; New York: Association Press).
1964   *Darius the Mede and the Four World Empires in the Book of Daniel* (Car-
         diff: University of Wales Press).
Russell, D.S.
1965   *The Method and Message of Jewish Apocalyptic* (Philadelphia: West-
         minster Press).
1981   *Daniel* (Daily Study Bible; Edinburgh: St Andrew; Philadelphia: West-
         minster Press).
Sachs, A.J., and D.J. Wiseman
1954   'A Babylonian King List of the Hellenistic Period', *Iraq* 16: 202-11.
Safrai, Z.
1996   'The Role of the Jerusalem Elite', in M. Poorthuis and S. Safrai (eds.), *The
         Centrality of Jerusalem: Historical Perspectives* (Kampen: Kok).
Sahlin, Harald
1969   'Antiochus IV: Epiphanes und Judas Mackabäus. Einige Gesichtspunkte
         zum Verständnisse des Danielbuches', *ST* 23: 41-68.
Schindele, Martin
1994a   'Möglichkeiten und Grenzen maschineller Befunderhebung zur Unter-
         suchung von Formeln und geprägten Wendungen mit Beispielen aus
         Daniel 8', in Bader (ed.) 1994: 31-38.

1994b   'Textkonstituierung zu Daniel 8', in Bader (ed.) 1994: 3-16.

Schwantes, S.J.
1978   ' '*EREB BŌQER* of Dan 8.14 Reexamined', *AUSS* 16.3: 375-85.

Schwartz, J.
1996   'The Temple in Jerusalem', in M. Poorthuis and S. Safrai (eds.), *The Centrality of Jerusalem: Historical Perspectives* (Kampen: Kok): 30-31.

Schweizer, Eduard
1975   'Menschensohn und eschatologischer Mensch im Frühjudentum', in Rudolph Pesch, Rudolf Schnackenburg and Odilo Kaiser (eds.), *Jesus und der Menschensohn* (Freiburg: Herder): 100-16.

Schweizer, Harald
1994   'Die Sprache der Zeichenkörper. Textinterne (Ausdrucks-)Syntax zu Daniel 8', in Bader (ed.) 1994: 17-30.

Shea, William H.
1982a   'Darius the Mede: An Update', *AUSS* 20.3: 229-47.
1982b   'Nabonidus, Belshazzar, and the Book of Daniel: An Update', *AUSS* 20.2: 133-49.
1983a   'A Further Note on Daniel 6: Daniel as "Governor" ', *AUSS* 21.2: 169-71.
1983b   'Wrestling with the Prince of Persia: A Study on Daniel 10', *AUSS* 21.3: 225-50.
1985   'Further Literary Structures in Daniel 2–7: An Analysis of Daniel 5, and the Broader Relationships Within Chapters 2–7', *AUSS* 23.3: 277-95.
1991   'Darius the Mede in His Persian-Babylonian Setting', *AUSS* 29.3: 235-57.

Shedl, Claus
1964   'Mystische Arithmetik oder geschichtliche Zahlen? (Daniel 8.14; 12.11-13)', *BZ* 8: 101-105.

Siegman, E.F.
1956   'The Stone Hewn from the Mountain (Daniel 2)', *CBQ* 18: 364-79.

Slotki, J.J.
1951   *Daniel, Ezra, Nehemiah* (Sontino Books of the Bible; Hindhead, Surrey: Soncino Press).

Smith, Mark. S.
1983   'The "Son of Man" in Ugaritic', *CBQ* 45: 59-60.

Smith-Christopher, David L.
1996   'The Book of Daniel', in *NIB*, 7: 17-152.

Sokoloff, Michael
1976   ' "*mar nᵉqē* ", "Lamb's Wool" (Dan 7.9)', *JBL* 95: 277-79.

Stahl, R.
1993   ' "Eine Zeit, Zeiten und die Hälfte einer Zeit": Die Versuche der Eingrenzung der bösen Macht im Danielbuch', in van der Woude (ed.) 1993: 480-95.

Steck, O.H.
1980   'Weltgeschehen und Gottesvolk im Buche Daniel', in Dieter Lührmann and Georg Strecker (eds.), *Kirche: Festschrift für Günther Bornkamm zum 75. Geburtstag* (Tübingen: J.C.B. Mohr): 53-78.

Stefanovic, Zdravko
1989   'Thematic Links Between the Historical and Prophetic Sections of Daniel', *AUSS* 27.2: 121-27.

1992   'Daniel: A Book of Significant Reversals', *AUSS* 30.2: 139-50.
Stensell, Gary
1995   'Honor and Shame in the David Narratives', in V.M. Matthews and D.C.
            Benjamin (eds.), *Honor and Shame in the World of the Bible* (Semeia, 68;
            Atlanta, GA: Scholars Press): 55-79.
Talmon, Shemaryahu
1987   'Daniel', in Robert Alter and Frank Kermode (eds.), *The Literary Guide
            to the Bible* (Cambridge, MA: Harvard University Press): 343-56.
Thomas, D. Winton
1955   'Note on *radda' at* in Daniel XII. 4', *JTS* 6: 226.
Toorn, Karel van der,
1998   'In the Lion's Den: The Babylonian Background of a Biblical Motif',
            CBQ 60: 626-40.
Towner, W.S.
1969   'The Poetic Passages of Daniel 1–6', *CBQ* 31: 317-26.
1984   *Daniel* (Interpretation Atlanta: John Knox Press).
Trevor, John C.
1985   'The Book of Daniel and the Origin of the Qumran Community', *BARev*
            48: 89-102.
Vasholz, Robert I.
1978   'Qumran and the Dating of Daniel', *JETS* 21: 315-21.
Wahl, H.-M.
1992   'Noah, Daniel und Hiob in Ezechiel 14.12-20', *VT* 42: 542-53.
Waltke, Bruce K.
1976   'The Date of the Book of Daniel', *BSac* 133: 319-29.
Walton, John H.
1986   'The Four Kingdoms of Daniel', *JETS* 29/1: 25-36.
Walvoord, J.F.
1971   *Daniel: The Key to Prophetic Revelation* (Chicago: Moody).
Weimar, Peter
1975   'Daniel 7: Eine Textanalyse', in Rudolph Pesch, Rudolf Schnackenburg,
            and Odilo Kaiser (eds.), *Jesus und der Menschensohn* (Freiburg: Herder):
            11-36.
Willi-Plein, Ina
1977   'Das Geheimnis der Apokalyptik', *VT* 27: 62-81.
1979   'Ursprung und Motivation der Apokalyptik im Danielbuch', *TZ* 35: 265-
            74.
Wills, Lawrence M.
1990   *The Jew in the Court of the Foreign King: Ancient Jewish Court Legends*
            (HDR, 25; Minneapolis: Fortress Press).
Wilson, Gerald H.
1985   'Wisdom in Daniel and the Origin of Apocalyptic', *HAR* 9: 373-81.
1990   'The Prayer of Daniel 9: Reflection on Jeremiah 29', *JSOT* 48: 91-99.
Wilson, Robert R.
1981   'From Prophecy to Apocalyptic: Reflections on the Shape of Israelite
            Religion', in Robert C. Culley and Thomas W. Overholt (eds.), *Anthro-
            pological Perspectives on Old Testament Prophecy* (Semeia, 21; Chico,
            CA: Scholars Press): 79-95.

1992   'Innerbiblical Interpretation of Prophecy', paper presented at Society of
            Biblical Literature Conference, 1992.
Winkle, Ross E.
1987   'Jeremiah's Seventy Years for Babylon: A Re-assessment. Part I: The
            Scriptural Data', *AUSS* 25.2: 201-14.
Wiseman, D.J.
1979   'Babylon', *ISBE*, I: 384-91.
Wittstruck, Thorne
1978   'The Influence of Treaty Curse Imagery on the Beast Imagery of Daniel
            7', *JBL* 97: 100-102.
Wolters, Al
1991   'Untying the King's Knots: Physiology and Wordplay in Daniel 5', *JBL*
            110: 117-22.
Woude, A.S. van der
1986   'Erwägungen zur Doppelsprachigkeit des Buches Daniel', in H.L.J.
            Vantisphout, K. Jongeling, F. Leembius and G.J. Reinik (eds.), *Scripta
            Signa Vocis: Studies about Scripts, Scriptures, Scribes and Languages in
            the Near East, presented to J.H. Hospers by his pupils, colleagues and
            friends* (Gröningen: Egbert Forsten): 305-16.
Woude, A.S. van der (ed.)
1993   *The Book of Daniel in the Light of New Findings* (BETL, 106; Leuven:
            Leuven University Press; Leuven: Peeters).
Yarbro Collins, Adela
1986   'Introduction: Early Christian Apocalypticism', in Adela Yarbro Collins
            (ed.), *Early Christian Apocalypticism: Genre and Social Setting* (Semeia,
            36; Decatur, GA: Scholars Press): 1-12.
Young, E.J.
1949   *The Prophecy of Daniel* (Grand Rapids: Eerdmans).
Zevit, Ziony
1968   'The Structure and Individual Elements of Daniel 7', *ZAW* 80: 385-96.
1978   'The Exegetical Implications of Daniel 8.1', *VT* 28: 488-92.
Zimmermann, Frank
1964   'The Writing on the Wall: Dan. 5.22 f.', *JQR* 55: 201-207.

INTRODUCTION

A. AUTHORSHIP AND DATE

Authorship

The traditional author of the book was a Judean named Daniel, who, according to Dan. 1.1, was taken to Babylon from Palestine in the third year of King Jehoiakim of Judah (ruled 609–598), that is 606. He flourished there, according to Dan. 10.3, until the third year of King Cyrus of Persia (ruled 559–30), a date probably reckoned from Cyrus's overthrow of Babylon in 539. If so, the date of 536 would be 70 years after Daniel went into exile. Nothing else really is known of him outside the book of Daniel, though Ezek. 14.14-29 and 28.3 list someone named Daniel as a righteous man alongside Noah and Job, two non-Israelite heroes of the Old Testament. Various scholars, (e.g. Bauer 1996: 36) think that the name 'Daniel' was simply lifted from Ezekiel, and that could be correct, but neither passage explicitly associates Daniel with the Exile. Ancient Canaanite texts also knew of a figure named Danel, but his relationship, if any, to the Daniel tradition remains obscure (see Dressler 1979: 152-61; and Wahl 1992: 542-53). In the book of Daniel, he appears as a wise man who rose through the ranks in the foreign court of Babylonia and remained a significant figure into the early Persian period.

Several problems call the traditional authorship into question. For one thing the book contains details whose historical accuracy has been questioned. A few examples will be noted here. The opening two verses appear to mention an invasion of Jerusalem by Nebuchadnezzar and the exile of Judeans to Babylon in the third year of Jehoiakim, events otherwise unknown for that year in the rest of Old Testament. The language of those two verses resembles 2 Chron. 36.5-7, which does speak of an incursion by Nebuchadnezzar against Jehoiakim. However, except for the note that Nebuchadnezzar bound Jehoiakim, 2 Chron. 36.5-7 agrees with what is known from 2 Kgs 24.2-6 about the siege of Jerusalem by Nebuchadnezzar in 598/7 and its surrender to Nebuchadnezzar by Jehoiachin, Jehoiakim's son, on 16 March 597 (cf. 2 Kgs 24.1-16).

Scholars defending authorship by Daniel (e.g. Baldwin 1978: 19-21; Hasel 1981a: 47-49; Mercer 1989: 179-92; and Waltke 1976: 325-26) attempt to relate the event to an attack of Nebuchadnezzar in the year 605 or 604, when he captured Philistia. They point out that the difference between Babylon and Palestine in reckoning when the new year began accounts for the minor difference in whether 605 was Jehoiakim's third or fourth year. Still, no clear record of such an attack on Jerusalem before 598 exists, either in biblical or Babylonian texts. If Dan. 1.1 does refer to an otherwise unknown attack, it does so using language from 2 Chronicles about a later siege and provides no dependable information about an attack in 605.

A second problem concerns Belshazzar, called the king of Babylon in Daniel 5, and whose father was said to have been Nebuchadnezzar in 5.2, 11, 13, and 18. Technically, Belshazzar was the vice-regent for his absent father Nabonidus, who usurped the throne from Neriglissar or his son Labashi-Marduk in 556. Thus, Belshazzar was not the king, though the distinction might well have been one of indifference to exiled Judeans. Alan Millard (1985: 77) points to a similar phenomenon in an Assyrian text from about 850, in which the Assyrian term for 'governor' is used in the official version, while the Aramaic term for 'king' was used in the version for the local subjects.

So, Belshazzar was not the successor son of Nebuchadnezzar. That son was Amel-Marduk (the Evil-Merodach of 2 Kgs 25.27, who ruled 562–60), from whom Neriglissar (560–56) usurped the throne. In an attempt to defend the accuracy of Daniel, traditional scholars sometimes claim a more general use of the term 'father' as 'ancestor'. Others follow D.J. Wiseman to the effect that Neriglissar had married a daughter of Nebuchadnezzar, through whom they speculate Nabonidus was descended.

A third problem is the mention of a king named 'Darius the Mede', who is said to have succeeded Belshazzar as king of Babylon (5.31, MT 6.1). The Persian King Darius I was neither Median nor the immediate successor of Belshazzar, so 'Darius the Mede' may have been a composite of that Darius and some other person(s) known to history, though not an outright fictitious person as is sometimes alleged. On the other hand, some scholars argue that 'Darius the Mede' was simply another name for a known historical figure. Nominees include Astyages, the last certain Median ruler; Cyaxares II, who is named as Astyages' successor by Xenophon (but unknown from Babylonian texts) and who is said to have been about 62 in 539; Cyrus, who is said to have been king of the Medes and also to have been the right age; his general Ugbaru, who actually captured Babylon for Cyrus and died a short time later; a man named Gubaru, said to have been governor over Babylon and the province Beyond the River; Cambyses, who bore the title 'king' even during Cyrus's lifetime; Darius I; and even Darius II. Traditional scholars in particular have championed one or another of the nominees as the real 'Darius the Mede', but none was ever called Darius in an extant text, nor was any the son of Ahasuerus (Xerxes). See the review of three such works by Grabbe (1988: 198-213), who concludes that none of the proposed identifications holds up under scrutiny.

A fourth historical problem concerns ch. 9, in which Daniel is said to have been reading the prophet Jeremiah concerning 70 years of servitude of Judah to Babylon (cf. 25.11-12 and 29.10). Daniel 9 interprets that time frame as 70 weeks of years. The interpretation, however, is filled with difficulty. First, one can not be sure when the 490 years begin, since the chapter is dated in the first year of 'Darius the Mede' and the weeks are to begin with the 'time that the word went out to restore and rebuild Jerusalem' That was perhaps 605, the date of the prediction in Jer. 25.11-12 that Daniel was contemplating. At any rate, the first seven weeks of years end with the coming of an 'anointed one' (probably Jeshua, the high priest). Some scholars suggest the starting date was the fall of Jerusalem, and think the 49 years were the period from the siege of Jerusalem to the Edict of Cyrus (587 to 538). Second, the next segment of time, during which Jerusalem is built, would last 62 weeks of years and end when another 'anointed one' was cut off. That 434 years apparently would extend from 538 to 104 BCE, but nothing is known of the assassination of an 'anointed one' in that year. Critical scholars often suggest that the 'anointed one' was Onias III, who was killed in 171 BCE (see 2 Macc 4.34), while traditional Christian scholars often see a reference to the crucifixion of Jesus. In either case, the number of years seems incorrect. Finally, the end of the time frame is also uncertain, since it looked forward to the end of foreign domination over Israel.

A fifth problem concerns the death of Antiochus IV Epiphanes, who is widely identified as the last 'king of the north' in Daniel 10–12. According to 11.40-45 he would die between the hill country of Palestine and the Mediterranean Sea, whereas actually he died in Persia under very different circumstances. He is also identified with the 'little horn' of Dan. 7.8 and 8.8, an identification traditional scholars some-times question (but see Walton 1986: 25-36, esp. 32-34).

In addition to possible historical inaccuracies, the use of the third person in the court narratives of chs. 1–6 calls Danielic authorship of those narratives into question. It is perhaps not impossible that someone would write about himself in the third person, but it does seem strange, especially when the apocalyptic narratives in chs. 7–12 for the most part employ the first person. Indeed, it seems more likely that another author would write in the first person singular as a kind of 'ghost writer' than that someone would write a personal narrative in the third person. Besides, if the use of the first person singular were decisive for authorship, Dan. 4.1-27, 34-37 should be attributed to Nebuchadnezzar.

Another whole set of problems arises from the switch from court nar-ratives to apocalyptic narratives after ch. 6. One encounters not only the shift from the third person to the first person singular, but also a shift in literary genres, and other differences as well. Gone is the more or less sympathetic portrayal of the foreign king encountered especially in Daniel 2 and 6, as well as the general hope that things would go well for Judeans in exile. Gone too is the portrayal of life in the Diaspora, and in its place is an overwhelming interest in Jerusalem and Judah. These differences also call into question the composition of the book by an exilic author. (For a thorough discussion of these problems from a traditional perspective, see Miller 1994: 22-42.)

Date
While the setting of the book of Daniel is the Exile, that is too early a date for the writing of the book. On the other hand, the discovery of eight fragments of the book among the Dead Sea Scrolls sets the last possible date. (For a discussion of the fragments, see Flint 1997: 41-45.) Based on the development of writing styles at Qumran, F.M. Cross Jr first dated the oldest fragment (4QDan^c) in the late second century (1961a: 43), then modified the date to c. 100 to 50 BCE (1961b: 190). Traditional scholars sometimes claim that the Qumran fragments pre-clude even a Maccabean date for the book as a whole, but that is not so since the book is likely to have been attractive to the peripheral com-munity responsible for the scrolls. Either date would allow ample time for the book of Daniel to find its way to Qumran.

The four apocalyptic narratives (7.1-28; 8.1-27; 9.1-27; and 10.1–12.13) provide internal evidence about the date of the book's final composition. If one follows the chronological notes in the book, the book presupposes a sequence of four kingdoms or empires, expressly interpreted as (1) Babylon (2.37), (2) Media, (3) Persia and (4) Greece (8.20-21). In addition, the 'little' horn of Daniel 7 and 8 follows ten other horns and is to be identified as Antiochus IV. Sachs and Wiseman (1954: 202-11; cf. *ANET*: 566-67) published a king list from the Hellenistic period compiled in Babylon. The list began with Alexander and included nine more kings before Antiochus IV: Philip, Alexander IV, Seleucus I, Antiochus I, Antiochus II, Seleucus II, Seleucus III, Antiochus III and Seleucus IV. Further indications that Antiochus IV was the eleventh horn are the references to his persecution of the saints and particularly to his desecration of the temple (8.13; 9.27; 11.31).

To be sure, traditional scholars typically (but not always, see Gurney 1977: 39-45; and Walton 1986: 25-36) interpret the kingdoms as (1) Babylon, (2) Media/Persia, (3) Greece and (4) Rome; but Rome is nowhere identified within the book as one of the four kingdoms. The only place Romans are mentioned at all is in 11.30, where they are called the Kittim. That verse says that they will restrain the advances into Egypt of the king of the north (Antiochus IV). Nor is the identification of the kingdoms offered here unique to modern scholars; it is very similar in places to the reading offered by Porphyry, a neo-Platonic philosopher of the third Christian century reported and reviled by St Jerome (see Casey 1976: 15-33).

A fairly precise date for the conclusion of the book of Daniel can be calculated from chs. 10–12. The message in 11.2–12.4 is an overview of the Persian and especially the Greek Empire with its various rulers, enumerating 23 events leading up to the end of time (see Kennedy 1956: 347-48). The first 20 reflect the history of that period with remarkable accuracy; the next two correctly predict the death of Antiochus, but under circumstances different from those of his death in November or December of 164. The final prediction (in 12.1-2) is of a period of extreme tribulation, followed by a resurrection. The narrative, however, does not mention the restoration of the temple on 14 December 164. Critical scholars conclude, therefore, that the narrative reached its final stage just before the death of Antiochus in 164. The addition in 12.5-12 was probably penned a little later, soon after the dedication of the temple (see commentary).

This conclusion does not mean that the entire book originated during those few years. The court narratives reveal no such preoccupation with the events of the Maccabean period and so presumably came from the Persian and early Greek periods. This conclusion does mean, however, that the book cannot have been the product of its exilic hero Daniel. The question of who did write it requires a complicated answer that involves some knowledge of the history of the postexilic period.

B. HISTORICAL BACKGROUND

The Fall of Jerusalem and the Period of the Exile

The literary setting for the book of Daniel is the Exile. According to Dan. 1.1-2, Daniel and his friends were taken to Babylon by Nebuchadnezzar 'in the third year of King Jehoiakim', presumably 606 BCE. As shown above this date is historically suspect, but that problem in no way affects one's understanding of the text. Whether the date was 606, 605 (the third year of Nebuchadnezzar's reign), 602 or 601 (when Nebuchadnezzar made forays into Syria and Egypt respectively), or 597 (which would corroborate better with the known history of Jerusalem), the setting is the Babylonian Exile.

In the chronology of the book of Daniel, the latest event occurred 'In the third year of King Cyrus' (10.1), 537 or 536, that is, 70 years after 'the third year of King Jehoiakim' (1.1). Thus, Daniel's career was made to last until the end of the '70 years' of the Exile. Not coincidentally, that date appears in the superscription immediately following the presentation in 9.21-27 of the 70 weeks of years leading up to the end of the devastation of Jerusalem.

Details about life in Babylon for the exiles themselves are somewhat obscure, but Ezek. 3.15 indicates that some of the early deportees settled in a place named Tel-abib (location unknown) on the River Chebar, usually identified as an irrigation canal known as the 'Kabar'. Archaeologists have uncovered a number of banking records with Hebrew names at Nippur, a city southeast of Babylon. These indications suggest that many of the exiles (perhaps all but the exiled King Jehoiachin and his family) lived outside Babylon, where country homes were sometimes set in irrigated gardens. Jeremiah admonished them to build houses, plant gardens, and marry (29.4-9). His admonitions suggest they were free to pursue normal life, though not to return to Jerusalem, a prospect held out by 'false prophets' among them (Jer. 29.8). Rather they lived as conquered aliens and bore the scorn of the Babylonian populace, as Psalm 137 makes clear.

The Neo-Babylonian Empire

The neo-Babylonian Empire was relatively short-lived. Its founding reached back to the rebellion against the Assyrian Empire instigated by Nabopolassar (reigned 626–606). His son Nebuchadnezzar (605–562) actually completed the conquest of Assyria and may be reckoned the first and only great neo-Babylonian Emperor. His exploits, especially his building projects in Babylon, are legendary. Those projects included the Hanging Gardens, described by Diodorus of Sicily (*History*, 2.10). Built for his wife Amyitis, who longed for her home in Media, the gardens covered an area a hundred feet square, and built in ascending tiers. Each tier was sealed to prevent moisture from leaking through, packed with enough dirt to allow even the largest trees to take root, and planted with all kinds of vegetation. The tallest plants towered above the city wall, and, when viewed from the outside, looked like a garden suspended from above.

It was Nebuchadnezzar who sacked Jerusalem in 597, 586, and (if one accepts the accuracy of Jer. 52.30) 581. He was succeeded by Amel-Marduk (the Evil-Merodach of 2 Kgs 25.27, who ruled 562–560), from whom Neriglissar (ruled 560–56) usurped the throne. Then, in 556, the last neo-Babylonian Emperor Nabonidus usurped the throne from Neriglissar or his son Labashi-Marduk.

The end of the reign of Nabonidus in 539 is described partially in the Babylonian Chronicles (*ANET*: 306-307) and the Cyrus Cylinder (*ANET*: 315-16). For reasons not specified in the extant texts, Nabonidus spent much of his reign at the city of Teima, worshipping foreign deities there, while neglecting the New Year ceremonies connected with the Babylonian deities. Meanwhile, by 550 Cyrus the Great began his expansion from Persia, taking the Median Empire, adding Upper Mesopotamia, and even Lydia in Asia Minor in 547/6, before expanding his power eastward to Hyrcania and Parthia and campaigning in Afghanistan. By 539 he conquered the province of Elam, and its governor, the Babylonian general Gobryas (or Gubaru), began attacking the city on behalf of Cyrus (see Bright 1981: 354, 360). Acting too late, Nabonidus returned to Babylon and had the images of the various Babylonian deities brought to the city from all over the country and the ceremonies observed. When Cyrus attacked the city of Opis on the Tigris, its defenders revolted and Nabonidus had them massacred. Two days later Gobryas entered Babylon without a fight. When Nabonidus returned there from Opis, he was arrested. A couple of weeks later

Cyrus entered Babylon himself. In his second year, he issued an edict allowing the exiles who wished to return to Jerusalem.

The Median Empire

According to Dan. 5.31, it was not Cyrus, but 'Darius the Mede' who followed Belshazzar to the Babylonian throne. Traditional scholars, desiring to defend the historical accuracy of the book of Daniel, and some critical scholars as well (e.g. Albright 1921: 112; and Koch 1983: 290) identify that 'Darius' with Gobryas or some other lesser-known figure at the transition from the Babylonian to the Persian periods. Information about this 'Darius' given in 9.1 is that he was the son of Ahasueras, the name in the book of Esther for the Persian king Xerxes I (486–65), and that he was a Mede by birth. The point was made earlier that 'Darius the Mede' is likely a composite character. Nothing else need be added here.

The land of the Medes lay between the Caspian Sea and the Persian Gulf, north of Elam. The Medes were an Indo-Aryan people who had been a constant threat against Assyria from the ninth century, and who, under Cyaxares II (c. 625–585), cooperated with Babylon under Nabopolassar to revolt against Assyria and ultimately destroy it. After the fall of Assyria in 605, Cyaxares built an empire from Iran through Armenia to Asia Minor and made Ecbatana its capital. In 585 Nebuchadnezzar intervened in his westward expansion and mediated the Mede-Lydian frontier at the Halys River. Cyaxares was succeeded by his son Astyages (585–50), during whose reign Median power reached its zenith and against whom Babylon built massive fortifications. In 550, however, the Persian leader Cyrus the Great revolted against Astyages and captured Ecbatana.

The Persian Empire

In the next 11 years Cyrus waged a campaign all the way to Lydia and back to Babylon, taking that city in 539. The next year he issued an edict allowing Judeans to return to Jerusalem if they wished (Ezra 1.2-4). Following the Edict of Cyrus, the focus of the Old Testament moved back to Jerusalem and Judah, except for Daniel 1–6 and the book of Esther. From the first Cyrus claimed to treat the Babylonians with kindness, but that is the claim of a ruler and might not have been shared by his foreign subjects. It is likely that subsequent Persian rulers raided Judah and in other ways displeased their subjects, but the Persians do seem to have been easier taskmasters than the Assyrians or Babylonians before them.

Cyrus was co-regent with and then succeeded by his son Cambyses (530–22), who added Egypt to the Persian Empire in 525. In 522 a rival to Cambyses, Gautama by name, appeared and claimed to be Camby-ses' brother (whom Cambyses may have assassinated already). Civil war broke out, during which Cambyses took his life. One of his officers, Darius I, himself a member of the royal family, but not through Cambyses, claimed the Persian throne and defeated Gautama. Rebel-lions flared from Asia Minor to the eastern edge of the Persian Empire and in Egypt as well. In Babylon a man claiming to be the son of Nabonidus set himself up as king and held out against Darius I for sev-eral months. By 520, however, Darius probably controlled the empire. He it was who organized the empire into twenty satrapies, an event per-haps reflected in Dan. 6.1. No later Persian is mentioned in the book of Daniel.

The Greek Empire
The battles between the Persians and the Greeks began at the battle of Marathon in 490 and ended with the rise of Alexander the Great, who conquered Egypt and Babylon en route east. Upon the death of Alexan-der, his half-brother Philip of Aridus became nominal king for seven years, with Alexander's generals serving as military satraps. Then the generals divided the empire among themselves, reducing their number to five and then four in 301, a situation alluded to in Dan. 11.3-4. These four were Seleucus in Babylon and Phrygia, Ptolemy in Egypt, Lysi-machus in Thrace and Bithynia, and Cassander in Greece and Macedo-nia. Of the four, the only two of importance in the book of Daniel are Seleucus and Ptolemy.

For a century the Ptolemies controlled Palestine. Very little is known about their rule, though clearly the impetus for translating the Hebrew Bible into Greek must have arisen during these years. In 198, however, the Seleucid ruler Antiochus III (223–187) wrested Judah from Ptole-maic control. Once again, Judeans in Babylon and in Judah were ruled by the same overlord. This fact perhaps made resettlement from Baby-lon to Jerusalem possible for any who wished to move. More will be said below about this possibility.

Antiochus III was succeeded by his son Seleucus IV (187–75) and in turn by Seleucus's son Antiochus IV (175–63). Because of Antiochus

IV's persecution of the worshippers of Yahweh, his reign was the subject not only of Daniel 7–12, but also of some of the Maccabean corpus and of Josephus. The most important of his actions are these. (1) He replaced the high priest Onias III with a man more to his liking, Jason the brother of Onias. (2) He established a gymnasium in Jerusalem and enlisted young men in its activities, which included participating in athletic games in the nude. In an effort to be accepted as Greek, some, possibly many, young males had their circumcision surgically altered. (3) While returning home from an invasion of Egypt in 169, Antiochus IV plundered the temple in Jerusalem. At that time he may have appointed a royal commissioner, as he did in Samaria, to aid the high priest in the Hellenization of the Judeans (so Bright 1981: 421). (4) Early in 167 he sent Apollonius to Jerusalem with a large army, resulting in an armed attack on its unsuspecting inhabitants. In addition, Apollonius looted the city and destroyed part of its wall. Then he built a citadel near the temple and garrisoned Syrian troops there, thus compromising the sanctity of the temple. (5) When Antiochus saw that opposition to his efforts to Hellenize Judeans was religiously based, he issued an edict that forbade some of the practices of Judean religion. Also, he had pagan altars erected and unclean animals sacrificed upon them. (6) The crowning sin, however, occurred in December 167, when he set up an altar (and perhaps an image) to Zeus. This was the infamous 'transgression that makes desolate' (Dan. 9.27; 11.31; 12.11; 1 Macc. 1.54). Ten days later he offered an unclean sacrifice, possibly a pig, on that altar (1 Macc. 1.59; 2 Macc. 6.4-5). According to C.C. Caragounis (1989: 302) Antiochus's purpose in these actions was to substitute for Jewish belief and dependence on Yahweh not reliance upon Greek gods, for whom the Greeks themselves had little use, but a spirit of self-sufficiency in the form of freedom from and arrogance toward the divine.

These actions led to acquiescence by some Judeans, but to armed rebellion by the Maccabeans, an effort perhaps referred to in Dan. 11.34 as 'a little help'. To the group responsible for the book of Daniel, the definitive defeat would come at the hands of God, to whom alone they should remain faithful. Hence, the more or less successful outcome of the Maccabean Revolt and the subsequent Hasmonean dynasty lie beyond the purview of the book of Daniel and require no discussion here.

C. UNITY, GENRES AND LANGUAGES

If the book was not written by Daniel, but originated over a long period of time, it does not constitute a unity in the traditional sense of that term. Rowley (1952: 249-80) argued, however, that it possesses a unity stamped on it by a final redactor living in the time of the Maccabean Revolt. Rowley's insistence on one ultimate redactor was opposed by H.L. Ginsberg (1954: 246-75), who argued that the book consists of a series of narratives in chs. 1–6 from the pre-Maccabean period and the work of no less than four apocalypticists in chs. 7–12. In the years since their debate, critical scholarship has leaned more toward Ginsberg than toward Rowley on the issues of multiple authorship and the date of composition. If one should indeed reckon with the accumulation of materials over a long period of time, can one nevertheless find some kind of unity behind the book? The answer to that question is bound up with the issue of the literary genres contained in the book and with the use of two different languages, Hebrew and Aramaic, in writing the book.

Unity and Genre

As noted above, in the first six chapters the book contains six narratives about court life. W. Lee Humphreys (1973: 211-13) classified these narratives under two main types. One type he calls 'tales of court conflict', narratives in which the hero is endangered by conflict among courtiers. Daniel 3 (the fiery furnace episode) and 6 (Daniel in the lions' den) belong to this type. P.R. Davies (1980) renames this category 'tales of deliverance', and Collins (1993: 45) calls them 'tales of the disgrace and rehabilitation of a minister'. Robert R. Wilson (1981: 89) calls them broken martyr stories, a description to which some scholars have objected, but which, nevertheless, makes clear the danger to which the Hebrew youths were subjected.

The second genre Humphreys calls 'tales of court contest', in which the hero outshines other courtiers by performing some task they are unable to complete. Daniel 2, 4 and 5 belong here (compare Davies [1980: 40-41] who speaks of 'tales of interpretation'). Susan Niditch and Robert Doran (1977: 179-93) argue that Daniel 2 fits a particular type of folk-tale in which a lower-class hero solves a problem for a higher-class person and is rewarded for doing so.

Collins (1975a: 225) thinks that in Daniel 4 and 5 the prophet's message overwhelms the element of competition and becomes the dominant motif. Further, (p. 224) he places Daniel 1 in the category 'tales of court conflict'. If so, one must say the element of danger to the hero is muted in comparison to the other two narratives. Perhaps it belongs instead to the category 'tales of court contest'. Humphreys (1973: 219) places it in neither category, but treats it as an introduction to the following five narratives, which is clearly its function.

Scholars trained in folklore have objected to these categories, arguing instead for a deeper-lying structuralist understanding of the genre. They contend that one structure underlies them all. Wills (1990: 10-11) adopts the following structure from H.P. Müller (1977: 77-98).

Introduction:

(1a)   Protagonist described in respect to his or her virtue (e.g. description of Job, Joseph's dream).

(1b)   Symbolic deed which arises from the virtue, and confirmation of its worth (e.g. Job's suffering, Joseph loved by father, resented by brothers).

(1c)   Antagonists introduced, with their intermediaries (e.g. Job's wife, interlocutors, Joseph's brothers as antagonists, and king in court legends as intermediary).

Body:

(2a)   Conflict arises, instigated by virtue (e.g. Job's arguments, Joseph's brothers' conspiracy, Joseph's restraint regarding Potiphar's wife).

(2b)   Testing and proving of the virtue (e.g. Job's despair, Joseph's sojourn in Egypt).

Conclusion:

(3a)   Confirmation of virtue of protagonist through punishment of antagonists (e.g. God's answers in Job, Joseph's superior position over brothers).

(3b)   Confirmation of virtue through rewarding of protagonist (e.g. Job upheld, Joseph benefactor of family).

(3c)   Confirmation of virtue sometimes through miraculous demonstrations (e.g. Job summons God, Joseph interprets dreams).

In an attempt to reconcile the differences between form and structuralist critics, Wills (1990: 37) offers a new definition for the wisdom court legend, which will be adopted here with reference to all the court narratives: 'a legend of a revered figure set in the royal court, which has the wisdom of the protagonist as a principal motif'. Further, E.M. Good (1984: 47-63) argues that the plots of the court narratives follow the pattern of a comedy, that is, they end up on a positive note, while the plots of the apocalyptic narratives do not (but see below under the heading 'E. Plot').

The four narratives in the last half of the book belong to the genre of 'apocalypse'. This genre emerged in the Mediterranean world at the time of Alexander's conquests (Willi-Plein 1977: 68). An apocalypse may be defined as 'a genre of revelatory literature with a narrative framework, in which a revelation is mediated by an otherworldly being to a human recipient, disclosing a transcendent reality which is both temporal, insofar as it envisages eschatological salvation, and spatial, insofar as it involves another supernatural world' (Collins 1979: 9). It is 'intended to interpret present earthly circumstances in light of the supernatural world and of the future, and to influence both the understanding and the behavior of the audience by means of divine authority' (Yarbro Collins 1986: 7).

Apocalypses typically exhibit a range of literary and conceptual characteristics found in the book of Daniel. Among the literary characteristics are visions with auditions (four, obviously, in Daniel 7–12); overviews of history (all four); paranesis (lacking in Daniel 7–12, but implied in the court narratives of Daniel 1–6); coded speech (e.g. animal symbols in Daniel 7); an interpretive angel to explain the visions (e.g. an attendant in 7.16; Gabriel in 8.16 and 9.21; and a 'man' clothed in linen in 10.5-6); the disclosure of secrets (12.4); preparations and reactions on the part of the seer (7.28; 8.16, 18, 27; 9.3; 10.2-3, 8-9, 11, 15-18), and pseudonymity (Daniel, the sage from the Exile). Conceptual characteristics include the periodization of history (e.g. four kingdoms succeeded by a fifth in Daniel 7; 70 weeks in Daniel 9); the expectation of the immanent end of the age (12.6-7); calculations of the end of time (8.14; 9.24-27; 12.11-12) with limited determinism inherent in such calculations; dualism (triumph of good over evil in all four narratives plus resurrection to everlasting life or everlasting contempt in 12.2); judgment (7.9-14); and angelology (10.13, 12.1). The primary task of apocalypses is exposition of mysteries (Willi-Plein 1977: 69).

Willi-Plein (1977: 79) described two categories of apocalypses: 'event apocalyptic' ('Ereignisapokalyptik'; e.g., *1 En.* 93 + 95; 135-140; the *Assumption of Moses*; 4 Ezra; and *2 Bar.*) and 'description apocalyptic' ('Beschreibungsapokalyptik'; e.g. *2 En.*; *1 En.* 17–36; 52–82; and *3 Bar.*). Daniel would belong to the first type. Two years later the Apocalypse Group of the Society of Biblical Literature published a sixfold typology based on a primary distinction between apocalypses with and without an otherworldly journey and a secondary distinction based on the presence of cosmic and/or political eschatology versus personal eschatology. In this typology, Daniel belongs to the type called 'apocalypses with a review of history but no otherworldly journey' (Collins 1979: 30).

Generally speaking, apocalypses arise from people of any background who perceive themselves to be disadvantaged (Wilson 1981: 21, 87). This simple sentence cut the Gordian knot between scholars who derived apocalyptic literature from prophecy (e.g. Rowley 1963: 15, 42; Russell 1965: 92-96; von der Osten-Sacken 1969: 11-12, 32-33; Hanson 1975: 6); and those who derive it from wisdom (e.g. Von Rad 1965: II, 303-304; and Otzen 1990: 227-28). Self-perception seems to be the key here; apocalyptic groups think of themselves as at least relatively deprived. A given apocalypse articulates a group's program to improve its situation. The specific shape of the program will depend on the background of the group itself (Wilson 1981: 84-87).

What kind of group stood behind Daniel 7–12, and was there any relationship between that group and the group standing behind Daniel 1–6? Plöger (1968: 7-9, 23-24) and Hengel (1974: I, 202-203) advance the position followed by a number of scholars (e.g. Lacocque 1993: 320-25; Hartman and Di Lella 1978: 43-45; Trevor 1985: 89-102; and Towner 1969: 6-8) that Daniel derived from the hasidim, a group known from the time of the Maccabean Revolt. Collins (1993: 67-69) shows, however, that the hasidim were far more militaristic and pro-Hasmonean than the group behind Daniel. John G. Gammie (1981: 282-92) pointed to the parallels between Daniel on the one hand and Job, Proverbs, Second Isaiah (cf. Nicol 1979: 501-505), and even the Priestly tradition on the other in a warning not to jump too quickly to a single origin for Daniel. It is necessary, then, to look further for the origin of the book.

Wilson (1981: 88) suggests that the book itself provides information helpful in that search. One should probably assume that the type of people most likely to cultivate narratives about Judean wise men succeeding in the courts of foreign kings were Diaspora Judeans trying hard to succeed in foreign cultures or even would-be Judean bureau-crats hoping to gain similar positions of service in foreign courts. Since the court narratives focus on Babylon, and since that city was the home of many Diaspora Judeans, one may probably assume the collectors of those narratives lived in Babylon (though the nearby city of Seleucia or even the western capital of Antioch can not be ruled out).

God granted the four young Judeans of Daniel 1 'knowledge and skill in every aspect of literature and wisdom' (NRSV), clearly skills valuable to any scribe. Daniel 2.21 records a prayer of praise to God for giving wisdom to the wise, and in Dan. 4.9 Nebuchadnezzar calls upon Daniel, for whom no mystery is too difficult, to interpret a dream his wise men could not interpret. The queen mother in Dan. 5.11 calls Belshazzar's attention to Daniel's wisdom, which the king acknowledges in 5.14. The point is clear: Daniel is a wise man, the ideal of the collector(s) of the court narratives.

The people for whom God sends messages to Daniel in Daniel 7–12 are also called the 'wise' in 12.3, 10. Hence, a number of scholars (e.g. Collins 1993: 66-67) have concluded that the 'wise' of Daniel 7–12 were the same group for whom the narratives of Daniel the wise man were collected. The differences were those of time (Dan. 7–12 focused on the Maccabean period, while Dan. 1–6 seems earlier) and locale (Dan. 7–12 focused on Jerusalem and Palestine, while Dan. 1–6 focus on the Diaspora). Also, H.P. Müller (1972: 268-91) and Reid (1989: 132-36) conclude the group may be called mantic in some sense, because its particular type of wisdom is divinatory. Reid (1989: 131) adds that Daniel 7–8, 10–12 manifested 'a quietistic, revolutionist/non-resistant perspective' (i.e., it anticipated a new world, but declined to fight for it). He also describes the group as anti-Seleucid and anti-Anti-ochen, though not anti-Hellenistic (p. 134). Bauer (1996: 199) argues that the chapter betrays a one-sided sympathy for the Ptolemies, supplemented by anti-Seleucid additions, but sympathy for Ptolemies is nowhere explicit. It is better to say that the whole chapter exhibits a one-sided antithesis against the Seleucids, which may be attributed to the circumstances in which the group for which it was written found itself.

It is possible to say more about the history of that group. Among the court narratives, Daniel 2 presupposes the Babylonian Empire and three successors kingdoms, understood by the final editor of the book to be

Media, Persia and Greece. One might assume, then, that Daniel 2 was composed during the last of those, the Greek period. Daniel 5 narrates events to explain the fall of the Babylonian Empire to the 'Median', and Daniel 6 speaks of the 'laws of the Medes and the Persians', so they presuppose dates of composition during the Persian Empire if not later. An ever-increasing number of critical scholars, therefore, conclude that the court narratives achieved their present form during the late Persian and the Greek periods, though some of them may be Israelite adaptations of earlier, even foreign, traditions.

The Judeans who collected and adapted these narratives would have experienced more or less benevolent treatment at the hands of the Persians (but see the caveat of Smith-Christopher 1996: 27-30, that scholars have seen the Persians entirely too kindly). When Antiochus III captured Palestine from the Ptolemies in 198 (to the great joy of the inhabitants of Judah, if Josephus [*Ant.* 12.3.3 line 138] is to be believed), the 'wise' would have taken advantage of the new political reality by moving there from Babylon, taking their court narratives with them. Unfortunately, any benefit they may have hoped to gain by moving to Judah was lost during the attempt to Hellenize Judeans by Antiochus IV.

U. Rappaport (1992: 222-23) calls attention to the intimate knowledge of Greek history in Daniel 11. It recounts event after event in the relationship between the Seleucids and the Ptolemies in remarkable detail. Such an interest is without parallel in other extant Israelite literature from the time; even the authors of 1 and 2 Maccabees showed far less concern. Rappaport also notes that those details are not simply reported in a straightforward manner, but in a disguised form. He suggests that the author may have adopted a non-Greek source or else have assembled the list of events himself. W.G. Lambert (1978: 15) argues that the closest parallels to Daniel 11 come from Babylon and could have been transmitted either in Greek or Aramaic.

It may be possible to push those observations a little farther for hints about the group behind the book. The fact that the historical information is disguised means, of course, that the author is not attempting to convey to the readers new information; instead he presupposes they will share and understand the references to the Seleucids and Ptolemies. If one asks what group of people in ancient Palestine would share such detailed information about the relationship between the Seleucids and the Ptolemies right down to 165, the answer probably is a group of Judeans employed by the Seleucids in some kind of scribal capacity (see Redditt 1998: 463-74). Heaton (1956: 22-24, 44) calls the group scribal, and distinguishes the author from Ben Sira, but does not identify the author or his group any further. If they were scribes, one can immediately understand their interest in narratives of Judeans in the employment of a foreign king. If they lived in Jerusalem, one can understand their abhorrence of Antiochus Epiphanes.

These observations correlate well with the views of Davies (1980: 33-53), who argues that the apocalyptic narratives represent an organic growth out of the court narratives during the Maccabean period. Moving a step toward Rowley from Ginsberg, Davies argues (p. 34) 'that the tales were re-read in the Maccabean period when they came to be understood in a slightly different way; and that the visions arise directly out of this re-reading and were composed as a contemporary application of the message of the stories, to which they were intended to form a sequel or supplement'. Further (p. 44), this sequel took the form of reviews of history, whose purpose was to reveal to 'the wise' the secret that the time in which the reader lived was the culmination of history, a history that began with Nebuchadnezzar and ended with Antiochus IV. Davies continues (p. 45) that the court narratives demonstrated both to Diaspora Judean and to Maccabean readers two points: (1) God was sovereign over history, and (2) God was able to deliver his servants in a time of danger. The court narratives also helped to answer new questions in the minds of Palestinian readers: Why this persecution? Why now when things seemed to be looking up? And why is there no divine deliverance? The answer to these questions was that they were participating in a universal historic drama, whose denouement was at hand in the imminent triumph of God's judgment and rule.

Davies (1993: 352-57) discusses three symbols used in the book of Daniel that help reveal more about this group. The first is the word 'book', employed in 1.4, 17 and 12.1, 4. The act of writing itself also plays a role, so that one may say that the book of Daniel often conveys significance by mentioning books or writing. Writing and reading books, however, was the prerogative of an elite group with the leisure to pursue the activity. Also, such activity was a means of wielding power, an attractive alternative to this group that, Davies argues, following the 'hunch' of Reid (1989: 135), constituted a 'falling elite'. While Davies refuses to call the group 'sectarian', one may add that the group certainly looks peripheral in its own society. (An excellent discussion of peripheral groups may be found in Cook 1995: Chapters 2 and 3.)

The second symbol was the court. Davies disagrees with Collins's view that the group had no political ambitions, noting that the court narratives certainly show they did not reject the lifestyle of the servant in the foreign court. Rather, 'the court is a positive symbol, the natural home and setting of the author's imagination' (1993: 356; cf. Wilson 1981: 88). Fewell even speaks of 'a politically aspiring Daniel', one who 'fully expects to participate in the establishment of God's kingdom and...in the physical, religious, and political restoration of Jerusalem' (1988: 158). To be sure, the book of Daniel does not advocate revolution, and its view of the future involves the intervention of God, but those features in no way preclude hopes for present and future participation in the political processes.

The third symbol was the device of the 'secret'. That device holds the two sections of the book together. In the court narratives God first reveals secrets to Daniel, who in turn reveals them to others, for example Nebuchadnezzar, and the emphasis lies on Daniel's public explanation of these secrets. In the apocalyptic narratives God still reveals secrets to Daniel, specifically through an interpreting angel, and the emphasis lies on the process of the revelation.

The knowledge of the secrets granted the group an alternative kind of power and led them to think that they might reasonably expect to gain power of a reconformed type. Davies (1993: 358-61) examines the nature of that power in connection with two institutions: monarchy and temple. In the court narratives the sovereignty of God could be exercised through a Gentile monarch, suggesting that the 'wise' may well have looked forward to a role in God's exercise of power in the future. In the absence of the temple during the Exile, the 'wise' turn to prayer; in the absence of sacrifice, they embrace suffering. Davis observes: 'In each case it is possible to detect both an adherence to the values of an established state of affairs and also the framing of an alternative' (p. 361).

Unity and Languages

As mentioned above, the issue of the unity of the book of Daniel is bound up also with the fact that the book was written in two languages, Hebrew (1.1–2.4a; 8.1–12.13) and Aramaic (2.4b–7.28). Scholars have debated the use of two languages for years, sometimes suggesting the entire book was written in Hebrew and partly translated into Aramaic or vice versa. The Aramaized Hebrew makes the first option unlikely, and neither option is really satisfactory. Why translate half a book?

The other way to account for the phenomenon is to assume that some of the materials were written in Aramaic and others in Hebrew. The issue then is how they were joined. James E. Miller (1991: 115-24) argues that an Aramaic document (Daniel 2–7) and a Hebraic document (Daniel 1–2, 8–12) were redacted along similar lines and united by 7.1-2a. He hypothesizes that Daniel 2, the chapter in which the transition from Hebrew to Aramaic is made, existed in both documents, with the result that the author could begin in one language and switch to the other.

Collins suggests that Daniel 1 was composed in Aramaic as an introduction to the court narratives and translated into Hebrew when the remaining apocalyptic narratives were added (1993: 24, 35-38). Collins also argues that Daniel 7 was composed in the Maccabean era and was dependent on Daniel 2. He adds that Daniel 8–12 was added slightly later by a different hand, and explains the switch to Hebrew as a result of the enthusiasm of the Maccabean period. For the most part, Collins seems to be correct. It is not clear, however, why someone who was producing a dual-language book would bother to translate a whole chapter from one language to the other.

A.S. van der Woude (1986: 305-16) agrees that the first vision narrative, Daniel 7, was composed and added to the other court narratives in the second century, but notes (p. 310) that redactional touches in ch. 7 were few and easily composed in Aramaic. (As will be shown below, those touches may well have been fewer even than van der Woude suggests.) He also agrees that an Aramaic-language introduction preceded the court narratives in Daniel 2–6. With regard to Daniel 1, however, he notes first that 1.1-2 was composed from 2 Chron. 36.6-7, which, of course, was written in Hebrew. Secondly, 1.8-16 is an addition to the account of the conscription of Daniel and his three friends to learn the Akkadian language and literature. Thirdly, 2.1-4a is a Hebrew-language lead-in to the first Aramaic-language court narrative. Thus, of the first 24½ verses of the book of Daniel, at least 14½ (1.1-2, 8-16; 2.1-4a) were composed by the author of the Hebrew sections of the book or adopted from Hebrew traditions (van der Woude 1986: 311-12). If, as seems likely, he worked from an Aramaic original of Daniel 1, that introduction was of an unknown length. Apparently, he chose to translate or rewrite only that part of the original introduction that he needed: namely, that Daniel and his friends had been students at Nebuchadnezzar's court. His decision to write in Hebrew probably was bound up with his rising nativism.

Summary
If the observations in this whole section are correct, the book of Daniel derived from a group of Diaspora Judeans who thought of themselves as 'the wise' and who moved from Babylon to Jerusalem after Antiochus III wrested Palestine from the Ptolemies. Unfortunately for them, conditions deteriorated in Judah and Jerusalem under Antiochus IV, causing the group to experience deprivation and to become apocalyptic. By the time of the 'transgression that makes desolate' in December of 167, the writer for the group switched from Aramaic to Hebrew, in which language Dan. 1.1–2.4a and Daniel 8–12 were composed. One may then perhaps speak of a unity of authorship in Daniel in terms both of an organic growth from the court narratives to the apocalyptic narratives and of an ongoing group with a final editor. As will be shown below, his hand can be detected throughout the entire book.

D. LITERARY HISTORY

Dates of the Individual Chapters
In view of these observations, it is time to sketch the major contours of the literary history of the book of Daniel. The place to begin is with the individual chapters themselves. The hypothesized Aramaic version of Daniel 1 was truncated and rewritten when it became the introduction to Daniel 2–12 and not just 2–7. Hence, the original version is almost impossible to date. The insertion in 1.8-16 about following dietary regulations could, of course, derive from the time of the efforts of Antiochus IV to force Judeans to consume meat, but Ginsberg (1954: 256) cautions that dietary regulations were strictly observed by some Judeans even in late Persian/early Greek times (cf. Tob. 1.10-11).

Daniel 2 is also difficult to date. Ida Fröhlich (1993: 266-70) argues that it was originally a sixth-century narrative about the history of the Babylonian Empire from Nebuchadnezzar to Nabonidus and that the stone that crushed the image would have originally been Cyrus. (See also Labonté, 1993: 283-84.)

As it stands, however, it deals with four empires. The background was the idea of four succeeding world ages, which idea predated the ancient Greek poet Hesiod (flourished c. 800). He modified a tradition that employed the four metals of gold, silver, bronze, and iron, metals of descending value. Further, a Persian text *Bahman Yasht* included the same four metals, with the added feature (like Daniel) that the iron was mixed with clay (see Collins 1993: 162-65).

These traditions help explain the sequence of empires in the book of Daniel. Assyria, of course, was replaced by Babylon due to the setting of the story during Babylonian Exile. Media, however, never ruled over Israel, so its inclusion suggests that the tradition originated somewhere in Persia, where the sequence Assyria → Media → Persia made good sense. Alternatively, C.C. Caragounis argues the inclusion of Media simply reflects the situation in Babylon as real power passed from the Babylonians to the Medes before the fall of the Medes to Cyrus in 550 (1993: 394).

Even the replacement of the four empires by a fifth was known in the ancient world. Collins (1993: 167) points out that Polybius, a Roman author from the late second century, was the earliest writer known today to add Rome to the sequence as a final empire and that Vellius Paterculus, from about the turn of the Christian era, named four kingdoms (Assyria, Media, Persia and Greece) as those that preceded Rome.

The author of Daniel 2 simply adapted the sequence to fit the history of Israel. Gese (1983: 143) thinks the mention in 2.43 of a marriage referred to that of Ptolemy V to Cleopatra, daughter of Antiochus III, in 194, the last dateable event in the chapter. That verse, however, is widely viewed as an addition to the text, meaning that the chapter itself is probably earlier, almost certainly before 200.

Perhaps the best reconstruction of the history of Daniel 2 is that of Davies (1970: 392-401). He begins at the end of that history with a redactor of the Maccabean period who inserted 2.13-23. These verses portray Daniel as one of the wise men at the court included in the king's threat to kill all the wise men for their failure to relate and interpret his dream, whereas the rest of the story assumes that he was unknown to the king. Also, Davies thinks (perhaps incorrectly) the note that this event occurred in the second year of Nebuchadnezzar's reign contradicts the three-year apprenticeship Daniel had served in the first chapter. Further, 2.13-23 and 2.49 are the only verses that mention the friends and presuppose ch. 1, which introduces the characters and gives their double names. Hence, 2.49 must be attributed to that redactor as well. (In this commentary, that redactor will eventually be called the second redactor, or R2.)

The next earlier version developed the idea that the statue represented four successive kingdoms, which were Babylon, Media, Persia and Greece. The identification with Greece had already been made prior to the addition in 2.41-43, which Davies (agreeing with Ginsberg) thinks referred to the marriage of Antiochus II and Bernice in 252, not the marriage in 194 between Ptolemy V and Cleopatra. If so, the narrative spoke of four kingdoms by the middle of the third century.

The earliest version of the narrative, however, appeared in the sixth century, before or after the fall of Babylon. In this version the motif of four successively inferior kings (not kingdoms) referred to Nebuchadnezzar, Amel-Marduk, Neriglissar and Nabonidus. The brittle toes of the statue, comprised of iron mixed with clay, referred originally to the kingdom in its last days under Nabonidus, when he sojourned in Teima and left Belshazzar in charge in Babylon.

Daniel 3 is likewise difficult to date, despite the attempts of traditional scholars to see Daniel as an office holder in the Babylonian Empire or of Rowley to see the image erected by Nebuchadnezzar as a substitute for the image Antiochus IV erected in the temple area. Persian influence may be detected in the preponderance of Persian titles among the list of officers in 3.2 (Collins 1993a: 182), while Greek influence appears in the list of musical instruments mentioned in 3.5, 7, 10 and 15, which Pierre Grelot (1979: 23-38) argues were common to Mesopotamia in the Seleucid period or in Hellenized regions of Syro-Phoenicia. Finally, F.H. Polak (1993: 259) points to the preference of verbs preceding objects in this chapter (and also the other 'martyr story' in Daniel 6), which he claims, following E.Y. Kutscher (1952: 123-27) is characteristic of Western rather than Eastern Official Aramaic, suggesting a Palestinian place of origin. By contrast Koch (1980: 46-47) used Kutscher's analysis to show an eastern provenance for the court narratives as a whole. Either way, Daniel 3 appears to have grown through the years, taking its present form in the Greek period, perhaps even in Palestine.

Of equal importance is the observation that Daniel does not appear in ch. 3. The heroes, rather, are Shadrach, Meshach and Abednego, who in the original form of this narrative may have been Babylonians. Their story was picked up and used here, among other reasons, to balance the story of Daniel in the lions' den. They were introduced to the reader in Daniel 1 and in 2.49, but were not mentioned again after ch. 3. The author 'Judaized' them by giving them the Hebrew names Hananiah,

Mishael and Azariah in Daniel 1, names Lacocque (1979: 29) thinks were taken from the lists of exiles who returned to Jerusalem in Neh. 8.4 and 10.3. Smith-Christopher (1996: 28) points out that name changing was one way to enforce the subordination of slaves and servants, so retaining their Babylonian names was possibly an indication that the authors of the book of Daniel felt bitter toward the Babylonians and the Persians.

The renaming of Daniel perhaps takes on an additional element in ch. 4, where Daniel is called Belteshazzar. It was not unusual in Hebrew Scriptures for a devout Yahwist to receive a Babylonian name (e.g. Zerubbabel), and dual names—one Hebrew and one foreign—appear in connection with Joseph in Gen. 41.45 and Esther in Est. 2.7. Further, Dan. 1.7; 2.26; 5.12; and 10.1 also equate Daniel with Belteshazzar. The crucial text, however, is Daniel 4, where Nebuchadnezzar says the name was taken from his god. 'Belteshazzar' was deliberately modified from its Akkadian form (*balat-su-usur* or *balat-sar-usar*) to include the name Bel or Marduk, the chief god of Babylon (Collins 1993: 141). Nebuchadnezzar's comment sets up the irony in the chapter; it will be Israel's God, not Nebuchadnezzar's, who will help Belteshazzar. The name, then, appears to be an ad hoc creation of R2 for polemical effect.

Daniel 4 is the story of Nebuchadnezzar's descent into the animal kingdom and return to the human level. The *Prayer of Nabonidus* discovered at Qumran contains a similar narrative about the seven-year madness of Nabonidus, the last Babylonian king, who was healed through the help of an unnamed Judean exile. (See Collins 1996: 83-93.) Its discovery confirms a long-held suspicion that Daniel 4 originally dealt with him rather than Nebuchadnezzar. That discovery does not help with the date much, except to suggest that the story would have originated in the Persian period rather than the Babylonian and the assimilation to Nebuchadnezzar would have come later still. Similarly, H.-F. Richter (1993: 246) argues that MT 4.7-14 (NRSV 4.10-17) was an earlier song about the fall of the Babylonian Empire reworked into a dream of Nebuchadnezzar.

Another possible indicator of a later date for the chapter is the use of the term 'Chaldean' to mean something like 'magician' instead of designating the ethnic identity of the rulers of the Neo-Babylonian Empire. Baldwin objects that the term already had this secondary use by Herodotus in the fifth century, so it does not prove a Maccabean date (1978: 28-29).

Of more help is the fact that Eusebius cites a Chaldean document from about 300 BCE that may well have been the source of 4.29-33a. Koch (1993: 86) argues that those verses constitute an addition, which would mean the chapter could have taken its basic shape earlier. By contrast, R. Stahl (1993: 494) thinks the reference to 'seven times' in verses 16, 23, 25 and 32 betrays a development of thinking dateable to c. 200 BCE. Perhaps the most one can say is that Daniel 4 probably underwent growth throughout the Persian period and took its final shape in the Ptolemaic period.

Daniel 5 tells of a feast at the court of Belshazzar. Traditional scholars (e.g. Hasel 1981: 43; Waltke 1976: 328; Miller 1994: 147-50; and Walvoord 1971: 114-15) point to the accurate preservation of the name Belshazzar as a figure in Babylonian history as an argument for the historicity of the chapter and then argue for an exilic date for the chapter, but the historical problems associated with Daniel 5 do not permit such a date. P.R. Davies (1980: 35), on the other hand, suspects the whole narrative may be Maccabean in date of origin, but it too probably underwent a long period of growth like the other court narratives.

Daniel 6 makes perfectly good sense as a narrative set in the time of Darius I (ruled 522–486), who was well known for dividing the Persian Empire into twenty satrapies or provinces. Indeed, but for the redactional notes in 5.31; 9.1; and 11.1 calling him 'the Mede', probably no one would have ever assumed any other setting. Thus, while there is no trace of any other hero in the story than Daniel, one should reckon again with the possibility that a story from the Persian period with a later Israelite (or even non-Israelite) hero was assimilated to the exilic figure Daniel.

The court narratives reveal themselves to have been narratives from the Persian and the Greek periods, with later editing. What is the situation with the apocalyptic narratives? The three Hebrew-language visions (Dan. 8.1-27; 9.1-27; and 10.1–12.4) focus on the events of the Maccabean period, but the outcome of those events was a matter of genuine prediction. The visions refer to the 'transgression that makes desolate' in 8.13; 9.27; and 11.31, but do not know the actual circumstances of the death of Antiochus or the cleansing of the temple, both in 164. Hence, they were written between the defiling of the temple in December of 167 and its cleansing in December of 164. Collins (1990: 97) suggests more specific dates: chs. 8 and 9 appear to have been written shortly after the 'transgression' with which they are so concerned;

vv. 10.1–12.4 comes a little later and take a broader picture; and 12.5-13 was written very soon after the temple was rededicated and the end did not come.

Collins (1993: 400) argues that Dan. 12.5-13 was secondary to the narrative in 10.1–12.4 on the basis of two observations. First, 12.10 picks up 11.35, which anticipates that some of the 'wise' who had been teaching the 'many' (11.33) would be martyred and thus 'refined, purified, and cleansed' presumably by their martyrs' death. In 12.10, however, the distinction between the 'wise' and the 'many' is blurred, suggesting a second hand. Secondly, vv. 11-12 recalculate the time of the end. Collins seems to be correct about 12.5-12, but v. 13 is another matter. While vv. 11-12 answer the question posed in v. 6, v. 13 actually refers to the doctrine of the resurrection discussed in v. 2, making the point that Daniel himself will be among those raised. It seems likely, therefore, that v. 13 originally belonged 10.1–12.4, but when 12.5-12 was added v. 13 was left at the end to conclude the book.

Two further observations can be made. (1) One may say that 12.5-12 *functions* as an epilogue to the book as a whole, not just 10.1–12.4 (13), because, for example, v. 7 reaches back to the phrase 'a time, times, and a half' in 7.25, and vv. 11-12 recalculate that timetable. (2) Verses 11-12 recalculate the time that would pass before the anticipated 'end', and constitute a single calculation, not two (Gese 1991: 417-21). The verses predict events that were to come to pass within 1335 days of the desecration of the temple. Thus, in its *present* form the epilogue originated before that day, that is before 5 August 163.

Daniel 7 is different from chs. 8–12 in that it makes no reference to the abomination; hence, it was likely written before 7 December 167. Gese (1991: 404), calculates the date of the chapter as early August 167. Scholars sometimes postulate numerous additions to an earlier narrative, but that conclusion is debatable. Ernst Haag (1993: 176-82) thinks in terms of a basic document from the Davidic Zion tradition, with elaboration first through the four kingdom tradition and secondly by means of the 'enemy of God' tradition. Haag overlooks several factors incompatible with his reconstruction. For one thing, the chapter builds on Daniel 2, which already provided the overall framework of four world kingdoms condemned by divine judgment and replaced by the kingdom of God, thus accounting for much in the chapter. Secondly, the scenes in heaven (7.9-10, 13-14) indicate the heavenly origin of the judgment on the fourth kingdom and are not additions. Thirdly, the chapter may have utilized images from Canaanite mythology (so Collins 1977: 104, but opposed by Ferch 1980: 75-86). If Collins is right, his observation would add weight to the suggestion that the chapter was composed in Judah (and, thus, after 198 or so) rather than Babylon. (See also Collins 1993b: 121-36, particularly 135.)

Van der Woude restricts the additions to the references to Antiochus Epiphanes in 7.8, 11a, 12, 20-21, 24-25. He thinks that without those verses the vision would have predicted the demise of the Seleucids, with the other successors to Alexander's empire continuing to exist a while. Even this limited excision of verses might be superfluous. Though van der Woude thinks the *Vorlage* preceded the Maccabean revision by some time, his truncated version would seem to imply special punishment of the Seleucids. It is not clear, though, that they had done anything deserving divine reproach before the time of Antiochus IV. To be sure, Seleucus IV had attempted to gain control of private funds left with the temple for security (2 Macc. 3.4-40), but he was such a weak man he would hardly be described as one who overthrew kings. If one is then left with the period of Antiochus Epiphanes as the subject of the original version of the narrative, why eliminate all verses that mention him?

It would appear, rather, that the chapter arose as a response to the actions of Antiochus IV in the early years of his reign, probably after he plundered the temple in 169 BCE but before December of 167. On the other hand, calling him a 'little horn' in v. 8 seems out of place in the middle of a description of his exploits and appears nowhere else in Daniel 7. It may have been read back from 8.9 to equate the two horns. Conversely, the phrase 'little horn' may have been original and only described the horn in its early stages. In that case, the author of 8.9 picked up the phrase to ensure that the reader identified the two.

Three Editions of the Book

How did these diverse materials come together to form the book of Daniel? A. Jepsen (1961: 391) concludes that the book underwent three recensions. The first included Daniel 4, 5, 6, and 10 + 12; the second added Daniel 2, 7 (in its original version), and 8, and the third added Daniel 1; 3; 7.7b-8, 11a, 18-26; 8.9-14, 23-26; and 11.2-45. The problem with his reconstruction is that it ignores differences in language and literary genre. Collins (1993a: 37) works with these two considerations in view. He suggests that chs. 4–6 may have constituted the first collection. The primary reason for this suggestion is that the Old Greek version of these three chapters diverges markedly from that of Theodotian and from the MT. This anomaly is best explained by the hypothesis that these three chapters circulated independently, developing different texts, before the remaining chapters were added to both text traditions. (See also Wills 1990: 144-47.) The redactor of this first edition will be referred to as R1.

The second edition probably would have included all the Aramaic materials, plus an introduction in Aramaic. This conclusion is debatable. Many scholars would separate Daniel 7 from Daniel 1–6, and that is certainly possible. On the other hand, the Aramaic narratives display a chiastic structure that suggests one redactor (= R2).

2.4b-49. A dream about four world kingdoms replaced by a fifth
   3.1-30. Three friends in the fiery furnace
      4.1-47. Daniel interprets a dream for Nebuchadnezzar
      5.1-31. Daniel interprets the handwriting on the wall for Belshazzar
   6.1-28. Daniel in the lions' den
7.1-28. A vision about four world kingdoms replaced by a fifth

This collection would also have had an introduction in Aramaic, but its length and full contents are now unknown, since it was incorporated into the new Hebrew introduction. Daniel 7 may well have been composed for its place in this edition. The date of this second edition would have been the same as Daniel 7, that is, between 169 and 167. That date also marks the point at which the 'wise' began expressing themselves in apocalyptic language.

R2 left several other indicators of his work. W.S. Towner (1969: 319-25) has shown that the doxologies inserted secondarily in 2.20-23; 4.3, 34b-35; and 6.26b-27 are Psalm-like songs composed for their place in Daniel. They offer praise to Israel's God, especially for God's eternality, and they express the import of what the celebrant has just learned from his experience. They deal with the question of theodicy, and proclaim that God, not evil, will triumph eventually. All but the first are placed upon the lips of unlikely speakers, namely foreign kings. What Towner does not note is that the language about God's eternality also shows up in the heavenly scenes of Daniel 7, particularly vv. 14 and 27. All these verses provide continuity in the second edition of Daniel.

Another trace of R2's work may be found in Dan. 1.3-7; 2.26, 49; 4.8, 19; 5.12. Daniel 1.3-7 appears to be a remnant from the Aramaic introduction, and those verses identify Belteshazzar with Daniel and

Shadrach, Meshach and Abednego with Hananiah, Mishael and Azariah. These identifications appear also in 2.26; 4.8, 19; and 5.12 as touches which should be attributed to R2. Also, Davies (1970: 394) shows that 2.49 belongs with the same redactor. The identification of Daniel and Belteshazzar also appears in 10.1, which was composed later. That verse came from the hand of the author of chs. 8–12 (to be called R3 in this commentary), who drew the identifications from the original version of Daniel 1, which he rewrote.

Daniel 4 betrays signs of further editing by R2. The Old Greek preserves what may have been R1's version of the narrative. It opens with Nebuchadnezzar having a dream about a great tree. In the dream an angel (not a watcher as in the MT) speaks, commanding someone to chop down the tree. Rising early in the morning, Nebuchadnezzar calls upon Daniel (who is not here called Belteshazzar) to interpret for him, which Daniel does. A year later, the dream came true. Nebuchadnezzar was shackled seven years, at which time he prayed to God. The narrative may have continued with God's forgiveness, but as it now stands it contains a one-verse description of Nebuchadnezzar reduced to a beast, apparently an addition from the MT version developing alongside of it. Upon receiving forgiveness, Nebuchadnezzar circulated a letter praising Yahweh and commanding people to sacrifice to him.

The MT shows considerable reworking. It opens (4.1-18) and closes (4.34-37) as a first person singular proclamation attributed to Nebuchadnezzar, into each section of which R2 has inserted a doxology (4.3, 34b-35. The letter is moved to the beginning of the chapter (becoming vv. 1-3) to tie it to Daniel 3. In 4.1-18 Nebuchadnezzar says he had suffered a bad dream, recounts the failure of his magicians to interpret it and the arrival of Belteshazzar, relates the dream to Belteshazzar, and requests that he interpret it. In 4.34-37 Nebuchadnezzar says that his reason and his kingdom returned to him. In between, 4.28-33 is a third person narrative of events a year after his meeting with Belteshazzar. It forms one piece with the interpretation of Nebuchadnezzar's dream in 4.19-27, the first verse of which made the switch from first to third person. The narrative came from R1, though in a somewhat different order from the MT. However, the moving of the original ending to the beginning of the narrative, the addition of the doxologies in vv. 3 and 34b-35, the appearance of the Babylonian wise men in vv. 6-7, references to the 'holy watcher' in v. 13 and the 'watchers' in v. 17, the reference to 'seven times' (not 'years' as in the Old Greek) in v. 17, and the behavior of Nebuchadnezzar in eating grass in v. 33 are revisions by R2.

A comparison of the MT and the Old Greek of Daniel 5 also reveals redactional additions that should be ascribed to R2. In 5.6, R2 added an insulting description of the physiological effect the writing on the wall had on Belshazzar. In 5.10 the queen mother comes to the banquet unbidden, while in the Old Greek Belshazzar sends for her. The list of officials in 5.11, missing in the Old Greek, is taken from 4.11. R2 adds vv. 18-21, which summarize Daniel 4, and also adds the transition sentence in v. 17b. Finally, R2 puts the actual words of the writing on the wall just prior to their explanation, whereas they appear only in the preface to Daniel 5 in the Old Greek.

R2's additions to Daniel 6 are fewer and less significant. In 6.5 those conspiring against Daniel explicitly state that they will be able to trap Daniel only through his pious lifestyle. In 6.13 the conspirators refer to Daniel as one of the exiles from Judah. Since the chapter nowhere explains the reference, it apparently presumes Daniel 1. Finally, the concluding doxology in vv. 26-27 is longer than the parallel statement in the Old Greek. It is the last of the doxologies isolated by Towner and reflects 4.2-3 in particular.

The third stage of the growth of the book of Daniel involved the addition of the Hebrew chapters to the Aramaic collection, probably though not necessarily by one hand (R3). Whether one person or several, R3 was both an author and a redactor. R3 composed Daniel 1 from Hebrew sources and the Aramaic introductory chapter. As mentioned above, 1.1-2 was composed from 2 Chron. 36.6-7; 1.8-16 was R3's own addition to the Aramaic account of the conscription of Daniel and his three friends to learn the Chaldean (Akkadian) language and literature; and 2.1-4a is his Hebrew-language lead-in to the first Aramaic narrative. He also truncated, translated or rewrote, and perhaps modified in other ways the original Aramaic version of Daniel 1.

He composed Daniel 8–12 in the present sequence. Daniel 8 presupposes the 'little horn' of Daniel 7; Daniel 9 presupposes the cessation of the sacrifice mentioned in Daniel 8; and Daniel 10–12 draws out in more detail the whole history the other narratives have alluded to (see Davies 1980: 36). To be sure, the prayer in Daniel 9 seems stylistically different from the rest of the chapter and probably was composed by someone else, but Davies (p. 62) shows that it fits its context because it too portrays the ravages of the temple by Antiochus in the context of the Exile. As mentioned above, Ginsberg (1954: 246-75) argued for four different hands in Daniel 7–12, and he points to 'revisions' in one or more narratives by each of the later apocalypticists. On the whole, it seems more likely that one hand generated these last three apocalyptic narratives (8.1–12.4) after the desecration of the temple in 167 but before its reconsecration in 164. That hand probably was responsible as well for the epilogue shortly after the rededication of the temple.

What is more, the arrangement of the narratives in Daniel 7–12 probably drew upon two patterns. Katrina J.A. Larkin (1994: 238-39) develops the view of Michael Fishbane that Daniel 7–12 constitutes a mantological anthology (i.e. a collection of exegetical passages designed to resolve cognitive problems). Such anthologies form a ring construction around a centerpiece, such as the Shepherd Allegory (Zech. 11.4-17) in Zechariah 9–14. In Daniel, chs. 7 and 8 offer symbolic visions, while Daniel 10–12 speak allusively about the history of Israel's experience in the Greek Empire. Daniel 9 stands as the centerpiece. Alone in Daniel 7–12 its point of departure is a passage of Scripture.

In addition, George G. Nicol (1979: 501-505) points to seven correspondences between Dan. 7.1–10.16 and the report of Isaiah's vision in Isa. 6.1-10 that guide the placement of materials within Daniel 7–12:

1.	The date formula	Isa.	6.1	//	Dan.	7.1
2.	The throne and its occupant		6.1	//		7.9
3.	The divine beings in attendance		6.2	//		7.10
4.	The confession		6.5	//		9.23
5.	The flight of a divine being		6.6	//		9.21
6.	The word about understanding		6.9-10	//		9.23
7.	The touching of the lips		6.7	//		10.16

(He notes that the seventh correspondence is followed in both cases by a long address from a divine being.) All but Dan. 7.9-10 derive from the hand of R3, who may well have seen in 7.9-10 the kinship to Isaiah 6 and built upon it.

The problem that Daniel 7 shares characteristics with both halves of the larger book of Daniel is now resolved. On the one hand, it was written in Aramaic and concluded the second edition in symmetry with Daniel 2. On the other hand, it was the last written chapter in that collection, in which chapter the move was made to make Daniel a seer of visions and not only an interpreter of the dreams of others.

Other notable concerns shared by Dan. 8.1–12.4 include (1) the 'transgression that makes desolate' (8.13; 9.27; and 11.31), (2) calculations of the end of time (the 'time, times, and half' of 7.25, 2,300 evenings and mornings in 8.14. and 70 weeks of years in 9.20-27), and (3) a concentration on Daniel. This last observation should not be overlooked. R3 inherited an Aramaic document that had perhaps assimilated narratives about a number of persons, reducing them to four heroes, the most important being Daniel. R3, however, added three more narratives about Daniel. The existence of the apocryphal materials Bel and the Dragon, Susanna, and The Prayer of Azariah and the Song of the Three Young Men suggests that R3 had other traditions to draw from. (In fact, J.C.H. Lebram 1982: 514 raises the possibility that the story of Susanna in the LXX of Daniel may have been the introductory story to the Aramaic collection.)

Characteristic of R3's work was the chronology supplied to the book as a whole. Superscriptions in Dan. 1.1-2; 2.1a; 7.1; 8.1; 9.1-2; and 10.1 are the most obvious examples. That chronology runs from the Babylonian Empire (represented by Nebuchadnezzar in Dan. 1–4 and Belshazzar in 5.1-29) to Media (represented by Darius 'the Mede' in the redactional note in 5.30-31 and in the narrative in 6.1-27), to Persia (represented only by the redactional note about Cyrus in 6.28). Then the chronology is repeated in the second half of the book with Babylon (Belshazzar in Daniel 7 and 8), Media (Darius in Daniel 9), and Persia (Cyrus in Dan. 10.1–12.4). R3 wrote no superscriptions for the Greek period, since it was clear Daniel could not have lived so late. The third year of Cyrus (10.1), that is, 537/6 or 70 years after the date in 1.1, probably was chosen to show that Daniel's career spanned the entire Exile (Jer. 25.11-12 and 29.10). Such a date may have been as late as believable. The unlikelihood that Daniel lived until the time of Darius I has already been mentioned. R3 avoided that problem by redefining who Darius was.

This redefinition occurs in 5.30-31 and 9.1. The narrative of the writing on the wall builds to a climax in 5.29 with Belshazzar's clothing Daniel in purple and elevating him to the 'third ruler in the kingdom'. Nothing in God's message suggests Belshazzar's imminent death; indeed, 5.29 would seem to imply that Daniel was rewarded in Belshazzar's court for his interpretation of the dream, a reward that would take some while to work out. The Old Greek makes no reference to how much time passed between the banquet scene and the fall of Babylon to the 'Medes and the Persians'. R3, however, was working with an existing collection in which Darius was the king in the next narrative (i.e., the present Dan. 6) and with Daniel 2 and 7, both of which utilized the Median-oriented succession Assyria (replaced by Babylon), Media, Persia. Furthermore, given his use of the book of Jeremiah in Daniel 9, R3 was no doubt familiar with the predictions in Jer. 51.11, 28 (and possibly with those in Isa. 13.17-22 and 21.2) that the Babylonian Empire would come to an end at the hands of the Medes. Hence, R3 gave the narrative in Daniel 5 a new ending by saying Belshazzar was killed that very night and was replaced by 'Darius the Mede'. The Old Greek reads 'Xerxes, king of the Medes'. The next verse (MT 6.1) introduces Darius, probably Darius I, but in smoothing out the connection between Daniel 5 and 6, R3 combined the two into 'Darius the Mede'.

In 9.1, R3 added that 'Darius' was the son of Ahasueras (the biblical name for Xerxes I) and a Mede by birth. These details do not match what is known of Darius I, who was instead the father of Xerxes, and who in any case did not follow Nabonidus on the throne in Babylon. In view of such a tangled history, scholars often suggest that the portrait of 'Darius' in Daniel was either a fictional creation or was derived from some other figure, whose identity can only be guessed. As mentioned earlier, suggestions include Astyages, Cyaxares II, Cyrus II, his general Gobryas (Gubaru), and Cambyses.

The source for Darius's genealogy in 9.1, however, might not have been ancient Babylonian or Persian documents, but traditions in Jerusalem or Judah in R3's own time. A witness to that tradition can perhaps be found in Tob. 14.15: 'But before [Tobit] died he heard of the destruction of Nineveh, which Nebuchadnezzar and Ahasueras had captured.' (RSV; some translations [e.g., NRSV, JB, NAB, REB] emend the text to the more historically correct reading 'Cyaxares of Media', but Greek mss. read 'Nebuchadnezzar and Ahasueras' or 'Ahikar'.) Scholars rightly note that the information is historically inaccurate, since actually Nabopolassar of Babylon and Cyaxares of Media (625–585) conquered Nineveh. What happened in this tradition, most likely, is that persons better known from the Old Testament were substituted for the lesser-known conquerors. If, however, one assumes that R3 shared that tradition, one can perhaps account for the detail that Darius was the son of Ahasueras. Since R3 thought Belshazzar was the son of Nebuchadnezzar, perhaps he concluded that Darius, in his mind a contemporary of Belshazzar who came to the throne upon the death of Belshazzar, was the son of Ahasueras. Then R3 could rely on 2 Chronicles,

Ezra, Haggai and Zechariah for his knowledge that Cyrus was the first Persian ruler.

James E. Miller (1991: 121-23) points out linkages between the beginning and end of the book that one should probably attribute to R3. Miller starts with Lacocque's observation (1988: 10-11) that the use of 'the wise' forms an inclusio in Daniel 1 and Daniel 11–12: i.e. between 1.4, 17 and 11.33, 35; 12.3, 10. Next, he mentions that Daniel 1 and 10 are the only chapters in which Daniel refrains from food. (It should be noted that he does so in Daniel 1 in vv. 8-16, which R3 wrote.) The Aramaic loan-word for the 'king's food', which appears five times in Daniel 1, also occurs in Dan. 11.26.

Miller also notes correspondences between the Aramaic court narrative in Daniel 2 and the Hebrew apocalyptic narrative in Daniel 9. They include the following. Only in Daniel 2 and 9 are the contents of Daniel's prayer reported. Both chapters also contain direct revelations to Daniel in response to those prayers. These correspondences would seem to indicate R3 constructed or modified Daniel 9 with Daniel 2 in view. In this respect R3 resembled R2, who composed Daniel 7 on the model of Daniel 2.

More difficult to ascribe to R3 alone is the phenomenon observed by Lebram (1975: 737-72), namely that the treatment of Antiochus IV in Daniel 7–12 is influenced not only by historical events, but also by literary typologies. In particular, 8.23-25 appears to employ the literary type 'the wise transgressor' encountered in various forms in Ahiqar, Tobit, and elsewhere. Further, Lebram argues that 7.11, 25 employs the type called 'the enemy of the godly order' and that 11.37-39 constitutes a previously existing Egyptian polemic against Antiochus as the enemy of the gods (and their priests and temples). This last suggestion, by the way, is completely compatible with the idea advanced above that scribes formerly in the service of the Seleucids produced the third edition of the book of Daniel. If Lebram is correct about these typologies, those in 8.23-25 and 11.37-39 would belong to R3. The typology in 7.11, 25 is more difficult to assign. It does appear in verses van der Woude considered secondary. It is, therefore, possible that R3 touched up the portrait of Antiochus in Daniel 7, but it is also possible that R2 originally used the typology.

Summary

One may summarize the literary history of the book of Daniel as follows. (1) Various court narratives arose over a period of time among the 'wise' in Babylon. At some point, before or after the 'wise' moved to Jerusalem, what became Daniel 4–6 was collected as three narratives about how to survive under foreign domination. (2) The group's experiences under Antiochus IV soon led to a second edition, this time including all the materials written in Aramaic, with an introduction of undetermined length knitting them together. The heroes were limited to four, with Daniel as the most important. Daniel 7 provides the date for this edition: after 169, when Antiochus turned against the inhabitants of Judah, but before December of 167, the date of the 'transgression that makes desolate'. (3) The third edition followed quickly, chs. 8 and 9 shortly after the 'transgression'; 10.1–12.4 (+ 12.13; see commentary) a little later, but before the death of Antiochus and the cleansing of the temple in 164; and 12.5-12 shortly after its rededication. (For a similar, though not so detailed discussion of the growth of the book of Daniel, see Bauer 1996: 35-45).

E. PLOT

The plot of the book of Daniel extends from the invasion of Judah by Nebuchadnezzar and the beginning of the Exile to the fall of the fourth kingdom and its replacement by God's kingdom. At least through Daniel 8, the plot can be called 'comedic' in the sense that things ultimately turn out right rather than tragically. E.M. Good (1984: 60-63) thinks Daniel 9–12 may move too far into determinism to justify calling it 'comedic', but the extent of determinism in those chapters is debatable and the outcome remains positive for the faithful.

F. THE FIGURE OF DANIEL AND THE READER

As noted above, the origin of the figure of Daniel is mysterious. He is mentioned elsewhere in the Old Testament—if at all—only in Ezek. 14.14, 20 and 28.3 as a wise man of old. This figure somehow attracted to itself a number of narratives set in the Babylonian exile. In the MT Daniel proves to be the ideal 'wise man', and in the addition to the book of Daniel known as Susanna, he plays the role of judge (as befits his name, which means either 'My judge is God' or 'judge of God').

Lacocque (1988: 191-96) describes this figure as a type of shaman with a speciality in the reading of signs. He is, however, not merely interested in mastering clever acts and words, but in testifying about the Hebrew God as the source of all wisdom. Adding to his mysteriousness,

Daniel hides himself behind God, the sole being worthy of worship and gratitude. Even when Nebuchadnezzar mistakenly commands that offerings be made in Daniel's honor (Dan. 2.46), the effect of that command is to show how badly the king had missed the point. As Lacocque puts it (p. 194): the story showed that the colossus has clay feet. Daniel is portrayed as Stoic-like in his patience, and his suffering (like that of the author and his group) vicariously blesses others, as in the case of the servant of Isaiah 53.

Davies (1985: 125-26) calls attention to the changing relationship between Daniel and the readers of the book. In the court narratives, the Maccabean reader observes the hero Daniel at work in a time and place far removed, but similar to his or her own: the reader is a religious alien in the presence of a Gentile king, albeit one more sinister than the king in the court narratives. In the apocalyptic narratives, however, Daniel is assimilated to the 'author' of the book by means of pseudonymity. The reader is now the 'confidant' of the hero, who is vexed and perplexed by the events he beholds.

G. CANON

Two issues of canon emerge with respect to the book of Daniel. The first is its position. In the English Bible, it follows the book of Ezekiel among the so-called 'major' prophets, but in the MT it is placed in the third section, the 'Writings'. Scholars typically attribute its place among the Writings to the fact that it is an apocalypse, which literary type the rabbis responsible for the Palestinian canon are supposed not to have liked. That dislike, however, would seem to have been reason for its exclusion altogether, rather than its placement among the writings. Davies (1980: 38) and especially Klaus Koch (1985: 117-30) note that early allusions to the book speak of 'Daniel the prophet', suggesting that its early readers did not recognize the distinction. In fact, its placement before the book of Ezra/Nehemiah in the MT suggests it was placed there because of the court narratives, that is, where the narratives would seem to fit chronologically if taken at face value.

The second issue is that the LXX (and the Roman Catholic) version of the book of Daniel is longer than the MT (and the Protestant version) by three narratives. These narratives go by the names of 'The Prayer of Azariah and the Song of the Three Young Men' (67 verses that appear between 3.23 and 3.24 of the MT), 'Susanna', and 'Bel and the Dragon', which two narratives follow Daniel 12 in the LXX and the Roman

Catholic book of Daniel. If they were composed in Aramaic, their omission might indicate that the Hebrew-language author/redactor of Daniel (R3 above), worked selectively in building the book of Daniel. On the other hand, it might have been the case that additional court narratives were attracted to the figure of Daniel after 163, of which these three were added to some editions of the book. In any case, this commentary will follow the MT.

H. MESSAGE

The various sets of symbols in the book of Daniel have been applied to various nations and governments for centuries. Koch (1997: 163-67) surveys part of that history and concludes that exegesis has been anything but the hodge-podge it appears. Readers have created and/or honed their own self image and national image in dialogue with the book. Still, much of that reading has been uncritical, so what is the message of the book if one takes seriously modern scholarship?

Stephen D. O'Leary (1994: 196-200) discusses four aspects of apocalyptic eschatology: time, destiny, suffering and evil, and spiritual authority. The book of Daniel addresses each aspect. First O'Leary notes that in apocalypticism, time must have an end, and soon. This motif stands front and center in the book of Daniel. For its second-century authors, things were going badly wrong; heathen kings worse than those of the Babylonians, Medes, and Persians were in charge of the world and attacking the structures of Israelite faith. Indeed, seen from the perspective of R3, both world events and the history of Israel seemed to point to the evil of humanity and the ineffectiveness of God's dealing with the various world empires (Steck 1980: 78).

The delay in righting these conditions, however, was not due to failure on God's part. Rather, God had revealed those very events to Daniel, which meant to the Danielic community that God was ultimately in control of things, appearances to the contrary notwithstanding. For R3, Daniel's 'visions of the future' were a reading of history, a looking back from the proper perspective. That reading, moreover, was fine-tuned as one vision after another unfolded. Daniel and his readers learned that despite the depiction of Nebuchadnezzar and Babylon as the golden head of the image in Daniel 2, neither they nor any other kings or governments were suitable objects for Judeans to trust.

O'Leary notes that in apocalyptic rhetoric, the solution to this problem is often articulated in terms of two periods, one before and one after the divine inbreak, and so it is in the book of Daniel in chs. 2, 7, 8, 9, and 10–12. He points out further that apocalypticists may find themselves caught in a dilemma. On the one hand, the need of their audience to know precisely 'how long' they must endure evil may lead apocalypticists to set a specific date or period when this age will end and the next will begin. However, the setting of dates is risky business, because if a date passes without the foreseen divine inbreak the message may be compromised. Daniel 7.25 may be read as an attempt to give a less than specific answer to the question of the time of the end, while 8.14 and 12.11-12 give a more specific answer, with 9.24-27 standing somewhere in between. R. Stahl (1993: 493) notes, however, that even though the calculations of the date were wrong, the authors were still correct that the space-time world is limited by God's world, which breaks into it.

H.S. Kvanvig goes further. She argues (1989: 46-47) that in apocalyptic literature history moves along the end, rather than simply toward the end. She writes: 'History moves on the border of chaos like a track...winding along a cliff... At one particular time, however, history will turn over the edge' (p. 47). This means that believers who thought they saw the end in various periods of tribulation 'were not mistaken. The signs of the end were present. The mistake was [made] if they thought that they could, through these signs, calculate the time when the real end time...would come'.

The second aspect of eschatology is the destiny of human beings. The rest of the Old Testament rarely considers this issue. Dead people, good or bad, would go to the underworld. On earth, people might well be punished collectively for misdeeds, but the idea of individual retribution was slow to develop. Jeremiah 31.29 and Ezek. 18.2 seem to be the first texts to argue for individual retribution, but the books of Job and Ecclesiastes raise serious questions whether such retribution actually existed. Hence, the book of Daniel takes the issue one step further. If retribution is individual, and evil people seem to have the upper hand in the world, where is God? The book as a whole answers this question in two ways. On the one hand, it expresses the hope that God would deliver the faithful from difficulty in this life (which God did in every case in the court narratives), while recognizing that God might not (3.17-18): 'If our God whom we serve is able to deliver us from the furnace of blazing fire and out of your hand, O king, let him deliver us.' But if not, they were prepared to die rather than commit idolatry. On the other hand, the book develops a double plot: virtuous people will be rewarded; sinners will be punished, if not in this life, then in the next. Daniel 12.2 articulates the dual fate as follows: some dead people would be raised to everlasting life and others to everlasting contempt. (See the commentaries for a fuller discussion of the meaning of this verse.)

Thirdly, O'Leary says that eschatology constitutes an attempt to solve the problem of theodicy, to account for the presence of evil and suffering in God's world. In the book of Daniel, the problems of death and foreign oppression in particular demand justification. The book of Daniel explains the presence of these two evils in the Seleucid period as the result of impious opposition to God's will by Antiochus Epiphanes (see 7.8; 8.9-12, 20-21, 24b-25), which will be redressed by God when the end comes. The question of theodicy was tied to the issues of time and destiny. The end would come soon. Then good people would be rewarded and sinners punished.

The fourth aspect of eschatology mentioned by O'Leary is the problem of spiritual authority. Max Weber identified three basic types of authority: rational, traditional, and charismatic. Any argument may appeal both to reason and to tradition. O'Leary notes (1994: 199), however, that charismatic authority, which is characteristic of apocalypses, properly speaking is not so much claimed by a document as attributed to it by its readers.

Perhaps to assure such attribution, the book of Daniel sometimes reports the conditions under which its hero receives his visions, conditions one might call charismatic. Further, the book clearly subordinates human authority (manifested in Antiochus Epiphanes) to divine. Further still, on the human level the book prefers the authority that accrued to the wise over either the operations of the priests (in which the book shows little interest) or the politics of the Maccabeans.

Rowley (1948: 406) argues that the abiding theological relevance of apocalyptic books, Daniel included, 'is not in the particularity that belonged to the circumstances of their day or to the form of their message, but in deep and enduring principles which can be applied to the circumstances of every generation'. He then enumerates seven such principles. (1) The future will be better. The authors of the book of Daniel had no hope of modifying conditions themselves, but they were optimistic and did believe God would set things right. (2) The true well-being of humans is found in following the will of God. (3) Obedience to

God will result not in quiet satisfaction in the face of turmoil, but in suffering for God's kingdom. (4) God, not human emperors or great nations, is in control of history. (5) The realization of hope also is in God's hands. (6) God's people should be loyal even in the face of persecution and death. (7) God's Golden Age has not come as long as any one is being persecuted for doing what is right.

COMMENTARY
ON DANIEL

FOUR WISE YOUTHS AT THE COURT OF
NEBUCHADNEZZAR
(1.1-21)

Daniel 1 functions as the introduction to the entire collection of narratives about Daniel and three other young men in exile. In doing so, it explains how they came to be in Babylon, who they were, how they got Babylonian names, and how they rose to prominence in a foreign court. Like the rest of the narratives in Daniel 1–6, its genre is 'wisdom court legend'.

The chapter may be analyzed as follows. It opens (vv. 1-2) with a description of its exilic setting. It continues with the complication (vv. 3-7) about four Hebrew youths assigned the task of learning 'the literature and language of the Chaldeans'. The climax comes much later in the chapter (vv. 17-19), where one reads that they learned both better than all the other foreign youths selected to serve in the Babylonian court. These verses read like a tale of court contest in that the heroes rise at the court by outperforming other candidates. The denouement (vv. 20-21) reports that Daniel continued at the Babylonian court until the reign of Cyrus. This structure is typical for descriptions of rites of passage, in which the subjects are removed from their normal lives, trained, educated, or initiated into special knowledge or a new status, and returned to normal life. Its structure will appear again in one form or another in chs. 4, 6, 7, 8 and perhaps 10–12.

In the midst of the narrative, the redactor of the book of Daniel as a whole (called R3 in the Introduction above) inserted a secondary complication (vv. 8-16) designed to explain that the four youths succeeded through an overly strict observance of the dietary laws of the Pentateuch, a matter of great concern to R3 and his audience in the Maccabean period. In this addition Daniel's request for a special diet implies danger to Daniel and his friends, and the narrative makes explicit the danger to the palace master (v. 10). Hence, there is an element of court conflict, but nothing so drastic as the broken martyr stories in Daniel 3 and 6.

THE SETTING: DANIEL AND FRIENDS
IN NEBUCHADNEZZAR'S COURT (1-2)

The setting explains the presence in Babylon of Daniel and other Judean youths (crucial for Daniel 3) and of vessels from the temple (important for Daniel 5). It also sets up a conflict in point of view within Daniel 1, as Fewell (1988: 35) points out. From Nebuchadnezzar's perspective, he was the primary mover in human affairs. He came to Jerusalem; he besieged the city; he took its vessels to Babylon; and he placed them in the treasury. From the redactor's point of view, Nebuchadnezzar simply functioned with the permission of God, who allowed Jehoiakim to fall into Nebuchadnezzar's power and—by implication—allowed these other catastrophes to happen as well, no doubt as punishment for sin.

Verse 1. The **third year of the reign of King Jehoiakim** was 606. **Nebuchadnezzar** is the typical form in the Hebrew Bible of the name Nebuchadrezzar, king of Babylon from 605 to 562. The discrepancy between 606 and 605 is sometimes explained as due to a difference in calculating the year's end in Babylon and Judah. Further, Mark Mercer (1989: 179-92) argues that 2 Chron. 36.6-7 refers to a minor siege of Jerusalem in 605/4. Neither of these positions resolves the real historical issue in this verse, namely that there is no record of a Babylonian incursion into Palestine in 605, let alone of the taking of captives to Babylon. If these scholars are correct, the Chronicler discussed a minor siege in 605 and omitted the major siege of 598. That is most unlikely. Rather, the first siege of Jerusalem occurred in 598/7 and resulted in the First Deportation, when King Jehoiachin and as many as 10,000 captives were taken into exile in Babylon (2 Kgs 24.14). Daniel 1.1 seems to have dated that event eight years too early.

Gese (1983: 141) notes that this discrepancy was not simply an error. The vision of the 70 weeks of years in Daniel 9 makes clear that the redactor was working with the notion from 2 Chron. 36.21 that the exile lasted 70 years (cf. Jer. 25.11-12 and 29.10). He apparently calculated those years as running from the third year of Jehoiakim to the third year of Cyrus.

Verse 2. According to this verse, **the Lord let King Jehoiakim fall into his power**... The somewhat garbled account of the First Deportation continues in 1.2. According to 2 Kgs 24.1, what actually happened was that Jehoiakim served Nebuchadnezzar for three years and then rebelled. Bright (1981: 327) reconstructs the sequence as follows. Jehoiakim probably transferred his allegiance to Nebuchadnezzar about 603 after Nebuchadnezzar invaded Philistia. The rebellion would have followed after Pharaoh Neco stopped Nebuchadnezzar in his bid to conquer Egypt in late 601. More pressing issues required Nebuchadnezzar's attention until late 598, when he turned against Jehoiakim. The king died during the siege and was replaced by his son Jehoiachin, who sued for peace and went into exile.

Daniel 1.2 continues by saying that Nebuchadnezzar took some of the vessels of the temple (cf. 2 Chron. 36.7) to **the land of Shinar** (or Babylon). He placed them in the **treasury of his gods**. The MT actually says he put them in the house of the treasury of his gods, which may combine two different traditions: (1) that he put them in a temple, and (2) that he put them in a treasury. The verse does not say that Nebuchadnezzar took Jehoiakim to Babylon, a point often made by traditional scholars who argue that Nebuchadnezzar invaded Palestine also when he invaded Philistia in 603 and that 1.1-2 is historically accurate. Of course, the verse also neglects to say that Nebuchadnezzar took Daniel to Babylon, though v. 3 clearly presupposes that he had.

COMPLICATION 1: COMPETITION TO LEARN THE CHALDEAN LITERATURE AND LANGUAGE (3-7)

The first complication appears in vv. 3-7. The king ordered that young men among the exiles be given the opportunity to rise to positions of influence in the Babylonian court. Their opportunity would involve learning a Babylonian language and Babylonian customs, and their success would inspire other Judeans desiring a position in a foreign court.

Verse 3. The king decided to make wise men out of the choicest Israelite youths. He directed the palace master to select youths from the royal family (literally, 'seed') and the nobles. The palace master was called **Ashpenaz**. The word is often understood as a proper name, but Collins (1993: 127) takes it as an Old Persian noun meaning something like 'major-domo'. The title was explained by a two-word Hebrew phrase translated **palace master**. Literally, that phrase may be rendered 'chief eunuch'. Eunuchs often served as guards of royal harems, and if they proved trustworthy they might acquire other responsibilities. The term may also have been used more generally to mean 'court official', as the NRSV translates. In any case, whether the major-domo was a eunuch plays no role in the narrative.

Verse 4. The qualifications of the potential servants were as follows: they were to be (1) without physical defect, (2) handsome, (3) well-educated, (4) knowledgeable, (5) insightful, and (6) competent to serve in the king's palace. Of these characteristics, the most striking is the first. Unlike some other servants at the royal court, these youth could not be eunuchs. The phrase also is familiar from the requirements that a sacrificial animal be without blemish. In other words, v. 4 already was working on the theme so crucial to the community of the book of Daniel, namely that Judeans serving a foreign king should nevertheless keep themselves ritually fit, a theme that would be made explicit by the addition in vv. 8-16.

The task of the potential servants was to learn both the literature and the language of the Chaldeans. The language in question was not the common Aramaic, but Akkadian, and the literature was that of the vast omen literature (Collins 1993a: 138). Despite this training, however, Daniel would interpret dreams not through the accumulated wisdom of the Babylonians, which fails in chs. 2, 4 and 5, but through revelations from God (2.28).

Verse 5. The apprenticeship of the Judean youths would have been typical for a rite of passage into adulthood or a profession. They would undergo physical separation from other countrymen. They would receive a different diet, namely, a daily portion of food and wine fit for a king. Also they would receive special instructions. The process was to last three years, after which they would enter the service of the king.

Verses 6-7. The narrator quickly focused on four of the Israelite youths: Daniel, Hananiah, Mishael, and Azariah. For each he reported a Babylonian name: Belteshazzar, Shadrach, Meshach, and Abednego, respectively. It was not unusual for a Judean youth in exile to receive a Babylonian name (cf. Zerubbabel), but it was an indication of sub-ordination and became a touchy issue in Hellenistic times. In the words of Lacocque (1979: 29), they would 'receive their new names by obli-gation, not by choice'. Here the giving of the new names also continues the account of the rite of passage. Their new identity warranted new names.

COMPLICATION 2: AVOIDING THE KING'S DIET (8-16)

Verses 8-16 constitute an addition to the original story of Daniel's apprenticeship (cf. van der Woude 1986: 310-11). They also present a second complication in this narrative. What vv. 8-16 add to the original story is an 'inside' explanation of how the four achieved their success:

not by capitulating to the lifestyle of the Babylonians epitomized by the king's food, attractive as that lifestyle may have been, but by remaining rigorously true to Torah and trusting in God.

Verse 8. Daniel determined not to defile himself by eating the king's food or drinking his wine and asked permission not to do so. Drinking wine was not prohibited in the Old Testament, of course, but Leviticus 11 prohibits eating certain kinds of meat, and Lev. 17.10-14 regulates the preparation of meat (Mason 1988: 84). There is no suggestion in v. 8 that the king's food violated those regulations. Some scholars have suggested that Daniel feared any food served by a Gentile, but in that case he could not have received his more meager fare from a guard later in the chapter. One is left, then, not with a regulation but an example. Daniel would succeed in the service of the foreign king without violating God's commandments in any way.

Verses 9-10. The narrator made it clear that God did not leave Daniel to face this situation on his own. Rather, God caused the major-domo to show favor and sympathy to Daniel, even though he did not agree to Daniel's request. Further, he explained his reluctance to agree to Daniel's request: he feared for his position and perhaps even his life if Daniel seemed less healthy than the other apprentices.

Verse 11. A new character appears abruptly in v. 11; the major-domo appoints a guard or superintendent for Daniel. While the introduction of the guardian is not worded smoothly, that alone is not evidence of a second hand. Indeed, such a functionary would be expected. Certainly a major-domo could not oversee personally everything about everyone in the palace.

Verses 12-14. A wise courtier knows the value of negotiation, so Daniel proposes a test to the new guard: let Daniel and his three friends (mentioned here for the first time in vv. 8-16) eat a different diet for 10 days and check to see who seems healthier. The guard apparently could see no harm in such a test, since 10 days would hardly be sufficient to destroy the health of the four. Besides, the guard could perhaps eat or sell the king's food.

The proposed diet was stringent, being comprised only of water and seeds. NRSV translates the Hebrew word for 'seeds' as **vegetables**, but, literally, it is related to the word for seed. Such a diet seems implausible; hence, translators typically render the Hebrew as 'vegetables'. The problem is that the translation understates the contrast between the king's fare and the diet they were proposing. Daniel is a book in which heroes emerge unscathed from a lion's den and a fiery furnace. Its authors clearly were not concerned about plausibility! Besides, in the history of religions such extreme diets are not unheard of. Some ancient Chinese Taoists, for example, thought they should give up meat, wine, strong-smelling plants and cereals, and live instead off herbs and minerals (Kaltenmark 1969: 124). Hence, one may conclude that Daniel and his friends committed themselves to the most severe diet imaginable, confident that God would care for such dedicated servants. That was, in fact, the outcome, as v. 17 makes explicit.

Verses 15-16. At the end of the 10-day trial, the four appeared **better and fatter** than all the remaining apprentices. In the West, where people have become conscious of the dangers of high cholesterol, being 'fatter' would no longer equate with being 'better' or healthier. In ancient Israel, however, a round, plump body was possible only for kings, nobles and those who had succeeded, and was deemed desirable. One need not ask how 'seeds' could make one fat; they could not, and that is the point. Daniel and his friends surpassed all the others precisely because they resolved not to defile themselves with improper food. The guard naturally decided to continue exchanging the king's rations for water and seed.

THE CLIMAX AND DENOUEMENT:
THE YOUTHS BEFORE THE KING (17-21)

The secondary nature of vv. 8-16 can be seen from the smooth connection between v. 7 and v. 17. Verse 7 names the four, and v. 17 reports that God gave them the knowledge and skill they needed to excel. Verses 8-16 could be left out entirely and a reader would never miss them. Verses 17-19, however, constitute the climax of the narrative, and vv. 20-21 form the denouement.

Verse 17. This returns to the first complication, the competition to learn the Babylonian language and culture. The four outstripped all other apprentices with the help of God. The verse takes a glance ahead to chs. 2, 4 and 7 with the note that God also granted Daniel insight into **all visions and dreams**.

Verses 18-19. At the end of the time for their training, that is, after three years (v. 5), the palace master brought all the students to the king for an examination by Nebuchadnezzar. The result was that Daniel and his friends were without equals, and Nebuchadnezzar rewarded them with the highest positions of all the students.

Verse 20. The ending of the original story compared Daniel and his friends favorably with all the enchanters and magicians in his whole court. The four were ten times better than any of the others. Among the other courtiers there were **magicians** and **enchanters**. Montgomery (1927: 137) explains that the word 'magician' refers to persons knowing Egyptian magic, while 'enchanters' designates those acquainted with Babylonian magic. He adds, however, that in Daniel 1 the words are probably not used with technical precision and do not prove the presence of Egyptians in Nebuchadnezzar's court. The claim simply is that the four excelled over all of the long-term professional 'wise men' in Babylon.

Verse 21. Daniel 1 ends with the chronological note that Daniel's career lasted until the first year of the reign of Cyrus the Great (537). That note foreshadows the latest-dated vision in the book (10.1–12.4a) and comes from R3.

THE THEOLOGY OF DANIEL 1

Since the book of Daniel was directed to people who perceived themselves to be disadvantaged in some significant way(s), some modern readers are prepared to dismiss its general applicability, but that is too extreme. This chapter makes at least two points of abiding relevance. First, biblical religion often stands at odds with its surrounding culture. To be sure, much of the Old Testament says that, and often it represented a minority report over against Israelite culture, including its religion. Daniel 1, by contrast, operates against the backdrop of a foreign culture. Even so, that culture was attractive because it offered a possible way of advancement. To advance would require the readers to walk a tightrope between acculturation to the foreign influences and fidelity to their own traditions. The temptations for religious compromise might lurk anywhere in a culture so far removed from hearing the word of God. The later experiences of the community under Antiochus IV proved just how deadly to the faithful a culture could become.

The second motif sounded by this chapter is simply this: ideally, Judeans would be able to thrive under foreign domination without compromising their faith, but if a choice had to be made they should choose God rather than material gains or even life itself. Later chapters develop the life-threatening nature of this choice. Daniel 1 makes it clear that social and/or financial advancement should not come at the expense of violating God's commandments, a word particularly relevant for affluent readers today.

NEBUCHADNEZZAR'S DREAM OF THE
STATUE OF FOUR METALS
2.1-49

Daniel 1 introduced the main characters of the book and explained how they came to Babylon. It also set out the theses (1) that God, not Neb-uchadnezzar, was in charge of the affairs of his people in Babylon, all appearances to the contrary notwithstanding, so (2) the way to succeed in the foreign court was by obeying God. Daniel 2 begins in the second year of Nebuchadnezzar, thus placing it in tension with the chronology of Dan. 1.5, which stipulated that the youths would undergo a three-year apprenticeship. Some scholars have suggested emending the word 'second' to read 'two and tenth' (i.e., 'twelfth'), a reading corroborated by Greek Papyrus 967 (Collins 1993: 154). Another alternative is to understand the chapter as a flashback to something that happened during the three-year trial period (Fewell 1988: 49).

As mentioned above, the language switches from Hebrew to Aramaic in 2.4b, so vv. 1-4a should be attributed in their present form to the author/editor of Daniel 1 (R3), though the original Aramaic story perhaps had a similar opening. A number of scholars suggest that the narrative itself probably originated in the late sixth century as a vision about the fall of the Babylonian Empire (cf. Fröhlich 1993: 266-68) rather than of four kingdoms, and it is easier to see a statue as referring to one empire than to a succession of empires. In addition, the fact that each succeeding metal is baser than its predecessor fits the succession of the four neo-Babylonian kings better than it does the succession of empires from the Babylonian to the Greek.

Hence, one should read vv. 39-40 and the fluctuation between 'king' and 'kingdom' in v. 44 as modifications to the original interpretation, making the dream refer to succeeding kingdoms rather than kings as it had originally. Since the idea that a fourth empire would replace three Mesopotamian empires arose during the Greek Empire, vv. 39-40 were added after Alexander's conquest of that area. Furthermore, vv. 41-43 built on that addition by alluding either to the marriage of Antiochus II to Bernice in 252 (so Ginsberg 1954: 250) or to the marriage of Ptolemy V to Cleopatra, daughter of Antiochus III in 194 (so Rowley 1952: 264-65). Thus vv. 39-40 appeared in the fourth or third century and vv. 41-43 in the third or early second century.

The image representing four kingdoms was destroyed by a stone, representing a fifth kingdom, the kingdom of God. The motif of the replacement of four previous kingdoms by a fifth, namely Rome, is attested as early as Polybius 38.22, from the late second century BCE, and the idea may have been earlier. Whether Daniel 2 drew upon that emerging Roman tradition or represented a parallel development cannot be determined.

Davies (1970: 392-401) argues that 2.13-23 is another late development, and Collins (1993a: 153) suggests that the verses resemble Daniel 7 and 8 and may have been inserted when Daniel 7 was added. Beginning with v. 13b, these verses portray Daniel as one of the wise men at the court included in the king's threat to kill them all for their failure to relate and interpret his dream, thus betraying familiarity with Daniel 1, whereas in the older story Daniel sought out the executioner to intercede on behalf of the sages. Besides, in the addition Daniel gains an audience with the king and promises to interpret the dream (v. 16), while in the older form of the story an official named Arioch introduces Daniel to the king as someone Arioch had found (v. 25).

One should also note in passing that 2.48 provides a suitable conclusion to the original narrative, while 2.49 (from R2) appears to relate the narrative to the larger Aramaic collection. In view of these observations, one may say that the original story would have included vv. 1-13a, 24-38, 44-48, with vv. 1-4a and 44 differing somewhat from the present text.

In terms of genre, Daniel 2 may be classified as another wisdom court legend, this one also having the characteristics noted by Humphreys in the tales of court contest: the hero outshines other courtiers by performing some task they are unable to complete. Davies calls it a tale of interpretation, and Niditch and Doran note that it fits a particular type of folktale, the success story of the wise courtier, in which a lower-class hero solves a problem for a higher-class person and is rewarded for doing so. Other examples of this type of folktale may be found among the stories of Joseph (e.g. Gen. 41).

The plot of Daniel 2 may be analyzed as follows. In v. 1a, the court setting is taken over from Daniel 1. The problem that must be solved is the meaning of King Nebuchadnezzar's dream (vv. 1b-3). That problem is complicated by his refusal to reveal its contents and his threat to destroy the Babylonian wise men if they fail (vv. 4-13a). Three times they ask him to relate the dream, and three times he refuses. The drama builds as Daniel is implicated in the threat (v. 13b) and seeks help from God, which he gains through a vision (vv. 14-23). Armed with the knowledge the king desires, he gains an audience with him (vv. 24-30). The plot reaches its climax when Daniel succeeds in relating both the dream (vv. 31-35) and its interpretation (vv. 36-45). In the denouement (vv. 46-48) Daniel receives his reward. The narrative concludes with a glance at the broader book of Daniel (v. 49). Towner (1984: 31) speaks of five scenes in this chapter. His headings are helpful in keeping track of the flow of the plot and will be employed here.

THE SETTING (2.1A)

The setting, taken over from the previous chapter, is the court of Nebuchadnezzar. The second year of his reign would be 604.

SCENE ONE: THE KING'S DREAM AND THE ORDEAL
OF THE MAGICIANS (1B-12)

Verses 1b-3. The king had a dream that upset him. On the one hand, he could not understand it; on the other he seemed to realize it boded evil for him. Consequently, he summoned the wise men at his court to interpret his dream for him.

Verse 1b. Nebuchadnezzar **dreamed...dreams**. The plural is used, despite the fact that the narrative focuses on only one dream. Scholars have offered various explanations for that anomaly. Slotki (1951: 7) mentions the possibilities that the plural is due to the fact that the dream had several scenes, or that the word also refers to Nebuchadnezzar's dream in Daniel 4. GKC §124 *o* cites this verse as an example of an indefinite singular noun. Perhaps the point here is that the dream kept recurring.

Both biblical and Babylonian stories featured dreams as omens or messages (see the Joseph stories in Gen. 37.5-11; 40.5-23; 41.14-36; cf. Gen. 20.3 and Mt. 27.19). Extant Mesopotamian texts describe royal dreams, and the Babylonian king Nabonidus was particularly interested in dreams. It is no surprise, then, when Dan. 2.1b depicts Nebuchadnezzar lying awake, worrying over the meaning of the dream.

Verses 2-3. Nebuchadnezzar called for **the magicians, the enchanters, the sorcerers, and the Chaldeans**. 'Magicians', whether in Egypt (Gen. 41.8; Exod. 8.3, 14, 15; 7.11) or in Babylon, were people who possessed occult knowledge, particularly the power to interpret dreams. 'Enchanters' were exorcists, while 'sorcerers' were specialists in dealing with evil spirits or evil consequences by means of magic (Oppenheim 1956: 219). 'Chaldeans' here carried the connotation of a group of wise men at the court as opposed to the name for the ethnic group by which the neo-Babylonian Empire was also known. It seems doubtful that these four terms were used with any technical precision here, because they are simply listed, because only Chaldeans are mentioned in vv. 4-11, and because a somewhat different list is given in v. 27 (**wise men, enchanters, magicians, and diviners**). Instead, the point of v. 2 was that Nebuchadnezzar summoned every person on his staff who might have the expertise to help him understand his dream.

Verses 4-12. How would the king know whether to trust the interpretation given by his wise men? If he did not know what his dream meant, how could he be sure that his counselors did? He hit upon the idea of making them divine the dream itself (cf. Flusser 1972: 156). Any one who could relate his dream to him could be trusted to interpret it properly. This understanding of the king's demand (vv. 5-6) seems preferable to another suggestion, namely that Nebuchadnezzar had forgotten his dream. In that case, he would have been at the mercy of his courtiers, who could have made up anything and told him it was his dream.

Verse 4. The sages request that the king relate the contents of the dream. Fewell (1988: 51) points out that the reader does not yet know the content of the dream either; the author does not divulge it until Daniel tells the king.

The point at which the narrative introduces their question is where the language of the book switches from Hebrew to Aramaic. The transition is marked by the note that the Chaldeans spoke to the king **in Aramaic**. Hartman and Di Lella (1978: 138) think the word was a gloss, and point out that in 1QDan[a] one finds only a space before the beginning of the Aramaic.

The word for **interpretation** is *pesher*. Outside of Daniel it appears only in Est. 8.1 in the Old Testament, but in the Aramaic section of Daniel it appears once as a verb (twice if one accepts the *qere* in 5.16) and 16 times as a noun (17 if one accepts the *qere* in 4.16). Students of the Dead Sea Scrolls are familiar with this term, where it is used in the so-called 'Commentaries' on biblical books. In those scrolls, interpretations seem to emphasize the meaning of a text for the specific community for which the commentary was composed. The word carries that same force here. This is no impersonal inquiry on the part of the king. He already believes what Daniel later tells him in v. 28, namely that God was communicating with him personally by means of the dream.

Verses 5-6. The king's response was anything but reasonable. Essentially, he threatened the sages with execution and dismemberment if they failed to relate and interpret the dream, and he offered to reward them handsomely if they succeeded.

Verses 7-9. The dramatic effect of the narrative is increased as the wise men repeat their question, and king accuses them of stalling for time and conspiring to lie to him.

Verses 10-11. The Chaldeans answered: No mere mortal could do as he asked, nor had any of the great kings of the Mesopotamian empires made such a request. Only the gods (no specific deities were envisioned here) could do as he asked, and they lived in heaven, not among humans. Of course, it will turn out that one specific God, Yahweh, will reveal the dream to Daniel, but even Yahweh will not be seen or heard explaining the mystery to Daniel (Fewell 1988: 54).

Verse 12. The king flew into a violent rage at their response and ordered all the wise men of Babylon to be destroyed. If one may anticipate for a moment the revelation of the dream and its interpretation, there is nothing about the king's conduct here that would distinguish him as a 'golden head'. If anything, he is exactly the opposite: a self-centered tyrant.

SCENE TWO: DANIEL'S INTERVENTION AND THE DISCLOSURE OF THE SECRET OF DANIEL'S WISDOM (13-23)

One would have expected the threat to include only the sages present, as v. 13a seems to suggest, and v. 24 continues the narrative with Daniel approaching Arioch with the information to save the Babylonian wise men. Verse 13b, however, broadens the scope of the threat, including Daniel and his friends under it.

The transitions between the older narrative and the addition are not smooth. In the transition to the addition, v. 13a seems to say that the killings were about to commence, but v. 13b says that indefinite persons ('they') were sent to find Daniel and his companions, presumably as the first sages to die under the king's order. The transition back to the original story is just as bumpy. When Daniel returned to Arioch, Arioch introduced Daniel to the king as someone he had found to reveal the dream (vv. 24-25). That would be unnecessary if the king had already granted Daniel time to learn the dream and its meaning (v. 16); nor would Arioch have claimed that he was the one who found Daniel (v. 25).

Verse 13. The author uses the passive voice to describe the order by the king to carry out the executions. This indirect mode of address does not hide the source of the order for execution, which must have come from the king, but allows the force of the verse to fall on the new twist being added to the plot in v. 13b, namely that the order for execution would include Daniel and his friends. Even the name of the executioner does not appear until the next verse. The point of the revised verse stands out clearly: the threat to Daniel and his friends came directly from the king. What is more, Daniel seems to have been intended as the first sage to die.

Verse 14. The nameless, faceless executioners 'they' are replaced in v. 14 by **Arioch**, the king's chief executioner, who had the good sense to listen to Daniel as he spoke with **prudence and discretion.** This was no time for Daniel to lose his wits!

Verse 15. Daniel asked why the decree of the king was so urgent, and Arioch explained to Daniel what had happened. The implied result of the conversation was that Arioch gave Daniel permission to gain an audience with the king.

Verse 16. At that audience, Daniel requested time to prepare himself to relate to the king both his dream and its interpretation. The sages had made the same request, and Nebuchadnezzar had accused them of stalling to buy time. Daniel's request met no such outburst, but received an affirmative reply.

Verses 17-18. Daniel then sought out his companions Shadrach, Meshach and Abednego and asked them to pray for him. On the one hand, these verses constitute a literary device with the transparent function of involving the three who had been introduced in Daniel 1 and who would be the heroes of Daniel 3. On the other hand, they allow the author to impress upon his readers the importance of intercessory prayer both in learning the mystery of the king's dream and also of gaining God's mercy in trying times.

The word for **mystery** in v. 18 is *rāzā'*, a Persian loan-word, meaning 'secret'. It is used eight times in Daniel 2. In v. 19 it is coupled with the verb **revealed**. In v. 22 Daniel says that God revealed deep and hidden things, but in v. 28 he tells Nebuchadnezzar that the revelation has to do with **what will happen at the end of days**. So the word **mystery** carries eschatological overtones in Daniel 2.

Verse 19. For the second time in only seven verses, the author uses the passive voice to describe a crucial point: **the mystery was revealed**. There is no question in the context about who revealed the mystery, just as there is no question why God did so. What is highlighted here is not the revealer, but the mode of revelation: **a vision of the night**. Still, as Fewell (1988: 53) notes, the actual content of the vision is not revealed even here. The reader will not learn the contents of the king's dream and its interpretation until the king does. On the other hand, the reader knows already the more important lesson the king will learn, namely that Daniel's God reveals mysteries; nothing is hidden from God.

Verse 20. With the words **Daniel said**, the author introduces a three-verse doxology (vv. 20-22) followed by an individual song of thanksgiving (v. 23; see Towner 1984: 33). Appropriately, the doxology blesses God, who had just revealed the mystery of the king's dream. The phrase **name of God** signifies the being of God, just as a human name signifies the person. The verse praises God for God's wisdom and power.

Verse 21a. God's power is manifested when God changes **times** and **seasons**. These are two loan-words denoting fixed times. Even they are not beyond the power of God to change. That power is also manifested when God deposes and sets up kings. This theme will be developed at length in Daniel 3, where Nebuchadnezzar thinks he is in control of things, only to discover that God is.

Verses 21b-22. God's power is also manifested when God gives wisdom to the wise. The book of Daniel repeatedly reminds its 'wise' readers that the source of their wisdom was none other than God. God reveals deep and hidden things, things like the dreams of kings and the meaning of those dreams. When Daniel says God knows what goes on in darkness, and that light abides with God, Daniel is speaking metaphorically.

Verse 23. The doxology is personalized in v. 23 where Daniel thanks God directly for revealing to him what he and the friends asked, namely the knowledge the king demanded. It is this verse, especially, that leads most commentators to say that vv. 20-23 were composed for their place

in this chapter, even though they may resemble passages such as Ps.
41.13; Job 12.12-13; Neh. 9.5; Est. 1.13.

SCENE THREE: DANIEL'S PROCLAMATION TO THE KING
AND THE REASON GOD REVEALED THE MYSTERY
TO DANIEL (24-30)

The older narrative resumes in v. 24 with Daniel seeking out Arioch
with a request to intervene on behalf of the Babylonian wise men since
he knows the meaning of the dream. In the older document it is not
clear how he came to that knowledge, but in the current state of the narrative he had learned it in a vision from God. In the older version,
Arioch introduced Daniel to the king (v. 25), unnecessary in the present
version in view of their meeting in v. 16. In v. 11, the sages had said
only the gods could meet the king's demands, and they did not dwell
with mortals. In v. 28 Daniel informed the king that one God had
indeed revealed to Daniel what the king wanted to know. God did so for
the benefit of Nebuchadnezzar (v. 30), implying both God's power over
and grace toward the king.

Verse 24. Reading v. 24 without the additions in vv. 13b-23, one
would assume that in the older version of the story Daniel was not
threatened by the king's order to kill the sages at his court, but had
come to rescue them, perhaps at peril to himself. Daniel 1.19, however,
mentioned that Daniel and his friends were appointed to stations in the
court, and 1.20 boasted that they were ten times better wise men than
all the Babylonian sages. The addition in 2.13-23, therefore, reconciles
the older story with its new context in the book of Daniel. In 2.24
Daniel asks Arioch to arrange an audience with the king, because he
can interpret the king's dream.

Verses 25-26. Arioch tells Nebuchadnezzar that Daniel can help the
king with his dream. His introduction of Daniel to Nebuchadnezzar presumes the men do not know each other, a presumption incompatible
with the narrative in its new context. Verse 26 adds the note that
Daniel's name was **Belteshazzar**, which links it with Daniel 1 and 4.
Nebuchadnezzar asks whether Daniel can tell both the dream and its
interpretation, the same demand he made on the Babylonian sages.

Verse 27. Daniel repeats the admission of the sages that no wise man
could do as the king demanded. By doing so, he denies that the sages
had hatched a plot against Nebuchadnezzar, as the king had claimed.

The inability of humans to meet the demands would stand in stark contrast to God's ability to meet them.

In his opening comment, Daniel lists four types of sages: **wise men, enchanters, magicians, and diviners**. When compared with v. 2, the new terms here are 'wise men' and 'diviners'. The first is from the noun meaning 'wisdom' and simply designates 'wise ones' in general. The second derives from a verb meaning 'cut' or 'determine', so it refers to persons who determine things, i.e. astrologers or soothsayers (*BDB*: 1086). As in v. 2, these terms do not seem to be used with technical precision here to denote particular types of sages, but are used to point to all types.

Verse 28. Daniel does not actually name the God who revealed the mystery to him, but that God is transparently clear to the reader. Daniel does give the first hint of the dream's meaning to Nebuchadnezzar in v. 28: it concerns events that will happen at the end of days. In point of fact, however, much of the dream and its interpretation deals with past history for the author and his community. That community is interested in the end of days, a subject in which Nebuchadnezzar may have had little or no interest!

Verses 29-30. God had revealed the mysteries of the last days to Nebuchadnezzar in the dream, and Daniel had come to disclose its meaning. First, however, he wanted the king to know what the reader learned in vv. 13-23, namely that the understanding of the mystery had been revealed to Daniel by God. On his own, Daniel was no wiser than other sages. Regardless of whether Nebuchadnezzar really understood (he worshipped Daniel in v. 46), the author was concerned that his 'wise' readers remember.

SCENE FOUR: THE DREAM AND ITS INTERPRETATION (31-45)

At last the narrative reaches its climax, the point at which the dream and its interpretation will be revealed. Daniel relates the dream in vv. 31-35 and its interpretation in vv. 36-45. The king saw a great statue composed of different metals: gold, silver, copper, and iron. While he watched divine hands cut a huge stone, which in turn smashed the statue at a single stroke. Perhaps originally the statue symbolized Babylonian kings, but in the chapter as it now stands the image referred to a sequence of four kingdom which would be replaced by a fifth: God's kingdom.

Verses 31-35. Daniel recounted the dream, which had been at the heart of the narrative to this point, in a mere five verses.

Verse 31. In his dream, Nebuchadnezzar had seen a great statue. Daniel gives no dimensions of the statue, in contrast with Daniel 3, where the height of Nebuchadnezzar's image will be given as 60 cubits (about 90 feet). Such precise measurements are more appropriate in a narrative than in a vision or dream. In 2.31, Daniel did single out three features of the statue for comment: its size was **huge**, its brilliance **extraordinary**, and its appearance **frightening**. E.F. Siegman (1956: 366) thinks the imagery was borrowed from the well-known colossi at Rhodes and Thebes or from the less-famous statues of Assyria and Persia. Regardless, it was not a vision to bring comfort to anyone, king or not.

Verses 32-33. As Daniel described the image, there emerged the familiar pattern of four metals, each more base than its predecessor. Its **head** was of fine **gold**, its **chest** (lit. 'breasts') and **arms** of **silver**, its **middle** (abdomen) and **thighs** (or hips) of **bronze**, and its **legs** of **iron**. Montgomery (1927: 167 n. 2) mentions the 'lavish' use of bronze in Babylon as a possible reason for its inclusion here, but Hesiod (*Works and Days*, 1.109-201), writing well before the neo-Babylonian period, also names bronze as one of the metals representing an empire.

A strange feature of the image, however, is that its **feet** were comprised of **iron** mixed with potter's **clay**. Collins (1993a: 163) points to a close parallel in the Zoroastrian text *Bahman Yasht*, a Zoroastrian apocalypse. It was written in the Pahlevi language, and did not achieve its final written form before about the tenth century. How much older material it may contain is uncertain (see Ringgren and Ström 1967: 283), so it is difficult to know whether the parallel verses were extant as early as the book of Daniel. Be that as it may, the mixed feet indicated an insubstantial base for the image.

Verse 34. The only action in the dream comes next. Speaking in the passive voice, Daniel tells the king that **a stone was cut out, not by human hands**... If the hands were not human, they were divine. The use of the passive voice to speak of God's actions without naming God is familiar elsewhere in the Old Testament. Somehow, the stone struck the image on its mixed toes, breaking them in pieces.

Verse 35. So struck, the image apparently fell and destroyed itself. Its destruction was so complete, indeed, that **not a trace** of its constituent parts **could be found**. In its place, the stone grew into a great mountain.

Verses 36-45. The dream ended as ominously as it had began. The king awaited Daniel's interpretation of its meaning for him, and the readers awaited its meaning for them.

Verses 36-38. Daniel addressed the king with appropriate decorum. He identified Nebuchadnezzar as **king of kings** and as the one **to whom the God of heaven has given the kingdom, the power, and might, and the glory**. It was God who made Nebuchadnezzar king, a point he would deny in 4.30, where he claimed to have built magnificent Babylon by his own power and for his own glory. Then Daniel told the king he was the gold head of the image.

Verses 39-40. If the head was Nebuchadnezzar, the lower parts of the image would originally have been the kings who followed him. The succeeding metals were less important than the first, just as the succeeding Babylonian kings (Amel-Marduk, Neriglissar and Nabonidus) paled in comparison with Nebuchadnezzar. Goldingay (1989: 51) objects to this view on the grounds that it would make Cyrus the rock that crushed the statue and his coming had no such impact. He argues that the four metals represented Nebuchadnezzar, Belshazzar, Darius the Mede and Cyrus, the four kings mentioned in Daniel 1–6. That would make Cyrus's reign the last before the inbreak of God's kingdom, but it is not at all clear why it would be described as having feet of clay. It is better to see the original form of the narrative as a portrayal of the kings of the Babylonian Empire.

In its present form and in the context of the whole book of Daniel, therefore, the lower parts of the body were associated with subsequent kingdoms (the Median, Persian and Greek Empires; see comments on 8.20-21) rather than kings. By implication, then, Nebuchadnezzar should be understood to represent the Babylonian Empire. This new reading of the image continued through the rest of the chapter.

The NRSV translates the end of v. 40 as follows: **it shall crush and shatter all these**. That translation implies that the Greek Empire would smash all the other empires; and Ginsberg (1954: 249-50) argues that the verse envisions and v. 41a presupposes a time when vestiges of the Babylonian, Median and Persian Empires all existed simultaneously, a condition that existed from about 307 or 306 until the Battle of Ipsus in 301. It is possible, however, that the crucial words translated **all these** actually belong to the description of iron, and not to the activity of the Greek Empire. The AV, for example, translated as follows: 'and as iron that crushes all these, it shall break in pieces and crush'. Taken this

way, v. 40 neither says or implies anything about whom the Greeks
defeated; it says only that the Greeks were invincible.

Verses 41-43. These verses interpret the toes of the image as a
divided kingdom, partly strong and **partly brittle**, a fairly obvious
reference to the division of Alexander's Empire among his generals
after his death. Verse 43 may allude simply to the uneasy alliance
among the generals that soon enough gave way to armed hostility. Or it
may allude to the frequent practice of intermarriage between the Seleucids and Ptolemies, or (as is often said) to a specific marriage, such as
that between Antiochus II and Bernice in 252 or of Antiochus III's
daughter Cleopatra to Ptolemy V in 193.

Verse 44. This verse interprets the stone cut by no human hand. At
the end of the days of the kings who **mix with one another in marriage** (i.e. the Seleucids and the Ptolemies), God will set up a new
kingdom. While Daniel does not say so, the kingdom in question is
Israel or a subgroup thereof. This development would have been of no
comfort to Nebuchadnezzar, but of immense comfort to the community
of Daniel either in the Diaspora or in Palestine. Hence, Daniel makes
two basic predications. (1) The new kingdom will never be destroyed,
unlike the old kingdoms of Israel and Judah which were overrun regu-
larly and substantially destroyed, Israel by Assyria and Judah by Babylon. (2) Nor would the kingdom be left to another people, unlike the
Judean kingdom, which had experienced a whole series of foreigner
rulers, one after another. Rather, the new kingdom would crush any and
every opposing army, and bring the opposing kingdoms to an end. In
saying so, Daniel was merely echoing the promise of Ezekiel 38–39,
the Gog of Magog passage.

Verse 45. This verse concluded Daniel's interpretation by repeating
that the stone would smash **the iron, the bronze, the clay, the silver,
and the gold**. These are the same elements as in the vision, though
almost but not quite in reverse order since clay was mentioned third
instead of first. It is doubtful that one should attach any particular
significance to the change. The real point is that Nebuchadnezzar could
rely on these things to come about as Daniel had said, because the God
who had interpreted the dream would also carry out the plan.

One last observation should be made here. Fewell (1988: 59-61)
notes that Daniel's reading of the dream is an underreading. That is,
there are several elements of the vision which are not explained, though
the reader will understand them. (1) The image is a singular construct

that stands and falls as one. To extend Fewell's observation here, one might say that the replacement of one empire by the next is not crucial; it is the elimination of those empires that the author and reader longed for. (2) Daniel never explains the significance of the image's human form and never points out that the stone represents a divine kingdom in contrast with human kingdoms (cf. Siegman 1959: 366). Rather, he distinguishes the stone as an eternal kingdom in contrast with the temporal kingdom represented by the statue. The image is, Fewell says, an idol of a humanity that is top-heavy and has overreached itself. (3) Daniel does not tell the king that his great empire rests upon an insecure base, and he minimizes Nebuchadnezzar's own failures.

SCENE FIVE: NEBUCHADNEZZAR PRAISES GOD AND ELEVATES DANIEL AND HIS FRIENDS (46-49)

The narrative ends quickly. Verses 46-48 form the actual conclusion, as the king recognizes Daniel and Daniel's God. Verse 49 ties the narrative to the rest of the book, as Daniel's friends are appointed over affairs in Babylon, where they are endangered by the king's erection of a golden statue (Dan. 3); and Daniel remains at the king's court, where he was available for consultation about Nebuchadnezzar's next dream (Dan. 4).

Verse 46. Despite the fact that Daniel had told Nebuchadnezzar that God rather than Daniel was the source of the interpretation of the dream, the king **fell on his face and worshipped Daniel** by offering grain and incense offerings to him. This action was clear evidence that Nebuchadnezzar did not fully understand what had happened and casts a shadow over the king's confession in v. 47.

Verse 47. The king then confesses that Daniel's God **is God of gods and Lord of kings and a revealer of mysteries**. Towner (1984: 33) notes that this confession constitutes a truncated version of a doxology similar to three others in Daniel 1–6 (4.1-3, 34-37; 6.25-27), all taken from the older psalmic tradition. Even so, it does not mean that Nebuchadnezzar has converted. As a polytheist, he always had room for one more god (Baldwin 1978: 95).

Verse 48. Since Daniel had proved so useful, Nebuchadnezzar promoted him. First, he made Daniel **ruler** (lit. caused him to rule) **over the whole province of Babylon**. No specific position for Daniel is named, and no title is given. It is pointless to try to determine exactly what his duties might have been; the issue is left completely open, presumably on purpose. Second, Nebuchadnezzar made Daniel **chief prefect over all the wise men of Babylon**. The word translated **prefect** is an Assyrian loan-word in both Hebrew and Aramaic. In late Hebrew it designates officials of various levels, some of them quite low, but in Daniel 3 it seems to designate fairly high-ranking officials, as it does here. His specific duties cannot, however, be determined from so general a title; nor are they important to the development of the book. What the author was interested in showing was that trusting in God could pay handsomely, even in a foreign court. The point of v. 48 was that Daniel went right to the 'top', just as in 1.20 Daniel and his friends went to the 'head of the class'.

Verse 49. The additional ending in v. 49 mentioned the friends again, making easy the transition to Daniel 3. The verse says that at Daniel's request, Nebuchadnezzar placed them **over the affairs of the province of Babylon**. Of course, the previous verse had made much the same claim about Daniel's new position. Is the reader to assume that the four shared power? that the friends ranked below Daniel? that they had separate spheres of authority? There is no way to know. All that is said is that they remained at court too. Hence, it is difficult to avoid the conclusion that very general claims are being made in v. 49 too.

THE THEOLOGY OF DANIEL 2

Once again the book of Daniel teaches that fidelity to Israel's God was the way for its readers to achieve success in a foreign court. In demonstrating that success, it makes three new points that warrant attention here. First, it claims that Israel's God could disclose the secrets of the future because God intended to intervene in history and correct its course. In the past, Israel had suffered; in the future, Israel would prosper.

The second point is more subtle. In his interpretation, Daniel identified Nebuchadnezzar as the golden head. Even in the context of Daniel 2, that identification is surprising, because the narrative supplied for the dream and its interpretation portrays Nebuchadnezzar as anything but golden or rational. Stated differently, the author had chosen to relate a dream of 'golden' Nebuchadnezzar, but the narrative he employed to introduce the dream and the interpretation belied them. Later chapters do the same thing. Nebuchadnezzar acts just as despotically and irrationally in the next chapter where he casts innocent men into the fiery furnace. In Daniel 4 he is reduced to the animal level. Nor

did his 'son' Belshazzar behave any better, so that no one would conclude that the Babylonian Empire as a whole deserved the title 'golden'
any more than did Nebuchadnezzar. As the book of Daniel progresses,
it will become clearer and clearer that no government made by human
hands deserved to be called golden.

Thirdly, as a document from the second century, Daniel 2 predicts
little more than that God will overthrow the system of world empires
and establish his own kingdom. Presumably that kingdom would be
Israelite, but that is not explicitly said in Daniel 2. Not until Dan. 12.1-3
does one find explicitly stated what is implicit here, and there little
more is promised to the 'wise' than 'brightness' that would attract others to God.

This limited articulation of the future stands in sharp contrast with the
attempt, repeated in Daniel 7, 8, 9 and 10–11, to read the past and present. In other words, the author was less worried about the future than
the present. He thought that if he could explain the past and the present
to the satisfaction of his readers, they would be confident and satisfied
with a brief glimpse of the future. Their problem was less what would
happen some time in the future than with the past events which led
them to their miserable present. If first they could understand how they
had come to their present situation, then they could see easily how God
would rectify things in the future.

If it is true as someone has joked that the people of Israel walked
through time looking backward, the author of the Daniel 2 turns out to
be thoroughly Israelite in his theology. More importantly, the fact that
he primarily looked backward ought to be the surest basis for not
attempting to use the book of Daniel as a blueprint for the future, either
by itself or in tandem with the New Testament book of Revelation or
other apocalyptic texts.

NEBUCHADNEZZAR'S GOLDEN IMAGE
AND THE FIERY FURNACE
(3.1-30)

Daniel does not appear in this chapter, and its heroes Shadrach, Meshach and Abednego fail to appear again in the book. It does, however, anticipate the danger that Daniel will face from the lions in ch. 6. Dramatically speaking, therefore, this narrative must precede Daniel 6. If not, it would be anticlimactic that the friends face such danger after Daniel himself had escaped. With the narrative of the threat to the friends coming here, the reader is warned that threats may come to Judeans in high places and is not surprised when Daniel too is endangered by his fidelity to God. The only way the tension could be higher in Daniel 6 is if the friends should actually die here, a possibility that is dealt with explicitly. The experience of the community in Babylon, however, is not so severe, so the friends escape through God's help.

This originally independent story was worked into the Daniel materials because it made a crucial distinction between allegiance to a king and worship of him. The means by which this story was integrated was quite simple. It begins with no superscription and no setting; instead, it is presented as the continuation of Daniel 2. Further, since Daniel 2 was tied to Daniel 1 by the common subject of dreams, Daniel 3 was tied to Daniel 2 by the common subjects of gold and statues (Fewell 1988: 65). Having seen himself as the head of gold in the statue of Daniel 2, Nebuchadnezzar commands that a statue of gold be made in his honor (Fewell 1988: 65). He summons his ranking officials (v. 3), and in an effort to ensure their subordination to him commands that they worship the statue (v. 6), both boosting his ego and proving that he has totally failed to understand the dream and its interpretation (Fewell 1988: 67). The narrative also revises the picture of Nebuchadnezzar in Daniel 2 as golden.

The complication arises in 3.8. When Shadrach, Meshach and Abednego refuse to comply with the king's command, he has them arrested. He threatens them with death, and brags in v. 15 that their God can not rescue them, words he has to take back in v. 28. The climax is reached in vv. 19-23, when the king orders the three friends cast into a fiery furnace. The denouement appears in vv. 24-30, where God rescues the friends and Nebuchadnezzar praises their God.

The LXX preserved a longer version of this narrative, with 68 verses inserted between 3.23 and 3.24, that is, between the climax and the denouement. That insertion consists of The Prayer of Azariah, The Song of the Three Young Men. In the MT the transition between v. 23 and v. 24 is abrupt, with v. 23 saying that the friends fell into the furnace and v. 24 describing the king's amazement that they had survived. The purposes of the additions were to explain why God came to intervene (because Azariah appealed to God's gracious nature), to exonerate God from any possible blame for their being placed in danger (the three were sinners), and to show proper behavior in the event of threats of martyrdom (praise God despite the circumstances). This commentary will deal only with the materials in the MT.

The genre of Daniel 3 is that of 'wisdom court legend'. Like Daniel 6, its plot leads toward martyrdom, which is averted by the intervention of God, resulting in a broken martyr story. In Daniel 1, any threat to Daniel and his friends was muted; here the threat is front and center. One might deduce that the community of the 'wise' had experienced or witnessed threats by a foreign king, a possibility they must have always known was possible. Even so, one message of Daniel 3 was the same as in Daniel 1, namely the means to higher office in the service of the foreign king was unswerving fidelity to the law of God. Under no other circumstance could God be expected to aid them.

A PUBLIC COMMAND TO WORSHIP A GREAT STATUE (1-7)

The narrative opens, without a new setting, by describing a public ceremony, which all the king's officials were required to attend. It was the type of public event that could easily lead an exiled Judean to ruin.

Verse 1. Nebuchadnezzar made a **golden statue**. The statue probably would have been made of wood and overlaid with gold (cf. Isa. 40.19). It measured **60 cubits** (about 90 feet) high and **six cubits** (about nine feet) wide, reflecting the Sumero-Akkadian sexagesimal number system (Baldwin 1978: 101). Its height would have exceeded the known size of other statues in the ancient world except the Colossus at Rhodes, which was 70 cubits high (Collins 1993a: 181). Its width of only one tenth of its height would have given it odd proportions, which has elicited

several explanations. One ancient papyrus simply corrects the width to
a more appropriate 12 cubits, while Goldingay (1989: 69) suggests it
may have been mounted on a large pedestal included in its overall
height. The point of the narrative, though, was the immensity of the
statue, so one should probably not press this detail.

Nebuchadnezzar set up the statue in the **plain of Dura**, the location
of which is uncertain. Following E.G. Kraeling, Baldwin (1978: 101)
suggests it is perhaps to be identified as Dura sha-karrabi, a suburb of
Babylon. Alternatively, E.M. Cook (1989: 115-16) suggests that Nebuchadnezzar set it up on the plain between the outer and inner walls of
the city.

Verse 2. Persons summoned for the dedication of the statue seem to
have been state officials, but the titles reflect those in the Persian
Empire. The first three offices formed a three-tiered structure, with **satraps** having overall responsibility for the satrapies or main divisions of
the Persian Empire, **prefects** or lieutenants assisting satraps, and **governors** as heads of the subdivisions (e.g. Samaria). The remaining four
were of lower rank, and the meaning of the titles is less clear, but perhaps they designate officials moderns would identify as counselors (or
informants, so Goldingay 1989: 65), treasurers, judges, and police
magistrates (Hartman and Di Lella 1978: 154-56). Similar lists appear
in Assyrian inscriptions, but their function here is largely for rhetorical
effect.

Hector I. Avalos (1991: 583-87) argues more precisely that the effect
is comedic. He points out that wherever the officials appear, they are
expected to genuflect *en masse*, mindlessly and automatically before a
lifeless statue. The repeated description of this behavior portrays them
as 'a version of Pavlov's dog' (p. 585). Their conduct stands in marked
contrast with that of the Judeans, who act as moral agents and give a
reasonable account for their actions when required.

Verses 3-4. According to v. 3 the officials assembled before the
statue, but according to v. 4 a herald commanded **all the peoples,
nations, and languages** to fall down and worship the statue at the
sound of music. Collins (1993a: 183) speaks of a tension between the
limited group assembled and the universal pretensions of the herald's
address; however, the broader assembly acts in v. 7, so the tension lies
within the narrative, not between the narrator and the herald. It may be
considered evidence that the story underwent changes during its

growth, but the narrative offers insufficient criteria for sorting out different strata in these verses.

Verse 5. The herald named six types of musical instruments by their Greek names. The KJV translated their names with instruments known from the Renaissance. Efforts to be more precise have met with mixed success. The instruments included the **horn**, the **pipe** (or flute or whistle), the **lyre** (or the higher pitched zither, see Collins 1993a: 184), the **trigon** (literally, 'sambuke', 'a triangular instrument of four strings with high notes', see Collins 1993a: 184), the harp (literally, 'psalterion', an instrument like a zither, see Collins 1993a: 184), and the **drum**. This last mentioned instrument translated the word from which the English word 'symphony' comes, and perhaps meant 'double-flute' (so Collins 1993a: 184; cf. Grelot 1979: 36-37), which would have been an instrument capable of playing two notes in harmony at once. Alternately, it might not have designated a musical instrument at all, but simply have meant something like 'et cetera' (so Baldwin 1989: 102).

All of the instruments would probably have been loud. Gammie (1976: 196-98) suggests that many of the instruments were associated with bawdy and lewd celebrations. Avalos (1991: 585-87) argues that the repetition of the list of instruments in vv. 7, 10 and 15 is, like the repetition of the lists of officials, part of the comedic effect of the chapter.

Ridiculous or not, at the sound of music, the throng was to **fall down and worship** the image. Herein lay the problem: idolatry. At any time Judeans in the service of a foreign king might be expected to affirm allegiance to the king or to his gods. While allegiance to the king could be gladly given, worship could not be, either to the king or his gods. Daniel 3 seems determined to make the distinction clear. It presented the issue in terms of bowing down and worshipping before an image of something on earth (namely Nebuchadnezzar), a clear violation of the second commandment (Exod. 20.4-5). As soon as allegiance to the king took on religious overtones, it became idolatrous. According to Lacocque (1979: 61), the required behavior was nothing other than 'religious parody become an affair of state'. The LXX of 3.1 makes the religious character of the act even clearer by dating the event in the eighteenth year of King Nebuchadnezzar. The date is taken from Jer. 52.29, which places the destruction of Jerusalem and the Second Deportation in that year. In other words, the LXX portrayed the statue as a commemoration of the destruction of the temple (Lacocque 1979: 56).

Verses 6-7. The command was followed by a threat that anyone who refused to worship would be thrown into a furnace of fire. The threat of being burned alive is mentioned elsewhere in the Old Testament (cf. Gen. 38.24; Josh. 7.15). It also occurred in various places in the ancient Middle East. J.B. Alexander (1950: 375-76) calls attention to an eighteenth-century command of a ruler named Rim Sin: 'Because they threw a young slave into an oven, throw ye a slave into a furnace.' Jeremiah 29.22 also alludes to two men Nebuchadnezzar burned to death. Since the threat would have seemed believable, the reader would not be surprised to learn that the 'peoples, nations, and languages' fell down and worshipped at the sound of the music.

THE FRIENDS' REFUSAL TO OBEY (8-18)

Verses 8-12. Shadrach, Meshach and Abednego refused. Their conduct was brought to the attention of the king. Since the purpose of the assembly was to dedicate the statue, one might have expected the king to be in attendance, and vv. 8-12 can be read from that perspective, though the verses might not require that reading. In v. 14, however, Nebuchadnezzar asks if the report was true. Had he been present, a more likely question would have been whether they were indeed the persons who refused to bow down. A consistent reading of vv. 8-15, therefore, requires the assumption that Nebuchadnezzar was not present at the ceremony.

Verse 8. Certain Chaldeans went to the king to report their behavior. Daniel 2.49 reported that Nebuchadnezzar had appointed Shadrach, Meshach and Abednego over the affairs of the province of Babylon, so in the logic of the connected narratives in chs. 2 and 3, the Chaldeans in question may have been magicians and enchanters displaced by the rise of the Judean youths. Consequently, they jumped at the chance and **denounced** the three for refusing to worship the king's statue. The Aramaic clause is quite forceful, and may be rendered literally as follows: 'they ate the Judeans to pieces'.

Verses 9-11. The Chaldeans began addressing Nebuchadnezzar with an appropriate blessing: **O king, live forever!** Then they reminded the king of his commandment and threat.

Verse 12. Next they accused Shadrach, Meshach and Abednego of not obeying the king's order, which presumably would have been obvious to all present. Hence, it would seem that all they needed to do was identify the offenders to Nebuchadnezzar, rather than inform him that the law had been broken. More importantly for the narrative, however, was their linking worshipping the statue with serving the Babylonian gods. In effect, the narrator had the Chaldeans themselves link the worship of the statue with the worship of Babylonian gods.

Verses 13-15. Nebuchadnezzar was outraged and offered the three a choice between worshipping the statue and refusing, that is, between life and death.

Verse 13. Nebuchadnezzar's anger was underscored by the use of two synonyms meaning 'rage', which NRSV translated **in furious rage**. His irrational anger dictates his behavior for most of the rest of the narrative. In anger he had the three brought to him for questioning.

Verse 14. Nebuchadnezzar links worshipping the statue with worshipping Babylonian gods.

Verse 15. This verse returns to the thrust of v. 13. Recognizing the guilt of the three, Nebuchadnezzar offers them one more chance to prove their loyalty to him and his gods. If they refuse, they will be thrown into a furnace of blazing fire. Then he defies them to name anyone, even a god, who could deliver them from his hands. (He is to receive his answer in v. 17.)

Verses 16-18. Shadrach, Meshach and Abednego declined to defend their behavior, but responded to Nebuchadnezzar's boast that no one could prevent him from carrying out the punishment.

Verse 17. Their response was not an unconditional declaration that God would save them. Instead, they responded that if God could, God would save them. NRSV renders the last phrase as a jussive: **let him deliver us**. Various ancient versions modified their statement into something more affirmative. Theodotion rendered it thus: 'For there is a god, whom we worship, capable of saving' (Collins 1993a: 187). Such modifications missed the point, which can only be seen in connection with v. 18. Coxon (1976: 400-409) reads the MT based on Akkadian parallels, and translates (p. 408): 'If our God is able to save us, he will save...but if not, let it be known to you...' In their peril, they did not know whether God could save them; perhaps there were reasons why not. However, in the narrative they did affirm their belief that if God could save them, God would.

Verse 18. This verse opens **But if not**... Even if it should turn out that God could not save them, they were unwilling to serve the Babylonian gods or to worship the golden statue. In other words, dying in faithfulness to God was preferable to living as a devotee of Babylonian gods, so they announced their intention to live for God whether it paid or not. Their commitment to God was unconditional, even if their confidence that God would deliver them was not.

THE FRIENDS THROWN INTO THE FIERY FURNACE (19-23)

The narrative reached its climax in vv. 19-23. Such effrontery would not be overlooked, and Nebuchadnezzar ordered the three bound and thrown into the fiery furnace. The heat was so intense it killed the guards who carried out the king's bidding, but Shadrach, Meshach, and Abednego remained unharmed.

Verse 19a. Nebuchadnezzar was so enraged by the friends' response to his demand they worship him that his **face** was distorted. The MT includes before the word 'face' the Aramaic word *ṣelᵉm*. It is the word for 'image' or 'statue' used in 3.1, 2, 3, 5, 7, 10, 12, 14, 15 and 18. The narrator was reminding the reader once more that the king resembled his statue.

Verses 19b-20. Nebuchadnezzar ordered the furnace heated **seven times more than was customary**, a detail supplied by the narrator for literary effect. There was no way to measure heat in an oven exactly, since thermometers were not invented until c. 1650 CE. The point was simply that the furnace was super heated, until it became, as Hartman and Di Lella (1978: 162) put it, 'as hot as possible'.

The narrator wanted the reader to understand that the king took no chances in having the prisoners bound. He did not simply order a few guards to arrest them, he had **some of the strongest guards in his army** bind the three. Collins (1993a: 188) notes that binding prisoners was customary to simplify the task of executing them.

The soldiers were to throw the friends into the **furnace of burning fire**. Furnaces were typically constructed either of brick or stone, and varied in size depending on their function: smelting ore, melting metal, firing pottery, firing bricks, or making lime (Funk 1962: II, 330). Montgomery (1927: 202) describes the furnace in Daniel 3 as similar to a lime-kiln, 'with a perpendicular shaft from the top and an opening at the bottom for extracting the fused lime'.

Verse 21. Typically, prisoners would be stripped before they were executed (Hartman and Di Lella 1978: 163), but not these three. The terms for their articles of clothing defy translation, though the NRSV calls them **tunics, trousers** and **hats**. Presumably the point was that the garments covered their whole bodies, including their heads.

Commentators sometimes suggest that the naming of their articles of clothing accentuates the miracle that will follow in v. 27, namely that neither a hair on their heads nor even their clothes were burned. In addition, one should remember the objection of the Hebrew Bible against public nudity. Exodus 20.26 warns priests against using raised altars, lest when they mounted the stairs they exposed themselves. In 2 Sam. 6.20 Michal chides David for dancing immodestly before the Ark (if that is the meaning of the verse, see Stensell 1994: 66-67). Also in Nah. 3.5-6 God threatens Assyria with pulling its skirts above its head to shame it. Perhaps, then, this detail was meant to assure modest readers that the intended martyrs were not subjected to public humiliation.

Verses 22-23. At the king's insistence the soldiers approached the raging furnace and pitched the friends into its top opening. The heat, ironically, was so intense it killed the executioners, while the friends themselves fell down the furnace shaft.

GOD RESCUES SHADRACH, MESHACH, AND ABEDNEGO FROM THE FIERY FURNACE (24-30)

The unthinkable had happened: the faithful servants of God had been hurled apparently to death in the furnace. Nebuchadnezzar's boast in v. 15 had apparently come true. Verses 24-26 describe the outcome.

Verses 24-25. Somehow the king could see the friends in the furnace. He was amazed because he had thrown three men, bound, into the fire, but he could see four men, unbound, walking around in the furnace. The fourth figure was described as a having **the appearance of a god** (literally, 'and the appearance of the fourth is like a son of a god'). The phrase has provided the occasion for debate. Some traditional Christian interpreters (e.g. Miller 1994: 123-24) translate the title 'the son of God', since the Aramaic word *'elāhîn* can be read as a proper name for God. They understand the figure as Jesus, but early Christians questioned how a pagan king would recognize him. (See Walvoord's rejection of this interpretation 1971: 91.) In light of Nebuchadnezzar's polytheism, the most obvious meaning is that the fourth figure was an angel, as he explicitly says in v. 28.

Verse 26. When Nebuchadnezzar discovered that the friends were unhurt, he approached the lower door of the furnace and commanded them to come out, which they did. He called the friends **servants of the Most High God**. The title occurs throughout Daniel 4 and is reminiscent of the name El Elyon, used of God in the Old Testament. It is also reminiscent of the title of the highest god in polytheistic religions. That god in some cultures was thought to be so far above mortals as to be uninterested in them. In ancient Ugarit, for example, the highest god was El, but other divinities, chiefly Baal, interacted with human beings and were worshipped by the Canaanites. The use of this title does not indicate that Nebuchadnezzar had converted, only that he recognized the power of the God of the Judeans.

Verse 27. Nor was Nebuchadnezzar the only one who witnessed the rescue. Verse 27 lists the first four sets of officials named in vv. 2 and 3 as present, and probably implies that the others were as well. Lest the reader miss the point, this verse insists that not only were the friends not killed or hurt, they did not even smell smoky!

Verse 28. Nebuchadnezzar blessed the God of the friends for sending an angel to deliver them from danger. The technique of having a pagan bless God appears elsewhere in the book in passages Towner (1969: 319-25) has shown were composed for and inserted secondarily in their contexts (2.20-23; 4.3, 34b-35; and 6.26b-27). It is likely that the same thing happened here. If so, given the mention of Michael as Israel's protector (12.1), the fourth figure might be conceived of as a guardian angel.

The doxology also extols the friends for their willingness to die rather than to worship the gods of the king and his court. In their case fidelity to God had required disobeying the direct order of the king, and their God had delivered them from harm.

Verse 29. Nebuchadnezzar ate his words from v. 15. There he had bragged that no god could deliver the friends from his hands; here he confessed that their God had done just that. He had thought that he was in charge of affairs in Babylon, but discovered that he could not carry out the execution of foreign servants without the permission of God. NRSV correctly translates the verb in his speech **utters blasphemy**. Shalom Paul shows (1983: 291-93) that the root *slh* is related to the Aramaic word *sillatu*, which was part of what W.G. Lambert (1960: 312 n. 28) called the 'Akkadian stock of terms for sinful speech'.

Verse 30. The narrative concludes with the note that Nebuchadnezzar promoted the faithful friends in the province of Babylon, over which 2.49 said he had already appointed them! Such conclusions also appear in 5.29 and 6.28. These conclusions appear to have been the narrator's way of saying the faithful heroes were rewarded for their fidelity.

THE THEOLOGY OF DANIEL 3

This chapter raises the issue of martyrdom. Perhaps Judeans in the exile and certainly Judeans under Antiochus Epiphanes had to face that possibility. The issue, therefore, was this: when, if ever, was one justified in bowing before other gods? If not in a situation like this, when? *4 Maccabees*, a later treatise from the middle of the first century CE, answered the question by focusing on the martyrdom of an old priest, a widow, and her seven sons at the hands of Antiochus IV. It seems to concede that the law would not condemn someone for recanting out of fear, but argued (8.1) that reason could overcome fear (see Redditt 1983: 253-54) and enable the believer to remain true in the face of death.

In Daniel 3, of course, the friends did not die; God could and did rescue them. That is its first answer to the question: God saves the faithful whenever possible. Verse 18 goes further to raise the issue of what to do when rescue is not possible. It affirms the superiority of death in obedience to God over life in the service of other gods. Ultimately, this chapter makes an argument for the superiority of God over the Babylonian divinities and life under Torah to life under any other religious system. If this verse is read in conjunction with 12.2, which seems to promise resurrection for martyrs, the message of Daniel 3 was reassuring to people facing martyrdom.

NEBUCHADNEZZAR'S DREAM OF
THE TREE AND HIS MADNESS
(4.1-37)

As seen in the Introduction, Daniel 4 probably opened the original edition of the book of Daniel, which included chs. 4–6, edited by a redactor called R1 in this commentary. (Meadowcroft 1995: 272-73 also begins his reconstruction of the history of the text of Daniel with the conclusion that chs. 4–6 formed the first version.) The chapter constitutes another wisdom court legend, in which Daniel competes with other courtiers and succeeds where they have failed.

The redactor R1 probably drew upon diverse traditions. For one thing, the original narrative may have concerned Nabonidus rather than Nebuchadnezzar, though P.W. Coxon (1986: 93) thinks such suggestions miss the point that Daniel 4 is a midrashic composition on various texts in the Hebrew Bible. Secondly, 4.10-17 [MT 4.7-14] may have been a song about the destruction of the Babylonian Empire, which was reworked into Nebuchadnezzar's dream (Richter 1993: 246). Thirdly, Eusebius cites a Chaldean document from about 300 BCE that may well have been the source of 4.29-33a (see Koch 1993: 86).

The opening verses, 4.1-3 [MT 3.31-33], suggest a complicated history of the chapter since they appear at the end of Daniel 4 in the Old Greek, which was their original setting. They were moved to the beginning of Daniel 4 by R2 to connect the first edition (Dan. 4–6) to Daniel 3. The song in 4.3, however, converts a promise to tell others about Israel's God into a doxology. It resembles other doxologies in the book of Daniel in which a character prays to and praises God: Daniel in 2.20-23; Nebuchadnezzar in 2.47; 3.28-29; and 4.34-35 (missing from the Old Greek); and Darius in 6.25-27 (see Towner 1984: 61, and earlier in 1969: 319-25). Since these doxologies appear throughout the Aramaic section of Daniel, they are best understood as the work of R2. It would follow, then, that the revision of 4.3 was his work when he moved the original conclusion of the narrative to the beginning.

One more problem in the MT. this one minor, can be solved by comparing it to the Old Greek. As the Hebrew text stands, the narrative switches its point of view from the first person to the third in v. 16 (NRSV v. 19) with the words 'The king said'. It switches back to the first person singular in v. 31 (NRSV v. 34). When R2 moved the ending of Daniel 4 to its beginning, he dropped the initial sentence of the chapter introducing what followed as something Nebuchadnezzar had said. Hence, the voice of the narrator was lost until v. 16 (NRSV v. 19). In the Old Greek Nebuchadnezzar also recounts his malady in the first person, but the MT (v. 30; NRSV v. 33) left it in the third person, resuming the first person account with the next verse.

The plot of Daniel 4 may be analyzed as follows. The transition verses, 4.1-3, provide the chapter with the appearance of an epistle. Verse 1 also repeats the list of people addressed by the herald in 3.4 and 7, leaving the reader with the preliminary impression that the letter was a response to the episode of the fiery furnace. That impression, of course, turns out to be mistaken, but the connection between the two chapters is established nonetheless. Verse 2, along with the doxology in v. 3, foreshadows the doxologies at the conclusion of the story in vv. 34-35, 37.

The narrative itself begins in 4.4, and relates in the first person singular a new episode about Nebuchadnezzar. Verse 4 establishes the setting: the palace of Nebuchadnezzar in Babylon. Verses 5-6 describe his situation: he had had a troubling dream and called on his specialists in interpretation for assistance. Verses 7-27 relate the complications. The Babylonian specialists fail (v. 7), Daniel/Belteshazzar arrives (v. 8), hears the dream (vv. 10-17), interprets it (vv. 20-26), and advises the king to atone for his sins (v. 27). The climax occurs in vv. 28-33, where Nebuchadnezzar leaves human society for seven years. Finally, vv. 34-37 relate the denouement, the return of Nebuchadnezzar to sanity and his praise of God. In this chapter it is Nebuchadnezzar who experiences the liminal experience in the form of his descent from palatial splendor into animal life, his discovery of the power of God, and his return to normalcy.

Shea (1985: 278) diagrams the narrative in a chiastic structure slightly modified here.

PROLOGUE (1-3)

Verses 1-3 introduce Daniel 4 and give it the appearance of an epistle. Verse 1 names both the sender and the recipients and invokes a blessing upon the latter; v. 2 states the purpose of the letter; and v. 3 breaks into a doxology.

Verse 1. It was standard practice among Babylonians and Persians to place the sender's name at the beginning of a letter, and the practice is attested also in Ezra 7.12. Here, the letter purports to be from Nebuchadnezzar and the recipients are all the peoples of the world, that is, the subjects of the Babylonian Empire. Such claims were fairly typical of ancient royal pronouncements.

Verse 2. Next, Nebuchadnezzar states the purpose of his letter: to extol the **signs and wonders** of God. The phrase is typically Hebraic (cf. Exod. 7.3; Deut. 6.22). Nebuchadnezzar identified God in vv. 2 and 34 as the **Most High God** and in v. 37 as the **King of heaven**. The further statement that he was pleased to relate the following matter anticipates the successful outcome of the episode, not the trauma he endured.

Verse 3. Next, the author places a doxology on the lips of Nebuchadnezzar. The doxology is echoed and expanded in 4.34-35, 37, thus forming an inclusio, opening and closing the chapter with praise to God. The name 'Yahweh' is not used, and there is no suggestion that Nebuchadnezzar converted to the worship of Yahweh alone, but the claim is being made that he recognized the God of Daniel as legitimate.

DREAM RECEPTION (4-6)

The narrative proper begins in v. 4, with Nebuchadnezzar at ease in his palace. As in Daniel 2, he had a dream, which disturbed him. Again, he called on his advisers to interpret it for him.

Verse 4. The setting is described in two parallel phrases: **at ease in my home** and **prospering in my palace**. One can easily imagine either phrase standing by itself. The claim that one was at ease at home conjures up warm images of a person at peace with himself in domestic surroundings. The claim that he was prospering in his palace conjures up stronger images of a powerful king ruling efficiently and perhaps ruthlessly. The interaction between the phrases suggests the best of both phrases, maximum success with minimal effort, a person who had it made, as only a victorious king now basking in his own glory could experience.

Verse 5. Three words describe the sight that terrified him: **dream**, **fantasies**, and **visions**. Dreams and visions can be distinguished, dreams being the ordinary experiences of people asleep, visions being the sensations of persons in an awake, but extraordinary state of consciousness. By contrast, the terms could be used in synonymous parallelism as they were in Joel 2.28 [MT 3.1] and Job 33.15. In addition, dreams could be seen as vehicles of revelation (as in the Joseph stories), as could visions (as in call visions and the visions of Isaiah, Ezekiel and Zechariah). On the other hand Jeremiah derided prophets who spoke on the basis of dreams and contrasted them with people who spoke the word of Yahweh (23.28); he also accused his opponents of prophesying on the basis of a lying vision (14.14). Hence, the meaning of the words fluctuated from context to context.

The word **fantasies**, however, appears only here in the MT, though its cognate appears in late Hebrew with a sexual connotation. Here it is variously translated: 'fancies' in the KJV; 'images' in the NAB; 'dread' by the NJB; and 'thoughts' by Hartman and Di Lella (1978: 171 n. 2). It is not clear that it necessarily carries the meaning of 'fantastic' or 'impure'; it does stand in synonymous parallelism with 'visions'.

The three terms, then, do not seem to carry a negative connotation here, but emphasize both the esoteric and nocturnal nature of Nebuchadnezzar's communiqué from God. Since he could not understand the dream, he was terrified of what it might portend.

Verse 6. In view of this fear, he summoned his sages to interpret the dream for him. It is not yet clear who these wise men are, but vv. 7 and 8 sketch out that information.

INSTRUCTIONS: KING TO DANIEL (7-9)

Complications arise at once (v. 7) when the Babylonian magicians are unable to interpret the dream, as in Daniel 2. This time Nebuchadnezzar makes no threats on their lives, because Daniel appears as the last among them (v. 8). Nebuchadnezzar instructs Daniel to interpret his dream (v. 9).

Verse 7. The list of officials in 4.7 differs from the list in 2.2 only in that 'sorcerers' are replaced by 'diviners' (as in 2.27). Here too these titles are probably used without precise meaning. Again the officials were unsuccessful in interpreting the king's dream.

Verse 8. Daniel enters the room after the king has told the Babylonian wise men his dream, and he has to repeat it to Daniel. He is further identified by his alternate name 'Belteshazzar', which Nebuchadnezzar explains was derived from the name of his god. Collins (1993a: 141) notes that the MT vocalizes the name so as to introduce the name of the Babylonian creator god Bel (also called Marduk). The mention of Nebuchadnezzar's god sets up the irony in the chapter; it will be Israel's God, not Nebuchadnezzar's, who will help Belteshazzar.

Nebuchadnezzar says that Belteshazzar was endowed with a **spirit of the holy gods**. The word for gods, *'elāhîn*, constitutes a pun. On the lips of a polytheist like Nebuchadnezzar, the word retains its grammatical force of a masculine, plural noun. On the lips of a monotheistic Judean, it is one of the names of Israel's God. In fact, the phrase 'holy God' is used of Yahweh in Josh. 24.19. The word **spirit** simply refers to the charisma or empowerment by God to perform a function.

Verse 9. Nebuchadnezzar addresses Belteshazzar as the **chief of the magicians**. In 2.48, the narrator called Daniel the **chief prefect over all the wise men of Babylon**. Since these titles are not official, probably no difference was intended. Nor is it likely that the author intended to say that Daniel was chief of the magicians only, and not the enchanters, Chaldeans, and diviners. Instead, he singled out Daniel as the chief of them all. (See the comments on 2.19 for a discussion of the word 'mystery'.)

DREAM RECITAL: KING TO DANIEL (10-17)

Nebuchadnezzar relates the dream to Daniel. Coxon (1986: 93, 107-109) argues that in the dream the author welds together the well-known image of the cosmic tree (vv. 10-12) with that of a shaggy beast-like creature, a symbol of humiliation (vv. 14-17). Thus, the first part of the dream (vv. 10-12) portrays Nebuchadnezzar as the cosmic tree, the source of life and blessing, while the second part (vv. 14-17) and the interpretation (vv. 28-33) make him a comic figure crawling around on all fours. The first is the type of portrayal of a king one would expect from his subjects; the second is a jarring rebuttal of that image, drawn as a consequence of the author's monotheism.

Verses 10-12. In his dream, Nebuchadnezzar had seen a great tree. Coxon (1986: 94-95) points to the use of tree symbolism in Genesis 3, where the human pair is to protect the tree in order to remain in paradise. More directly, wisdom is called the tree of life to those who lay hold on 'her' (Prov. 3.18; cf. 11.30; 13.12; 15.4); and Ezek. 17.24 utilizes the symbol by speaking of Israel as the small tree God will elevate above all the others. It is clear, then, that Dan. 4.10-12 portrays Nebuchadnezzar in a favorable light as the source of blessing for his people.

Verse 10. As the king lay on his bed, he dreamed of a lofty tree at the center of the earth. The concept of the cosmic tree is one form of the more generic notion of the 'center of the earth'. In some cultures that center could be a mountain; in others a sanctuary, a leader's house, or even a person. Assyrian and Babylonian ziggurats (temple towers built of successively smaller square platforms one on top of another and topped by a sanctuary) may have constituted another example. The fluidity of the concept lay behind the transference of the tree to Nebuchadnezzar in Daniel's interpretation.

Verse 11. The top of the cosmic tree **reached to heaven**; that is, the tree functioned as the 'navel of the earth', the means by which the blessings of the gods reached earth. The comment that it was visible to the whole earth was simply a pre-scientific way of extolling its height and majesty.

Verse 12. As the cosmic tree, its foliage was beautiful. As the earth's navel, its fruit was abundant. **All living beings** (literally, 'flesh') fed from it; birds nested in its branches, and animals sought its shelter.

Verse 13. This verse juxtaposes the perspective of the Judean redactor R1, who has Nebuchadnezzar continue to narrate his dream, with a second image, quite opposite in content to the first. In the first part of the dream, Nebuchadnezzar describes what he saw. In the second part, Nebuchadnezzar relates what he hears, namely a voice giving a series of commands about what is to be done to the tree.

The voice was that of a **holy watcher**. The term 'watcher' is widely attested in intertestamental literature, particularly in *1 Enoch* 1–36 and *2 Enoch* 18. 'Watcher' seems to be a term for 'angel', including fallen angels. Here in Daniel 4, the 'watcher' is called 'holy', and is said to come down from heaven. Verse 17 makes it clear that the 'watcher' is a representative of a larger group and has come on God's business.

Verses 14-17. Nebuchadnezzar hears a decree that the tree be cut down, though not destroyed. The fact that the tree symbolized a human is made clear in v. 16, which commanded that his human mind be replaced by that of an animal. Nebuchadnezzar was sentenced to live in that state **seven times**, in order to teach him that God, not he, ruled the world.

Verse 14. The watcher commands that the cosmic tree be felled and its branches stripped off. In such a condition, it could no longer function as the earth's navel, so the animals would leave it. Who was to carry out the commands of the watcher? Daniel 4 offers no definite answer, but the reference to watchers (plural) in v. 17 suggests that the watcher of v. 14 may have been thought of as a high-ranking angel with subordinates who would do his bidding.

Two passages from Ezekiel illuminate this action. First, Ezek. 17.3-4 speaks of an eagle (Nebuchadnezzar) topping a huge tree, which symbolized King Jehoiachin. Secondly, in predicting the downfall of Egypt, Ezekiel 31 draws upon the downfall of Assyria to Babylon. Assyria, like Nebuchadnezzar in Dan. 4.10-12, was beautiful (Ezek. 31.3), grew tall, with its tops among the clouds (vv. 3-5), and provided shelter for birds and animals (v. 6). God handed over Assyria to the 'prince of the nations'—that is, Nebuchadnezzar, king of Babylonia, 'the most terrible of the nations' (v. 12)—who punished it appropriately for its deeds (v. 11). Verse 14 states the purpose for the fall of the tree representing Egypt: 'All this is in order that no trees...may...set their tops among the clouds.' That purpose applies equally well to Nebuchadnezzar.

Verse 15. The tree is not to be killed. Rather, its stump and roots are to be left in the ground, so it can put out shoots again when bathed by the dew. The idea that a tree stump can put out new shoots is used elsewhere in Hebrew Scriptures. Job 14.7-9 expresses the thought poetically:

> For there is hope for a tree, that if it is cut down, it will sprout again, and
> its shoots will not cease.
> Though its root grows old in the earth, and its stump dies in the ground,
> yet at the scent of water it will bud, and put forth branches like
> a young plant (NRSV).

To return to Dan. 4.15, the phrase **with a band of iron and bronze**, literally 'in binding of iron and bronze', is enigmatic. Scholars typically take either of two approaches. The first is to understand the phrase to mean metal bands placed around the stump, but there is no evidence of such a practice in the ancient Near East. The second is to suppose that the depiction of the tree turns into a depiction of Nebuchadnezzar, who might have been bound.

If one adopts the second suggestion and reads v. 15b as a reference to Nebuchadnezzar, one might also adopt the recommendation of *BHS* to amend the verb **bathed** (literally, 'let it/him be made wet') to read 'let it/him be fed', both here and in v. 23 (MT v. 20), agreeing with the interpretation in v. 33, which says that Nebuchadnezzar ate grass. On the whole it seems better to adopt this second interpretation and read v. 15b as a reference to Nebuchadnezzar. The following two verses also have him in mind.

Verse 16. In v. 16, the watcher commands that the tree have its **mind** (literally, 'heart') changed from that of a human to that of an animal. Ancient Israelites did not share a modern, scientifically informed, understanding of human anatomy. The word translated 'mind' referred to the inner person Only the context can make clear exactly what aspect of the person was in question.

Traditional scholars (e.g. Walvoord 1971: 108-10; Miller 1994: 142) take this verse to mean that Nebuchadnezzar was eventually overtaken by the delusion that he was an animal. One problem with trying to take the text literally, however, is that vv. 25 and 33 speak of his eating grass, which is not digestible by humans, since they lack the enzymes to break down cell walls of grass. Humans could extract vitamins from grass, but not sugar. Hence, it would be possible for Nebuchadnezzar to live on grass until his body burned its supply of sugar, but no longer.

The duration of this malady was to be **seven times**. The word 'times' is sufficiently ambiguous that it could refer to any measure of time (e.g., weeks, months, seasons, years); the Old Greek simply uses the word 'years'.

Verse 17. The source of the decree was the **watchers** themselves, further identified here as **holy ones**, or angels. The purpose of the decree was that **all who live**, Babylonians and their subjects, would recognize the sovereignty of God, again called the **Most High**, over all the nations. The Most High demonstrates divine power by making the lowliest people sovereign, a statement probably meaning that God had the power to elevate the exiles over the Babylonians and Nebuchadnezzar.

DIALOGUE: KING AND DANIEL (18-19)

Having finished reciting the dream, Nebuchadnezzar directs Daniel to interpret it (v. 18). Daniel is reticent to do so because of the implications of the second part of the dream for Nebuchadnezzar (v. 19a). The king, however, acts as every messenger must have wished for a king to act; he directs Daniel to tell him what the dream means without fear of reprisal (v. 19b).

Verse 18. Nebuchadnezzar is confident that Daniel/Belteshazzar can interpret his dream, because Daniel has been **endowed with a spirit of the holy gods**. (See comments on v. 9.)

Verse 19. Daniel was still reluctant to obey the command, so Nebuchadnezzar pressed him for an interpretation. Daniel, ever the diplomat, offered a brief wish that the dream and its interpretation would come true for the king's enemies instead of the king.

DREAM INTERPRETATION: DANIEL TO KING (20-26)

The next major section of this narrative is the interpretation of both parts of the dream.

Verses 20-22. First, Daniel identifies the tree as King Nebuchadnezzar himself. Verses 20-21 repeats the essence of vv. 10-12, while v. 22 makes the identification.

Verses 23-25. Likewise, v. 23 repeats the essence of vv. 14-16. In particular, Daniel says that the king will be driven away from human society. Biblical Hebrew frequently used the passive voice when the subject of an active verb would be God. That is probably what was implied here, though the watchers might have been God's agents.

In parallel clauses Daniel says the king will **be made to eat grass like oxen** and **be bathed with the dew of heaven**. On the issue of a human's eating grass, see the comments on v. 15. In areas of sparse rainfall like Babylon and Israel, dew was necessary for an abundance of crops. Hence, it can be used as a symbol of God's blessing (Ps. 133.3) and even resuscitation or resurrection (Isa. 26.19). Here, however, it functions as part of the description of how low the king would fall: the cosmic tree would lie in the dew; the king would have only dew for his bath.

Nebuchadnezzar's sentence was for **seven times**. The use of the term 'years' in the Old Greek suggests that the use of 'times' here is a deliberate, redactional element originating with R2 and anticipating the use of the term in 7.25, where the author was probably being deliberately vague about the time Antiochus IV would rule.

Verse 26. This verse repeats and applies v. 15a to Nebuchadnezzar. Just as a stump will again put out shoots, so his kingdom will come alive again when the king had learned that it was God who had put him on his throne.

INSTRUCTIONS: DANIEL TO KING (27)

Daniel advised Nebuchadnezzar to make atonement for his sins with righteousness and mercy, thus avoiding the punishment portrayed in the dream. He was not told to offer sacrifices, nor in the MT did he do so even after he suffered his downfall and redemption. By contrast, in the Old Greek version, he promised to offer daily sacrifices upon his restoration to power. This difference suggests that R2 entertained no notion of converting foreign sovereigns, but did still hope for justice and even mercy from their hands. It also shows that in Daniel 4 Nebuchadnezzar, the head of the statue in Daniel 2, was no longer golden.

The Old Greek also emphasized the guilt of Nebuchadnezzar, but by a different means. As evidence of Nebuchadnezzar's arrogance, Daniel tells Nebuchadnezzar that God saw how he 'desolated the house of the living God', a detail that fit Nebuchadnezzar perfectly and would have retained its force after the 'transgression that makes desolate' at the hands of Antiochus IV.

DREAM FULFILLMENT UPON KING (28-33)

Verses 28-33 constitute the climax of the narrative. The king would not learn from his dream, refused to recognize the sovereignty of God over him (vv. 28-30), and suffered the ignominy the dream had warned him about (vv. 31-33).

Verse 28. This verse seems almost out of place, because it says that Nebuchadnezzar suffered all that Daniel had warned him against before it relates why that punishment came upon the king. The author, however, reports first what was most important to him: the punishment was the fulfillment of God's word relayed to Nebuchadnezzar through the dream and its interpretation by Daniel.

Verses 29-30. The narrative jumps ahead a full year. Apparently, God granted Nebuchadnezzar that much time to repent and change his behavior toward both God and Israel. The night the dream came true the king was walking on the roof of his palace, surveying his capital city and congratulating himself for his work on it.

Imaginative as the scene was, it was true to life. During Nebuchadnezzar's reign, the city of some 3.2 square miles straddled the Euphrates River with inner walls 21 feet thick and towers every 60 feet rising 30 to 60 feet high. A double outer wall and then a moat surrounded the city, with yet a third wall enclosing a plain where people in the surrounding area could take refuge. Inside, Nebuchadnezzar had built a citadel to help defend the palaces. The city's opulence rivaled its magnitude, with great thoroughfares lined with bas reliefs and the famous Hanging Gardens visible above the walls when viewed from the outside. Temples to Marduk and at least 50 other gods dotted the city, along with statues to more than two hundred additional divinities (Wiseman 1979: I, 386-89).

Verses 29-30 picture Nebuchadnezzar taking credit for the grandeur of the city in words that emphasize his role: **I have built**; **my mighty power**; **my glorious majesty**. He clearly had not learned who was in charge of the nations in the time God had granted him.

Verse 31. As Nebuchadnezzar bragged about his power, his words stuck in his throat. He heard a voice from heaven. Slotki (1951: 36) compares the voice to the *bath kol* (daughter of a voice) from rabbinic literature, and Collins (1993a: 231) notes that such heavenly voices are also widely attested in Hellenistic literature. The voice told Nebuchadnezzar his kingdom had departed from him. The MT says nothing more about who would administer the kingdom, but the Old Greek says the kingdom would be given to a despised person in his household.

Verse 32. This verse essentially repeats v. 25, except for substituting 'animals of the field' from v. 23 for 'wild animals' in v. 25. In another echo of v. 25, God told the king that the punishment would last **until you have learned that the Most High has sovereignty over the kingdom of mortals and gives it to whom he wills**. These words both echo and parody the pronouncement of Jer. 27.5-7, where Jeremiah says that God had made the world and put Nebuchadnezzar in charge, not only of the people, but even of the animals.

Verse 33. While v. 32 predicts what would happen to Nebuchadnezzar, v. 33a announces that it was carried out. Verse 33b adds the details that **his hair grew as long as eagles' feathers and his nails became like birds' claws**. The description of the transformation was even more pronounced in the Old Greek, where Nebuchadnezzar's nails are compared to lion's claws. These details seem to pick up on the motif of 'wild animals', so that both v. 23 and v. 25 are carried out. They betray a literalist tendency to see that each detail of prediction has its corresponding detail of fulfillment.

EPILOGUE (34-37)

The denouement, which returns to the first person singular, announces Nebuchadnezzar's return to his senses. Having learned his lesson at such a fearful price, Nebuchadnezzar was quick to extol the power of God, lest an even more serious tragedy befall him!

Verse 34a. This verse opens with a temporal note: **when that period was over.** The period is clearly the 'seven times' mentioned in vv. 23 and 32. Suffice it to say that extant Babylonian records say nothing of Nebuchadnezzar's loosing control of or vacating his throne for a significant period of time.

It is worth noting that Nebuchadnezzar's cure does not come automatically. Rather, he first **lifted** his **eyes to heaven,** that is, he acknowledged the power of God over him and looked to God for help. This acknowledgment was the condition specified in vv. 17, 25 and 32 for his restitution to human society and his throne.

Verses 34b-35. Appropriately, R2 places a doxology on the lips of Nebuchadnezzar. In it, he blesses the **Most High.** (See comments on v. 2.) He confesses that God does what God wills both with the host of heaven and with the inhabitants of the earth. In adding **the host of heaven** (based on his contact with the watchers and the voice?), he went further than the watcher required in v. 17 or than Daniel and the voice specified in vv. 25 and 32.

Verse 36. Nebuchadnezzar's sanity returned, and along with it the majesty and splendor requisite for him to reign. Hence, Babylonian officials sought him out and re-established him on his throne with more power than before.

Verse 37. No longer did Nebuchadnezzar brag about himself, however. Now he praised God, whom he called **the King of heaven.** If Nebuchadnezzar was king of the known earth, he nevertheless recognized God as his king. Nebuchadnezzar praised two characteristics of God in particular: **truth and justice.** These were not abstract characteristics. Rather, Nebuchadnezzar experienced God as truthful in that God acted as promised, and Nebuchadnezzar also experienced God as just in punishing the haughty king for his pride.

THE THEOLOGY OF DANIEL 4

Once again, the primary theological point of the narrative was monotheism. Marduk, the god of Babylon, and Nebuchadnezzar, Marduk's man on the throne, were no match for Israel's God. The cosmic tree, the self-styled king of the world, was reduced to the level of an animal walking on all fours, eating grass, and sleeping outside where he would be covered by the dew. Only when he recognized the sovereignty of Israel's God even over the Babylonian Empire would that God restore him to his throne.

Secondly, the metal of the head was certainly not golden. R1's depiction of Nebuchadnezzar's madness made such an idea seem preposterous; the king was an arrogant fool who thought he ran the world. R2 shared that same opinion, clearly, since his hopes for the kings were no higher. As he saw it, the best one could hope for was that foreign kings acknowledge God and be just and merciful to Judeans in their kingdoms.

Thirdly, since Judean readers and not foreign kings were the intended audience of this narrative, what would this view of kings mean to the readers? It would mean that the way for Judeans to prosper in foreign service was by acknowledging God. Obedience to their God was their best hope, no matter how attractive assimilation to the foreign culture might seem.

BELSHAZZAR'S FEAST AND THE WRITING ON THE WALL (5.1-31)

Daniel 5 is simply juxtaposed to Daniel 4; the transition between the two chapters could hardly be more abrupt. Daniel 4 ended on a note of praise offered by Nebuchadnezzar; Daniel 5 opened with a blasphemous act committed by Belshazzar, who is not even introduced at the outset. Nor is there a historical note indicating the difference in times of the two events. In fact, the time of the narrative is not indicated until the last verse!

Despite the abruptness of the transition to Daniel 5, the concluding doxology in Daniel 4 expresses the theme of the narrative in Daniel 5:

> for all [God's] works are truth,
>> and all his ways are justice;
> and he is able to bring low
>> those who walk in price.

In addition, the chapter includes a number of details tying it to the previous narratives. Daniel 5 opens with wording identical to Daniel 3: '(So and so) the king made...', and both chapters open abruptly (Fewell 1988: 114). Daniel 5 and 6 both draw upon Jeremiah 27. Daniel 4.30 does so in connection with Jeremiah's view of Nebuchadnezzar as expressed in Jer. 27.5-7; Dan. 5.2 does so by speaking of the vessels Nebuchadnezzar took from the temple. Jeremiah warned that they (like the exiles) would not soon be brought back; instead Nebuchadnezzar would return to Jerusalem and remove the vessels he had left the first time (27.16-27).

Davies (1985: 48-50) notes recapitulations of earlier stories. In 5.11, the queen mother speaks in words that echo the list of wise men in 2.2, 10, 27 and in 4.7. In v. 13 Belshazzar remarks that Daniel was one of the exiles from Judah that Nebuchadnezzar brought to Babylon, information from Daniel 1. In 5.18-21 (missing from the Old Greek) Daniel summarizes ch. 4 and warns that Belshazzar was repeating Nebuchadnezzar's mistakes. Davies argues that these recapitulations prove that the chapter was written during the Maccabean period. What they probably prove, however, is that a Maccabean redactor (R2 in this commentary) inherited Daniel 4 (from R1) and reworked it. They add details to the narrative, but are not essential to it.

Herodotus (*Histories* 1.191) and Xenophon (*Cyropedia* 7.5) report a widespread story that when the Medes and Persians captured Babylon with a surprise attack the Babylonian king and nobles were carousing at a banquet. That story probably forms the basis for Daniel 5, to which the early redactor (R1) added a Judean explanation for the event, namely the blasphemy of Belshazzar in drinking from the temple vessels. He also converted it into another wisdom court legend, in which Daniel succeeded in reading the handwriting where the other courtiers had failed.

Shea (1985: 290) offers an analysis of Daniel 5 that underscores its chiastic structure, reproduced here with a few modifications.

A   (1)   Description of the banquet (1-4)
    (2)   Handwriting on the wall (5)
    (3)   Offer of honors for its interpretation (6-7)
    (4)   Failure of the king's wise men (8-9)
          B   Queen's speech: Nebuchadnezzar, Daniel and the
              spirit of interpretation (10-12)
              C   Daniel arrives and the king offers gifts (13-16)
              C' Daniel declines gifts (17)
          B' Nebuchadnezzar's dream interpreted (18-21)
A' (1)   Interpretation of the banquet (22-23)
    (2)   Interpretation of the handwriting (24-28)
    (3)   Bestowal of honors for interpretation (29)
    (4)   Fall of Babylonian Empire (30-31)

My comments on Daniel 5 will follow this analysis.

DESCRIPTION OF THE BANQUET (1-4)

The setting of Daniel 5 is a festival, the precise nature of which is not specified. The picture it paints is one of a crowd whose partying led it into a blasphemous use of utensils from the temple in Jerusalem. Bentzen (1952: 49) thinks the description of the banquet was drawn from Isa. 21.5, which is part of a passage about the fall of Babylon (21.1-10). The implied date of the banquet (from vv. 30-31) was the fifteenth day of the seventh month of the seventeenth year of the reign of Nabonidus, that is, the night before the Persians entered Babylon in October 539.

Verse 1. Daniel 5 opens with a reference to **King Belshazzar**, whose name meant 'Bel, protect the King'. Verse 2 says that Nebuchadnezzar was his father, a conclusion the author perhaps drew from Jer. 27.7, which speaks of the end of Babylonian hegemony after the reigns of Nebuchadnezzar, his son, and his grandson (so Mason 1988: 89).

Actually, Nabonidus not Nebuchadnezzar was the father of Belshazzar, so some translations (e.g. NIV) offer alternate meanings for the word 'father' like 'ancestor' or 'predecessor'. Nabonidus had usurped the throne from Labashi-Marduk, the young son of Neriglissar, who himself seems to have usurped the throne from Amel-Marduk, his brother-in-law, so it is unlikely that Belshazzar even descended from Nebuchadnezzar. Hence, some scholars suggest that the word 'father' means Belshazzar was of the same 'class' as Nebuchadnezzar (Owens 1971: 404) or that the terms 'father' and 'son' were only used 'figuratively' (Baldwin 1978: 22), and CEV includes a footnote that previous kings could be called 'father'. All of these suggestions are attempts to get around the apparent view of the R1 that Belshazzar was the actual son of Nebuchadnezzar. Recognizing that historical lapse, others (e.g. Goldingay 1989: 108) repeat the possibility that Daniel 4 originally referred to Nabonidus, not Nebuchadnezzar, and suggest that the confusion carried over into Daniel 5. Jeffery (1956: 422) agrees and holds that the relationship was already incorrectly assumed before the tradition reached the author of Daniel 5.

The 'Nabonidus Chronicle' (*ANET*: 306-307) records the events leading up to the fall of Babylon. It reports that Belshazzar ruled Babylon during the frequent absences of his father. While the 'Chronicle' reports that Nabonidus was arrested in Babylon after its capture by Cyrus, it does not report Belshazzar's fate. Daniel 5 does, of course.

The festival was attended by **a thousand of his lords**. Scholars have sometimes questioned the accuracy of the number, and they may be correct. Certainly a large hall would have been required to hold so many people. Montgomery (1927: 250), however, finds nothing surprising about the number and notes that Ctesias reported that a Persian king fed 15,000 guests at a feast and that 10,000 guests attended a wedding celebration held by Alexander. In addition, a document entitled 'The Banquet of Ashurnasirpal' claimed that the king fed a total of 69,574 persons at the dedication of his palace, though not in one hall (*ANET*: 558-60).

The purpose of the festival is not mentioned. L.M. Wills (1990: 123-

24) suggests that it was the *akitu* festival observed the year of the fall of Babylon, but v. 1 provides no such information. Miller (1994: 151-52) lists three other possibilities. (1) The celebration may have been held to build morale in light of the impending attack on Babylon by the Persians. However, Daniel 5 gives no hint that the city was under attack. (2) Perhaps it was a coronation ceremony for Belshazzar, who had heard that the Persians had defeated Nabonidus at Sippar and hastily named himself king (cf. Shea 1982: 142). Unfortunately for this view, 8.1 speaks of the third year of the reign of Belshazzar. (3) Xenophon (*Cyropedia* 7.5.15) implies that the Babylonians were observing a traditional festival that fell at that time. This view is the most plausible of the three, but again Daniel 5 ignores such information and simply says that Belshazzar drank in front of his guests.

Verse 2. Under the influence of wine, Belshazzar ordered that the vessels of gold and silver Nebuchadnezzar had taken from the temple be brought to the banquet hall for his guests (the nobles, their wives, and their concubines) to use in their drinking. Commentators often assume that the author meant that Belshazzar was already drunk. Fewell (1988: 118) disagrees and points to a contrast between Nebuchadnezzar and Belshazzar in Daniel 4 and 5 that is pertinent to the issue. As Daniel 4 depicted him, Nebuchadnezzar was proud of his considerable achievements. As he surveyed Babylon, he could justly, if nevertheless arrogantly, brag about his achievements. In Daniel 5, by contrast, Belshazzar simply appears, and the author attributes no great accomplishment to him. He is proud nevertheless, but he has to vie with the reputation of his putative father. In view of this implicit contest, Fewell argues, Daniel 5 portrays Belshazzar's conduct at the banquet as carefully planned, not as the result of a drunken impulse. If that is correct, the phrase 'Under the influence of the wine' might mean simply that his inhibitions were lowered or that he was emboldened to act as he planned.

Verse 3. This verse repeats the description of the vessels from v. 2, except that in the MT the word 'silver' is omitted. NRSV adds it from v. 2. Verse 3 adds that the temple was **the house of God in Jerusalem**. The contrast between the intended function of the vessels and the use to which Belshazzar ordered them put, though not drawn, is obvious. They were intended for use in a temple by consecrated priests in the worship of Israel's God; he ordered their use in a banquet hall by an unconsecrated throng engaged in a secular Babylonian festival.

Verse 4. This verse continues to contrast the intended use of the vessels and the use to which Belshazzar put them: the drinkers praised **the gods of gold and silver, bronze, iron, wood, and stone.** This praise of the gods is not evidence that the banquet was a religious observance; a toast to the various divinities of Babylon would have been appropriate at a secular festival like a state banquet.

HANDWRITING ON THE WALL (5)

In the eyes of the author, this public misuse of the temple vessels was blasphemous, and it was answered at once with a public reprimand. **The fingers of a human hand appeared and began writing...** The hand looked like a human hand, but it was not connected to an arm and body. Clearly, this was 'no human hand', but the hand of God. In typical fashion for the court narratives in Daniel, the author postpones divulging the message until later in the chapter.

The writing appeared on a plaster wall **next to the lampstand,** which would throw light upon its surface. Montgomery (1927: 252) envisions a large banquet room, with the royal table located on a dais next to a wall and with a lampstand nearby.

The king watched as the **hand** wrote. The Aramaic word used here is often translated 'palm', but it designates the 'hand' from the wrist down. Lacocque (1979: 95) argues that Belshazzar was the only person in the room to see the hand and the writing: 'to everyone else the palace wall stays blank, there is no message'. Anderson (1984: 54) rejects this interpretation, and rightly so, because the remainder of the story presupposes that the Babylonian sages and Daniel can see it. One might understand v. 5 to mean that no one else could see the hand that did the writing, though even that is not necessary. The author's point was that the king had sinned, and he watched the hand as it wrote.

AN OFFER OF HONORS FOR ITS INTERPRETATION (6-7)

The king was terrified at the sight of the hand and at the possible meaning of the message written on the wall. He summoned his wise men, and promised a huge reward to any one who could interpret it.

Verse 6. This verse describes the king's physiological responses to the sight: **the king's face turned pale, and his thoughts terrified him. His limbs gave way, and his knees knocked.** All of these phrases are self-evident except for the third: 'his limbs gave way'. Wolters (1991:

117) argues that the phrase is a word-play on vv. 12 and 16, where Daniel is said to be able to 'loose knots', which means to 'solve riddles'. He suggests (p. 118) that the phrase be translated 'loosening the knots in the loins', which amounted to something quite different, specifically to losing control of the sphincter muscles. If Wolters is correct, the phrase not only ridicules the pompous king but also rankles with bitterness at foreign rulers. Its absence from the Old Greek lends weight to those who suppose that this addition was motivated at least in part by an aversion to Antiochus.

Verse 7. The king called for **the enchanters, Chaldeans, and the diviners**. This is by now a stereotypical list of wise men (cf. 2.2). The reward for interpreting the writing consisted of purple clothing, a chain of gold around the neck, and high rank in the government. Purple was the royal color among the Persians (see Xenophon, *Anabasis* 1.5.8), the Medes (Xenophon, *Cyropedia* 1.3.2), and the Seleucids (1 Macc. 10.20). In 1 Macc. 10.20, King Alexander gives Jonathan a gold crown as well, but it signified only that he was a friend of the king. The gold chain offered by Belshazzar would mean the same.

The rank of third in the kingdom (cf. vv. 16, 29) is a bit more obscure in meaning. Smith-Christopher (1996: 82) suggests that Daniel would rank third behind Belshazzar and the queen mother, while Shea (1982: 139) thinks he would rank behind Nabonidus and Belshazzar. Rashi and Ibn Ezra thought he would rule over a third of the country (so Slotki 1951: 41). Similarly, some scholars have joined this verse with 6.2, which says Daniel was one of three officials over the satraps established by Darius. Perhaps the best suggestion is that the word *taltî* is a later version of the old Babylonian word *salsu*, the title of a high official. *Salsu* in turn corresponds to the Hebrew word *šālîš*, which designates a military officer or a court attendant (Slotki 1951; and Collins 1993a: 247).

THE FAILURE OF THE KING'S WISE MEN (8-9)

Despite these rewards the Babylonian wise men were unable to understand the message on the wall. Belshazzar's terror at what the message might portend grew more intense.

Verse 8. This verse says that the wise men entered the room, a contradiction of v. 7, which already said that Belshazzar spoke to them. The contradiction, however, also exits in the Old Greek. Perhaps it was simply a slip-up by the original author.

Verse 9. This verse completes the initial scene in the narrative, with the king as terrified as before and the wise men thoroughly baffled. Action in the plot had ground to a halt; a new direction was needed.

THE QUEEN'S SPEECH: NEBUCHADNEZZAR, DANIEL
AND THE SPIRIT OF INTERPRETATION (10-12)

The 'queen' offered that direction by coming to the banquet hall uninvited and reminding Belshazzar that the best interpreter in the land (Daniel of course) had not been summoned. She advised Belshazzar to call him. In the Old Greek Belshazzar himself summoned the 'queen', which implies a different relationship between the two than in the MT.

Verse 10. The **queen** is not identified, but she is not one of Belshazzar's wives, who according to v. 2 are already in attendance. The next most obvious candidate to be called 'queen', then, was the queen mother, but her identity remains a subject of debate. Baldwin (1978: 121-22) notes that the real queen mother (i.e. the mother of Nabonidus) had died during the ninth year of her son's reign, according to the 'Nabonidus Chronicle'. Baldwin thinks the queen of 5.10 was probably the wife of Nabonidus and the mother of Belshazzar. Lacocque (1979: 97), however, correctly notes that the author of Daniel 5 thought Belshazzar was the son of Nebuchadnezzar, so Nebuchadnezzar's widow Nitocris would be the queen mother (cf. Collins 1993a: 248). Bentzen (1952: 49) mentions that possibility without accepting or rejecting it. Nitocris was widely reputed as a wise woman, so she seems to be the model for the queen mother in this episode.

Verse 11. After appropriate greetings (v. 10b), she calls Belshazzar's attention to Daniel, who was **endowed with a spirit of the holy gods**. The term 'spirit' simply meant that Daniel had a specific power or charisma. The queen mother was a polytheist, who would attribute Daniel's gifts to her gods, not to Daniel's God. The whole phrase had already appeared on the lips of Nebuchadnezzar in 4.18. Not surprisingly, then, she next spoke of Daniel's role in that event. During the reign of Belshazzar's 'father' Nebuchadnezzar, Daniel had proved himself wise. As a consequence, Nebuchadnezzar had appointed him **chief of the magicians, enchanters, Chaldeans, and diviners**. This list, missing from the Old Greek, appears in Dan. 4.7, further tying the two chapters together.

Verse 12. The queen mother makes two statements about Daniel in v. 12. First, she notes that he had been found able to interpret dreams

(Daniel 2 and 4), explain riddles, and solve problems. Belshazzar had a riddle to solve if there ever was one. Secondly, she adds that **the king** had named Daniel 'Belteshazzar'. In saying that she makes explicit what Nebuchadnezzar implies in 4.8, where he says in the passive voice that Daniel 'was named' after Nebuchadnezzar's god. Then the queen mother advises Belshazzar to summon Daniel to interpret the message on the wall.

It is not unusual for interpreters to ponder why Belshazzar does not know, or at least know of, Daniel. Fewell (1988: 123-24) contends, however, that those interpreters misread the interpersonal dynamics of the chapter. It is clear, she thinks, from Daniel's statement in v. 22 that Belshazzar knows all about the events of Daniel 4, but refused to learn from them. Hence, when Belshazzar says in vv. 13-14, 'So, you are Daniel, one of the exiles whom my father the king brought from Judah? I have heard of you', he is not referring simply to what the queen mother had told him, but is admitting that he already knew who Daniel was.

Why would the king behave in such a fashion? Because, Fewell argues, Belshazzar was battling the memory of Nebuchadnezzar who had accomplished so much, and he had done so little. Hence, he had ignored Nebuchadnezzar's counselor, just as he tried to belittle Nebuchadnezzar's conquest of Jerusalem by defiling the vessels from its temple. Of the queen mother's relationship to Belshazzar here, Fewell writes: 'She is the voice, and perhaps not the welcome voice, of the dead king Nebuchadnezzar' (1988: 123).

DANIEL ARRIVES AND THE KING OFFERS GIFTS (13-16)

Daniel appears before Belshazzar, who offers him the same reward for interpreting the writing that he offered the Babylonian wise men: purple clothing, a gold chain, and the third position in the kingdom. Much of the King's speech is simply a repetition of what was said in previous verses (5-12) and will require no further discussion here.

Verse 13. In Belshazzar's greeting he acknowledges Daniel as **one of the exiles of Judah, whom my father the king brought from Judah**. That is information the queen mother did not give Belshazzar in vv. 11-12. It could, of course, simply be an editorial linkage to Daniel 1, and it is that. It is also possible, in view of v. 22, to see it as evidence in favor of Fewell's reading. Taken at face value, it implies that Belshazzar knew of Daniel before they met. Further, calling Daniel an exile rather than a counselor is a put-down (Fewell 1988: 125). Why would Daniel not be one of the king's advisers, as he was already in 1.20? Precisely because he was an adviser to the 'father', the 'son' wanted nothing to do with him. Read in this light, the greeting smacks of antagonism rather than of friendliness as Lacocque says (1979: 92).

Verses 14-16. In v. 14 Belshazzar repeats what the queen mother said about Daniel, and in v. 15 he tells Daniel about the failure of the Baby-lonian wise men. Verse 16, then, reads like a challenge to Daniel to see if he can do any better.

DANIEL DECLINES THE GIFTS (17)

Given this understanding of their meeting, there is little wonder that Daniel's reply is gruff in the extreme. He rejects the king's gifts (as nothing more than a bribe?) and promises to render faithfully the mean-ing of the writing anyway. As Lacocque says: 'When the Word is spo-ken, it requires an interpreter and an interpretation' (1979: 101). Any reading that sees Belshazzar's overture as friendly stumbles over Daniel's apparent anger.

Daniel's refusal to accept the king's rewards in v. 17b stands in ten-sion with v. 29, which says he received them. The effect of his refusal of the rewards at least is to point out to the reader that one may not allow the promise of reward to influence the delivery of God's word, and Daniel does not. In the end, the king rewards him for his work anyway.

Further, v. 17b and the recapitulation of Daniel 4 which follow in vv. 18-22 are missing from the Old Greek. They are part of the work of R2. In vv. 18-22, Daniel sounds more like a prophet than a wise man. Robert R. Wilson (1978: 90-91) finds in Daniel 2 and 4 a similar pattern of a wise speaker standing in the court of the Babylonian kings deliver-ing such prophetic messages. Daniel's prophet-like demeanor here pre-pares the way for a more thoroughgoing shift to prophetic elements in Daniel 7–12, which elements suggest a change in the composition of the group responsible for Daniel in the Maccabean period.

NEBUCHADNEZZAR'S DREAM INTERPRETED (18-21)

Daniel's response to Belshazzar (vv. 18-23) may be divided into two parts. In the first (vv. 18-21, missing in the Old Greek) he reminds Belshazzar what happened when Nebuchadnezzar became haughty and

refused to acknowledge God. In the second part (vv. 22-23), he charges
Belshazzar with having learned nothing from his father's mistakes (v.
22). Then the older story resumes briefly with a description and interpretation of the banquet scene (v. 23).

Verse 18. There had been no salutation glorifying Belshazzar like
those Daniel offered to Nebuchadnezzar: 'O king, the king of kings—to
whom the God of heaven has given the kingdom, the power, the might,
and the glory…' (2.37). Even less did Daniel raise the possibility that
the impending doom would fall on the king's enemies, as in 4.19.
Instead, he moved straight into his prophetic critique. His first words
would have been as unwelcome as those of the queen mother, and for
the same reason: Daniel spoke about Nebuchadnezzar. To him, God had
given **kingship, greatness, glory, and majesty**, a not-so-faint echo of
2.37.

Verse 19. Because God had blessed Nebuchadnezzar, **all peoples,
nations, and languages** (i.e. the known world) **trembled and feared
before him**. They had cause to do so. Nebuchadnezzar had killed or
kept alive, honored or degraded people as he saw fit. While this comment may indicate how Nebuchadnezzar exercised his God-given
power, it probably does not express approval of that conduct. The very
next verse, in fact, articulates disapproval for failure to acknowledge
God, though it primarily had 4.28-33 in mind.

Verses 20-21. Nebuchadnezzar's refusal to acknowledge God's
power over him was the reason for his malady. Daniel made that point
to Belshazzar by reviewing what had happened to Nebuchadnezzar.

THE INTERPRETATION OF THE BANQUET (22-23)

The second part of Daniel's speech also begins with a direct address to
Belshazzar: **and you, Belshazzar, his son**. The structure of vv.
18-23 carries an echo of David's encounter with Nathan (Smith-Christopher
1996: 83). In 2 Sam. 11.27b–12.4 Nathan tells David a parable and then
in 12.7-12 accuses David of sin. In Belshazzar's case, the 'parable' was
an event from his father's reign which the king knew well, and in 5.22-
23 Daniel accuses Belshazzar of sin.

Verse 22. The contrast between the successful father and the
unproven son comes to the fore in v. 22. As great a sinner as Nebuchadnezzar could be, he could also repent. Belshazzar failed to learn
from the mistakes of his father because he had been intent on outdoing
his father and shaming his lingering reputation. Consequently, he had

not humbled himself, that is, acknowledged God's sovereignty.

Verse 23. What Belshazzar had intended as a put-down for his father turned out to be gross blasphemy. He had exalted himself against the one true God in a toast to all **the gods of silver and gold, of bronze, iron, wood, and stone**. Those gods were as blind as the materials from which they were made, and Belshazzar had honored them. Daniel implied that the real God saw everything Belshazzar had done, and that God he had not honored. His father's malady should have been warning enough to him, and he should have learned as Nebuchadnezzar had. Belshazzar would get no second chance, as the interpretation of the writing would make clear.

THE INTERPRETATION OF THE HANDWRITING (24-28)

At last the narrative reported what the hand had written (vv. 24-25). (The Old Greek, by contrast, disclosed the message at the time it reported the hand's appearance.) This way of building suspense had appeared earlier in Daniel 2 (also ultimately from R2), which postponed revealing Nebuchadnezzar's dream until the time to disclose its meaning. R2 followed the same pattern here, with Daniel explaining the meaning of the message in vv. 26-28.

Verse 24. This verse made clear what v. 5 had intimated: the hand that did the writing had been sent from the presence of God. Unlike Exod. 31.18, which attributed the writing on the two tablets to the finger of God, this verse did not ascribe body parts to God.

Verse 25. The message consisted of four words: **MENE, MENE, TEKEL AND PARSIN.** They are pointed as nouns in v. 25, but treated as verbs in the interpretation (vv. 27-28). The most widely held explanation of the words is to understand them as the names of weights. **MENE** (or mina) was a weight known from 1 Kgs 10.17, Ezra 2.69, Neh. 7.71-2, and Ezek. 45.12). **TEKEL** seems to be the same as 'shekel'. Its value was about one-fiftieth of a mina. **PARSIN** is a plural form of the noun *p*ᵉ*rēs*, which designates a 'half mina'. Baldwin (1978: 124) suggests that one might expect to see such a list of measures in a steward's room, and even speculates that the king caught sight of one and mistook it for writing on the wall.

Verse 26. The interpretation uses *m*ᵉ*nē*' only once, as do the preface to Daniel 5 in the Old Greek and Josephus (*Ant.* 10.11.3 lines 243-44), suggesting that the message originally may have contained only three words (see Montgomery 1927: 262; Hartman and Di Lella 1978: 189;

Lacocque 1979: 103; and Collins 1993a: 250). The words originally
may have been in a different order too; the Old Greek switches the last
two. Whatever the original wording might have been, the problem is to
understand their meaning in their context.

Daniel listed and interpreted each weight in succession. He construed
MENE as *m^{e}nāh*, an Aramaic peil (or passive) verb meaning 'number'
or 'reckon', with God as its subject. The idea of numbering a kingdom,
like numbering the days of someone's life, suggests an end. Hence,
Daniel interpreted MENE to mean **God has numbered...your kingdom and brought it to an end**. In other words, Belshazzar had run out
of time.

Verse 27. Similarly, Daniel construed TEKEL as *t^{e}qilta'*, a peil (or
passive) verb meaning 'weighed'. Weighing something presupposes
scales or balances. One places a known weight (e.g. a shekel) on one
side and grain or whatever is to be measured on the other. Hence,
Daniel interpreted TEKEL to mean **you have been weighed on the
scales and found wanting**. Rashi derives from the word *teqilta'*
(weighed) from the root *qll* (which could mean 'to make light'), and
treats it as a pun to the effect that Belshazzar was too 'light' to handle
the kingdom (see Collins 1993a: 252).

Verse 28. Finally, Daniel substitutes the singular noun PERES for
the plural noun (U)PARSIN (the first letter being the conjunction 'and')
and construed it as *p^{e}rîsat*, a peil verb meaning 'divided'. What did
Belshazzar have that could be divided? Many things, possibly, but the
most important was his kingdom. UPARSIN already facilitated a pun
on the name Persian. The Persians, in turn, were closely associated with
the Medes. Hence, Daniel interpreted PERES to mean **your kingdom is
divided and given to the Medes and the Persians**.

Scholars have suggested different renderings from the one given
here. For example, Zimmermann (1964: 201-207) proposes a reading
which he translates 'Set (or appointed) is the Persian trap'. Others have
tried to identify the weights with different people: for example, Nebuchadnezzar as the mina, Belshazzar as the shekel, and the Medes and
the Persians as half-minas (Eissfeldt 1951: 109).

At a minimum one must admit that the meaning of the message was
less than self-evident! In the reading given above, one has to fill in the
logic between the name of the weight and the interpretation given by
Daniel. Other explanations for why the message was so obscure have
been proposed. Two examples will suffice. (1) According to Jewish

tradition the words were written down instead of across, arranged in five columns of three letters each. The first three columns contained the letters *m-n-a, m-n-a, t-k-l*, while the last two columns contained the letters *u-p-r* and *s-i-n* (Slotki 1951: 45). (2) Pierre Grelot (1985: 200) suggested instead that it was hard to read because it was written in cuneiform.

THE BESTOWAL OF HONORS FOR INTERPRETATION (29)

The king kept his promise to reward Daniel for interpreting the writing, despite Daniel's rejection of such rewards (v. 17). He clothed Daniel in purple, put a gold chain around his neck, and made a proclamation appointing him to a high rank in the kingdom. (See comments on v. 7.)

THE FALL OF THE BABYLONIAN EMPIRE (30-31)

The conclusion of Daniel 5 is the fall of the Babylonian Empire, in fulfillment of the interpretation of the writing. Verse 28 had announced that the kingdom would be given to the Medes and the Persians, and vv. 30-31 (MT 5.30–6.1) reports the death of Belshazzar and the passing of the kingdom from the Chaldeans to the Medes.

Verse 30. Verse 29 conveys no sense of urgency. Indeed, one might imagine the proclamation being made at a public ceremony the next day or week. The Old Greek reports the fall of Babylon, but does not mention how much time elapsed between the banquet and that event. Verse 30 of the MT, by contrast, says that Belshazzar was killed **that very night**. This phrase perhaps suggests that the king was stricken before the assembled crowd. If so, it adds a detail of immense dramatic effect. Alternatively, the verse may mean that Belshazzar died that night after the banquet. Either way, the hand of God answered Belshazzar's blasphemy at once, and his predicted demise came soon. What is not said is who killed Belshazzar. Given what is known about the fall of Babylon, one might more easily guess palace intrigue than the Persian army. However, the use of the passive voice is often a way of ascribing an action to God, and that is highly likely here. If so, who God's agent might have been, if anyone, was of no interest; the point was that God punished Belshazzar's blasphemy.

Verse 31. This verse (MT 6.1) poses a historical problem, namely that Cyrus, not Darius the Mede, conquered Babylon. The Nabonidus Chronicle says Gobryas (Gubaru), the governor of Gutium, entered the city with the army and held it for Cyrus until he arrived. Still, there is just enough murkiness in the Babylonian and Persian chronicles about the fall of Babylon to give rise to a plethora of scholarly identifications as to who Darius the Mede might have been. This issue was discussed in the Introduction and need not be reviewed here. Suffice it to say that none of those nominated (Cyaxares II, Cyrus, Ugbaru, Gubaru, Cambyses, Darius I or Darius II) is ever called Darius the Mede in extant literature from that time.

Having said that, one may suggest that the description of 'Darius' in 5.31 and 6.1 (MT 6.1-2) was a composite from various sources, rather than simply the creation of the author. First, Darius I was the probable source of the name. He divided the empire into 20 satrapies, each with a satrap or governor. This action perhaps stood behind 6.1 (MT 6.2), which credits Darius with setting 120 satraps over his empire. Indeed, the original setting of Daniel 6 may have been the court of Darius I, since the title 'Mede' is not used in the rest of the story. Secondly, Jer. 51.11 says that Yahweh stirred up the king of the Medes to end the Babylonian Empire. That verse perhaps caused the writer to call Darius a Mede. Darius's genealogy in 9.1, which also calls him a Mede, may have rested on a tradition articulated in Tob. 14.15 that Nineveh was captured by Nebuchadnezzar and Ahasueras (not Cyaxares, as was the case historically). If the author of v. 31 thought Ahasueras was a contemporary of Nebuchadnezzar, he also probably supposed that his 'son' Darius was the contemporary of Nebuchadnezzar's 'son' Belshazzar. Thirdly, the note that he was about 62 years of age perhaps fit Cyrus at the time of the fall of Babylon. Finally, Darius I suppressed two revolts in Babylon, so a story of one of those battles might have been confused with Cyrus's conquest of Babylon (so Collins 1993a: 254).

THE THEOLOGY OF DANIEL 5

Daniel 5 offers a glimpse into the authors' theology in the restricted sense of the doctrine of God. R1 and R2 portray God indirectly. God sends a hand to write on the wall. Belshazzar is killed in fulfillment of the writing, but the agent is not specified, though God must have been responsible. The chapter reflects a growing awareness of God's transcendence, though not aloofness. Also, it remains uncompromisingly monotheistic, and presents blasphemy as the worst sin.

In the broader sense of the word 'theology', Daniel 5 completed the process of rethinking the Babylonian Empire. It certainly was no longer golden; nor did Nebuchadnezzar emerge unscathed, though he continued to rank well above Belshazzar. Nor was Nebuchadnezzar mentioned again in the rest of the book. Daniel 7 and 8 were set in the first and third years of Belshazzar's reign, but there could be no questioning of his worthlessness.

In addition, one gains the impression from the death of Belshazzar that R2 had abandoned hope that the foreign king would acknowledge God, though not the conviction that he should. Belshazzar is presented with none of the conciliation granted to other kings down to Antiochus Epiphanes. Whether R2 deliberately colored Belshazzar in hues of Antiochus may remain open, but the narrative would have seemed relevant indeed to second-century readers even if he did not.

A fourth feature of this chapter is its emphasis upon the necessity for interpreting God's word. That might be taken as evidence that the authors thought prophecy was still alive, but that seems unlikely. It is more likely that they wanted to emphasize that people (obviously Belshazzar, but Nebuchadnezzar before him, and even Daniel in chs. 7–12) need an interpretation to make clear the meaning of what they read or see.

Fifthly, the animosity of the foreign king to things Judaic demanded a fearless response. Such battles were no place for cowards. Daniel serves as a hero and a role model for such fearlessness. The issue was not what paid the most dividends, but what God said.

Finally, the chapter promised rewards to God's people who remained faithful to God. On the other hand, these rewards did not yet include resurrection for the martyrs (12.2), perhaps because at the time of writing of Daniel 5 there had been none in the redactor's community.

DANIEL IN THE LIONS' DEN
(6.1-28)

Daniel 6 begins with a reference to Darius. In the context of the book of Daniel, Darius must be understood as 'Darius the Mede', the putative successor to Belshazzar and predecessor of Cyrus (6.28). (See the comments on 5.31 for a discussion of 'Darius' and Cyrus.) The story itself is known from different cultures, so the only issues here are when people in the Diaspora began to tell the story and when its hero became Daniel. Hartman and Di Lella (1978: 197) argue for a date in the Persian period because of Persian loan-words. That does not help much, however, because Dan. 5.39 precludes a date earlier than 539.

F.H. Polak (1993: 259) points to the preference of verbs preceding objects in this chapter, which he claims, following E.Y. Kutscher (1952: I, 123-27), is characteristic of Western rather than Eastern Official Aramaic, and argues for a Palestinian place of origin. By contrast Koch (1980: 46-47) uses Kutscher's analysis to show an eastern provenance for the court narratives as a whole. At the present, it is not possible to establish either the date or the provenance of a passage on the basis of its use of the Aramaic language.

One is left with the following conclusion: the dates the narrative arose and was attached to Daniel are irrecoverable. A date in the Greek period should be posited for R1 (represented in the Old Greek). Further, R2 made his additions in the second century. This narrative, with its sympathetic portrait of the ruler, must have reached its present form before the abuses that led to the Maccabean revolt, but late enough to misunderstand when Darius I reigned (see Collins 1993a: 273).

The Old Greek version of Daniel 6 differs from the MT, but not nearly so significantly as in Daniel 4 and 5. Based on a comparison of the two, Collins points to three redactional additions in the MT. In 6.5 those conspiring against Daniel explicitly state that they will be able to trap Daniel only through his keeping of his law. In 6.13 the conspirators refer to Daniel as one of the exiles from Judah. Since the chapter nowhere explains the reference, it presumes Daniel 1. Finally, the concluding doxology in vv. 26-27 is longer than the parallel statement in the Old Greek, reflecting the other doxologies on the lips of foreign kings, particularly 4.2-3.

The narrative can be analyzed as follows. The setting (vv. 1-2, vv. 2-3 in the MT) is the court of Darius, where Daniel enjoys the high position of 'president' (NRSV). Jealousy by the two other presidents only (Old Greek) or by the presidents and the 120 satraps (MT) leads to conspiracy against Daniel's life, from which Darius is unable to extricate him (vv. 3-18). The climax comes when Darius approaches the lions' den at the break of day, discovers Daniel still alive, and casts the conspirators and their families into the den (vv. 19-24). In the denouement Darius commands all his subjects to worship God, whom he himself praises (vv. 25-27); then the redactor adds a concluding, chronological note about Daniel's continuing career (v. 28).

Bentzen (1952: 55-56) suggests that behind this narrative stood the story of the descent of a hero (king?) into the underworld and his return. He thinks that the lions are the narrative's version of the demons who attacked the hero in the netherworld. Porteous (1965: 88) rightly rejects this suggestion on the grounds that martyrdom (or the threat of martyrdom) is quite a different thing to the cultic dying and rising or humiliation and exaltation of a king. Karel van der Toorn (1998: 638-40) argues that the author of Daniel 6 simply mistook a metaphor for a difficult situation for a literal description of what happend to a figure in a Babylonian narrative—*Ludlul bel nemeqi*—and used it as his model for telling Daniel 6. Be that as it may, the author had real lions in mind in Daniel 6. On the other hand, Daniel 6 does exhibit the basic structure of the tales of court conflict, as described by Humphreys (1973: 211-13), in which the hero is endangered by conflict among courtiers. In addition, Fewell (1988: 152) understands the structure of this chapter in terms of a rite of passage. Daniel is separated from society, sent down to the pit, and then brought back among the living. One should note, however, that the plot takes a twist: it is not Daniel who is changed during the liminal period, but society itself in the person of the king.

The dramatic tension of Daniel 6 was set up by Daniel 3. The friends Shadrach, Meshach, and Abednego had been tested for their faith; now Daniel would be. The friends had escaped. Would he escape too, or would he fare worse?

THE SETTING IN THE COURT OF DARIUS (1-2)

The setting of the narrative is the court of the putative 'Darius the Mede' soon after the fall of Babylon in 539. If the narrative originally dealt with Darius I, it would have come early in his reign (522–486). Perhaps Darius was the model for the king because of his role in rebuilding the temple (Ezra 6). Neither Dan. 6.1-2 nor 9.1-2 (also set in the reign of Darius the Mede) names the city where the king was living, but the connection with 5.31 might imply that the authors of Daniel 6 thought it was Babylon.

Verse 1. The chapter opens with a note on the administration of Darius. According to v. 1 he set 120 satraps over his kingdom. (Actually, the number for Darius I was 20.) Each satrap was appointed by and answerable to the king, but had local authority. According to Est. 1.1 and 8.9, Ahasueras (Xerxes I, the son and successor of Darius I) divided the kingdom into 127 satrapies from India to Ethiopia. The Old Greek of Daniel 6 uses that number.

Verse 2. This verse envisions three **presidents** serving in the court of Darius. No such officials are known to have existed in the Persian Empire, though Darius did appoint a commandant and a civil servant in each province to act as checks on the power of the satraps (Goldingay, p. 126). Regardless, according to v. 2 Darius appointed three 'presidents' to whom the satraps gave an **account**. Others translate the noun $t^{e'}\bar{e}m$ as 'counsel'. At issue is the role of the presidents. Did they simply offer counsel, or were they overseers? The rest of the narrative seems to suggest more administrative responsibility on their part than simply giving advice.

The idea that Daniel was one of three ranking officials may have been suggested by the word *taltî* (third rank) in 5.7, 29, but that is by no means clear. (See comments on 5.7.) Regardless, Daniel was one of the three, so Daniel 6 is much more a contest among court officials than the narrative of a young unknown rising through the ranks. Daniel had risen through the ranks in chs. 1 and 2; in Daniel 5 he was known to Belshazzar, but out of favor. Here he is both known by and in the favor of the king.

THE PLOT AGAINST DANIEL (3-18)

Unlike Belshazzar in Daniel 5, Darius is portrayed as a friend of Daniel, albeit one who let himself get tricked into issuing a decree that meant the death of his friend and courtier. In many folk traditions, the king or ruler is portrayed as neutral or even kindly disposed toward his subjects. The danger lay among his subordinates. Goldingay (1989: 122) speaks of the wisdom triangle here: Darius is the powerful but witless dupe, Daniel is the righteous wise man, and the conspirators together play the role of conniving schemers.

Verses 3-5. As in Dan. 1.18-19 and 4.6-17, Daniel surpasses the other wise men, so that the king plans (literally, 'is inclined') to elevate him further. Acting out of jealousy and/or a desire to preserve their posts, the other two presidents plus all the satraps seek a weakness in his character to entrap him. Finding none, they determine to find a way to derail his promotion though his observance of the law of his God.

Verse 3. The cause of Daniel's success was **an excellent spirit** within him. This 'spirit' was the empowerment by God to perform the tasks of the office. (See comments on 4.8.)

Verse 4. The other two presidents learned of the king's intentions, though the text does not say how. They conspired with the satraps to find something wrong with the way Daniel conducted the affairs of his office, but were unsuccessful. Because of his faithfulness to the king and to his office, he was guilty neither of negligence nor corruption.

The Old Greek actually says only that the other two presidents plotted to eliminate Daniel. On the surface that makes more sense than a conspiracy involving 127 additional people, whose status would not be affected anyway. Also in v. 24 of the MT the conspirators as well as their wives and children were thrown into the den. That would add up to a crowd of five hundred or more people! It is hard to imagine a den large enough to accommodate such a crowd, so Wills (1990: 137-38) observes wryly that the people were more likely to suffocate than be killed by lions. Montgomery (1927: 276) describes the den as 'a deep, cistern-like cavity, the mouth of which above could be closed with a stone, and so sealed'.

Verse 5. The conspirators concluded that their only hope was to find a way to get at him through his fidelity to the law of God. Many religious Judeans in the Diaspora must have harbored the fear that their religious observance would cause them trouble. That would have been particularly true of any Judeans seeking public office, as the members of the Danielic group seem to have done. They would need to face that possibility without caving in to the pressure to assimilate. While there is no allusion to Antiochus IV in Daniel 6 (as even Rowley admitted,

1952: 277-78), the narrative would retain its relevance in the face of Antiochus's persecution.

Verse 6. The presidents and satraps hatched a plot to rid themselves of Daniel. They **conspired and came** to Darius. BDB gives 'be in tumult' as the meaning of the verb *rᵉgaš*, and translates it here 'shew tumultuousness, come thronging' (BDB: 1112). That translation is favored by Slotki (1951: 48) and Collins (1993a: 256). Porteous (1965: 89-90) rejects it as inappropriate, especially for v. 15, where the conspirators appear before the king. He accepts 'came by agreement' but prefers 'watched for'. Hartman and Di Lella (1978: 192) translate 'went in collusion' (cf. Montgomery 1927: 272-73; Baldwin 1978: 128). Goldingay (1989: 121) agrees that they act on the basis of prior planning, but objects that these last two translations miss the point that their action is peremptory and translates 'mustered'. The word is so rare that no decision is possible here, but the context makes clear that they had conspired together to trap Daniel and now were coming to the king to put their plan in action, as the NRSV says.

The officials greet the king with an appropriately polite salutation: **O King Darius, live forever**. It is difficult to imagine a tumultuous throng speaking so properly. Nor is it clear that they speak as intemperately in vv. 11 and 15 as is sometimes alleged.

Verse 7. The list of conspirators grows in v. 7, where it includes not only the two presidents and the satraps, but also **the counselors and the governors**. The word for 'counselors' appeared in 2.28, where the NRSV translates Daniel's title as 'chief Prefect'. These 'counselors' or 'prefects' apparently are the class of officials over whom Daniel previously had control. The **governors** appeared in 3.24 as attendants to Nebuchadnezzar whom he asked if they had not cast three men into the furnace, and all four kinds of officials appear in 3.2, 3, and 27 (see comments on 3.2). That fact may account for the inclusion of the counselors and governors here. They are not mentioned again.

The conspirators had devised their plan to trap Daniel and began to put it into effect. To do so they had to appear to be acting on the king's behalf. They made it seem they wanted to help him unite his kingdom behind him. Hence, they suggested that he issue an edict forbidding his subjects to pray to anyone but himself, divine or human, for 30 days. They put forward their suggestion as a protection against conspiracy, but actually it was a vehicle for their conspiracy against the king and Daniel (so Fewell 1988: 146).

They knew perfectly well that Daniel prayed to God three times daily and would continue to do so no matter what the law said. Their plan was foolproof if they could persuade the king to go along with it. The king may have known about Daniel's prayer life too, judging from the fact that he accepted the word of the conspirators in v. 13. That may constitute too close a reading, however.

Violators of this new law would be thrown into a pit of lions. Assyrians and Babylonians hunted lions, and even kept them in cages until they could be released at hunts (Collins 1993a: 267). The Persians also kept lions in their zoos (Slotki 1951: 49). There is, however, no record in the ancient Middle East of lions being kept in pits and used to execute criminals. Perhaps this instance was conceived of as exceptional, just like the law.

Verse 8. The conspirators insisted that Darius sign the document so that it could not be changed (literally, 'so that it not be changed, according to the law of the Medes and the Persians, which does not change'). The MT diverges from the Old Greek, in which the conspirators ask the king not to change his mind later (which was always the king's prerogative according to Herodotus *Histories* 3.31 and which Darius eventually does). Collins (1993a: 267) suggests that the MT may have been influenced by Est. 8.8: '(A)n edict written in the name of the king and sealed with the king's ring cannot be revoked.'

Verse 9. Darius is portrayed as signing the document with little thought about its implications. Thus, the king was implicated in the threat to Daniel, but through a failure to think through an act suggested by subordinates, not out of malice to Daniel or to exiled Judeans.

This episode offers an interesting perspective on guilt. Since the king issued the edict, he was technically guilty of any harm that might befall Daniel, but morally he was not at all or at least not solely responsible. On the other hand, the conspirators were technically blameless, but morally responsible for the anticipated death of Daniel.

Verses 10-11. Undaunted by the king's proclamation, Daniel continued his practice of praying to God. Since he did so daily, his opponents watched for him, waiting for the opportunity to report him to the king.

Verse 10. Daniel knew of the king's proclamation, and recognized its threat to him. It would have been easy for Daniel to avoid capture. All he needed to do was pray in secret. Indeed, that very fact has caused some critics to question whether a Persian king would have bothered to issue such an edict. It would have been one thing to forbid the public observance of religion, but quite a different thing to forbid even private petitions. This question overlooks the author's purpose in telling this story: to portray this event as a clash between God's law and the foreign ruler's law. The narrative presents Daniel as the model of Judean piety. (See the discussion in Montgomery 1927: 274.) Similar prayers may be found in Ezra 9.7-15; Neh. 1.5-11; and Dan. 9.3-16.

Daniel went to his house, **which had windows in its upper room open towards Jerusalem**. Once again the Old Greek and the MT diverge over a detail. The MT uses a passive verb, suggesting that the windows were already open. The Old Greek, though, says specifically that Daniel opened the windows. Smith-Christopher (1996: 91) concludes from this difference that the Old Greek has Daniel deliberately commit an act of passive resistance in praying to God, and he points (p. 94) to M.K. Gandhi's appreciation of Daniel as 'one of the greatest passive resisters that ever lived'.

Daniel faced Jerusalem to pray. The origin of this practice is unknown, but its scriptural basis is the prayer of Solomon in 1 Kgs 8.30: 'Hear the plea of your servant and of your people Israel when they pray toward this place...' Daniel prayed three times a day. The custom of praying in the morning, the afternoon, and the evening is also old and may be mentioned in Ps. 55.17:

> Evening, morning and at noon
> I utter my complaint and moan,
> and he will hear my voice.

Daniel got **down on his knees...to pray to his God and praise him...** The original meaning of the root for 'pray' was 'bend'. It appears, then, that Daniel was following the three acts of prayer: kneeling, bowing down, and praising (Slotki 1951: 50).

Verse 11. The conspirators **came** to Daniel's house to catch him in the act. The word translated 'came' is the same as in v. 6. The meaning 'thronged' or 'came tumultuously' is inappropriate here too. They could scarcely come tumultuously to spy on him! Rather, they had come by prior agreement and found Daniel praying and seeking mercy from God.

Verses 12-13. The trap for displacing Daniel had been cleverly set, and it worked. The conspirators rushed to Darius with the news. The verb $q^e r\bar{e}b$ is used here in the sense of 'bring a lawsuit' (Hartman and Di Lella 1978: 195). Again they spoke to the king. While the author does not repeat the polite salutation 'O King Darius, live forever', he may have omitted the words for the sake of the flow of the story. The conspirators still needed Darius to find Daniel guilty, and could ill afford to offend him with victory almost within their grasp. They began by asking him to affirm his prohibition against praying to anyone but himself, which he did, agreeing with them that the rule could not be broken. Then they reported the news that Daniel continued to pray three times daily to his God.

Verse 14. The king received the report with sadness. The NRSV reads: **he was determined to save Daniel**. A more literal translation would be 'he set his heart to save Daniel'. In the biblical understanding of human nature, the term 'heart' included not just the heart muscle or the seat of one's emotions, but the center of volition, purpose, and even intellectual activity. To say that he **made every effort to rescue him** probably meant that Darius explored every way he could think of to extricate Daniel from the death sentence. He struggled with the issue **until the sun went down**. Goldingay (1989: 121) notes that the meaning 'until high noon' is etymologically possible and would give time for Daniel to be arrested and imprisoned before nightfall, but concludes that 'until the sun went down' is the better translation.

Verse 15. For the verb **came** (by agreement) Slotki (1951: 51) again reads 'came tumultuously' and suggests that the conspirators had been dismissed after the interview in v. 14. He posits their return in v. 15 to press their case and makes the point they do not salute the king, but speak forthrightly. Montgomery (1927: 275) concurs that they returned that evening and spoke impudently. He has Darius consult lawyers and browbeat the conspirators. But how could he browbeat them if he had dismissed the conspirators, and where is there mention of lawyers he consulted? It is better to construe v. 15 as an exposition of his discussion with the conspirators in v. 14. In the intensity of the debate, they pressed their case that the law was irrevocable.

Verse 16. Unlike Nebuchadnezzar, who told the three youths no god could rescue them (3.15), and who cast them into the fiery furnace in a rage (3.19), Darius unwillingly sentenced Daniel to the pit of lions and added a blessing if not a prayer: **May your God, whom you faithfully serve, deliver you**.

The threat of martyrdom was as pronounced as in Daniel 3, but the attitude of the kings was quite different. The Nebuchadnezzar of Daniel 3 and 4 was not golden, and neither, perhaps, was Darius. He was, however, a sympathetic villain at worst, or perhaps only a well-intentioned monarch who was no match for his cunning subordinates.

Verse 17. The pit that held the lions apparently had a fairly small opening that a stone could cover. When it was in place, Darius sealed it with his own signet and those of his lords as well. A signet was an engraved emblem set on a ring, which might be worn on the finger or hung on a cord around one's neck. It would be pressed into a dab of hot wax, leaving a permanent impression of a person's distinctive mark or 'signature' on the seal. The Old Greek explains that the purpose of the seal was to detect whether anyone had moved the stone to remove Daniel from the pit.

Verse 18. The king retired to his palace and spent the night fasting. During the night **no food was brought to him**. The word translated food was *dah^awān*, the meaning of which is widely debated. Rashi suggested 'tables', Ibn Ezra 'musical instruments', and Saadya 'dancing girls' (Slotki 1951: 52). Others have suggested 'concubines' (NJB), 'woman' (REB) 'diversions' (RSV), 'entertainments' (NIV), and 'entertainers' (NAB). 'Food' or 'tables' was suggested by the context. 'Musical instruments' was taken from an assumed meaning 'to strike (strings)'. The translation 'concubines' came from an attempt to derive the word from an Arabic root. At least the NRSV translation does not add possibly incorrect connotations to the verse. Besides, the overall sense of the sentence is plain: Darius spent the night in misery and without sleep.

GOD'S RESCUE OF DANIEL (19-24)

The king need not have agonized. God was able and willing to protect Daniel as he had protected the three friends in the fiery furnace. Darius responded by punishing the conspirators with the punishment they had arranged for Daniel.

Verses 19-20. After a sleepless night, Darius rose **at break of day** (literally, 'at dawn, in the brightness'). He **hurried** to the lions' pit to learn what had happened to Daniel. He **cried out anxiously** (literally, 'with a pained voice') to Daniel, asking if his God had kept him alive. If the conspirators had labelled Daniel simply 'one of the exiles from Judah' (v. 13), Darius called him a **servant of the living God**. As in v. 16, Darius emphasized here that Daniel continuously worshipped his God. The martyr story was broken; God turned out to be the 'living God' as Darius had hoped (v. 16).

Verse 21. Daniel answered Darius at once: **O King, live forever,**

which was the same salutation the conspirators had used in v. 6 and the Babylonian magicians had used in 2.4; 3.9; and 5.10. Here in Daniel 6 the author made a word-play with the adjective 'living' in v. 20 and the verb 'live' in v. 21.

Verse 22. Daniel told Darius that God had sent an angel to the shut the lions' mouths so they could not hurt him. Similarly, the fourth 'man' in the fire (3.25) was an angel (3.28). In both stories God intervened through an angel. God had acted because Daniel was **blameless** (legally innocent) before God and Darius. If v. 9 dealt with the guilt of Darius and the conspirators, v. 22 deals with the innocence of Daniel. In doing so it concludes the study of guilt and innocence in this chapter. Technically, of course, he was guilty of breaking the king's law, but he was not disloyal to the king in doing so. It was his competitors who were guilty of conspiracy to subvert the well-being of the king. Before God as well, Daniel's conduct was blameless. On the other hand, had he obeyed the king's law, he would have been guilty before God.

Verse 23. In a scene reminiscent of 3.27, where Nebuchadnezzar released the three friends from the fiery furnace and not one hair was singed, here Darius freed Daniel, who did not have so much as a scratch on him from the lions. Why was he unscathed? He had trusted in God. If it was obedience to God's law that landed him in the pit in the first place, it was trust in God that delivered him in the second place. The lesson was not subtle: Judeans living in a foreign court had better trust God, even if keeping the law got them in trouble.

Verse 24. What follows is one of the bloodiest scenes in the Hebrew Bible. In the Old Greek, the conspirators include only the other two presidents, so the number executed is small. In the MT, however, the conspirators include the other two presidents and 120 satraps. They and their families were thrown into the pit. According to v. 24b, the lions attacked them **before they reached the bottom**. While that is conceivable for two families, it is unimaginable for 122.

The principle invoked here is familiar in the Hebrew Bible. According to Deut. 19.18-19: 'If the witness is a false witness…then you shall do to the false witness just as the false witness had meant to do to the other.' In other words the penalty for perjury was the same as for the act the perjurer accused someone of committing. A similar reversal appears in Esther 9, where the Judeans were allowed to execute all those people who had planned to execute them the next day. In Dan. 6.24, the families too were included. A similar outcome met the family of Achan in Josh. 7.24. These three passages (Deut. 19.18-19; Josh. 7.24; and Est. 9) would seem to account for the scene described in Dan. 6.24, but Smith-Christopher (1996: 95) may also be correct when he attributes the savagery of the scene to the simmering anger of the dispossessed.

THE CONCLUSION (25-28)

Darius's reaction was to order his subjects to worship Daniel's God. His proclamation was not a requirement that everyone in the Persian Empire convert, but a command to add the God of the Judeans to their pantheon.

Verse 25. The address of the proclamation is almost identical to 4.1 (from R2). It includes everyone under his rule. He salutes his subjects with a wish for their prosperity.

Verses 26-27. The essence of the proclamation was that they all **tremble and fear** God. Darius acknowledges God and commands his subjects to do likewise. Fewell (1988: 152) notes that this new decree effectively sets aside the old one proscribing prayer to anyone but himself. Hence, it turns out the issue in v. 15 was not whether the law *could* be set aside, but whether it *should* be. (Besides, as several scholars have pointed out, the notion of a law valid for only 30 days that nevertheless could not be changed is self-contradictory.) The proclamation concludes with another doxology like those in 2.47; 4.3; and 4.34-35. It was composed for this place in Daniel (cf. Towner 1969: 320), and praises God for rescuing and delivering people in need.

Verse 28. This verse may be called an epilogue. It says that Daniel prospered during the reign of Darius and during the reign of Cyrus the Persian. It was added by R3 to help fit Daniel 6 in the chronology of the book of Daniel. Thus far in the book, that chronology has included the following empires and emperors: the Babylonian Empire (Nebuchadnezzar and his 'son' Belshazzar); the Median Empire (Darius the Mede); the Persian Empire (Cyrus); and the Greek Empire (the legs and feet of the image in Daniel 2).

THE THEOLOGY OF DANIEL 6

Anderson (1984: 71) calls the phrase **the living God** in v. 20 profoundly theological. He writes: 'That the God of Israel is such a God, alive and not dead, enduring and not ephemeral, has to be brought home to the author's compatriots, and how better to proclaim that truth with unparalleled effectiveness than to have it come from the lips of a pagan.'

Daniel 6 also emphasizes that Daniel is the model Judean in his rigorous keeping of the law, even in the face of death. The chapter makes one thing perfectly clear: trouble will come one way or another, so the Judean in the foreign court had better trust God.

Finally, Smith-Christopher (1996: 90) points out that Daniel's confinement in the lions' pit functioned as a symbol for the exile. Imprisonment was not a typical form of punishment in ancient Israel; it occurs almost exclusively in the context of the treatment of people by kings or conquerors. This narrative reflected the experience of every Judean in the Diaspora.

DANIEL'S VISION OF THE FOUR BEASTS (7.1-28)

Daniel 7 is often called the most important chapter in the book of Daniel. That is so partly because of the appearance in 7.13-14 of 'one like a son of a man', who receives dominion over all nations. Many scholars, both Jewish and Christian, have seen that figure as the Messiah, while others, again both Jewish and Christian, have seen him as an angel or a collective figure for the people of Israel. Closely related is the identity of 'the saints of the Most High' and 'the people of the saints of the Most High'. Who are they, and what are their relationships to each other and to the one like a son of a man? These questions are best answered in their context in Daniel 7, and will be taken up where they appear in the chapter. First, however, it will be useful to examine the relationships of the chapter with the book of Daniel as a whole.

Daniel 7 shares significant features with Daniel 1–6. First, of course, it was written in Aramaic, and concluded the second recension of Daniel (Dan. 1 in some form, plus Dan. 2–7). Secondly, it borrowed the four-kingdom motif from Daniel 2. Thirdly, it borrowed the device of dreaming from Daniel 2 and 4. Neither the noun nor the verb for 'dream' appears outside those two chapters and 7.1, except for 1.17, which was written by R3 with Daniel 2–7 in hand. The word 'dream' was a deliberate linking device to Daniel 2 and 4. Fourthly, it was set in the career of Belshazzar, forming a direct link with Daniel 4. Finally, the Aramaic narratives display a chiastic structure that suggests this chapter was placed here to balance Daniel 2.

2.4b-49.   A dream about four world kingdoms replaced by a fifth
   3.1-30.   Three friends in the fiery furnace
     4.1-47.   Daniel interprets a dream for Nebuchadnezzar
     5.1-31.   Daniel interprets the handwriting on the wall for Belshazzar
   6.1-28.   Daniel in the lions' den
7.1-28.   A vision about four world kingdoms replaced by a fifth

On the other hand, Daniel 7 marks a significant turn in the book of Daniel. For one thing the interpreter of dreams, visions, and strange handwriting becomes a visionary. Now, however, he cannot interpret his own vision, but needs an interpreting angel to help him understand. Theologically expressed, the God who had revealed meanings directly to Daniel in chapters 2, 4, and 5, now uses an intermediary. Literarily expressed, the genre of Daniel 7–12 is apocalyptic narrative. The narratives report the visions of Daniel and their meaning. Secondly, the primary focus of the book shifts in Daniel 7 from the foreign setting in Babylon to the fate of Jerusalem and the community living there, a focus which does not change for the rest of the book. This shift in focus is one piece of evidence that the group behind the book of Daniel had relocated to Jerusalem. (See Redditt 1998: 468-70; see also Collins 1993b: 135.) Thirdly, while Daniel 7 clearly builds on the dream of Daniel 2, there are differences between them. For example, in Daniel 2 Nebuchadnezzar and the Babylonian Empire could be symbolized as a golden head, albeit with subsequent empires becoming baser. In Daniel 7 all four empires are subhuman beasts that arise from the sea; none is golden, none behaves properly.

The arrangement of the narratives in Daniel 7–12 probably drew upon two patterns. Larkin (1994: 238-39) develops the view of Michael Fishbane that Daniel 7–12 constitutes a mantological anthology (i.e. a collection of exegetical passages designed to resolve a cognitive problem). Such anthologies form a ring construction around a centerpiece, such as the Shepherd Allegory (Zech. 11.4-17) in Zechariah 9–14. In Daniel, chs. 7 and 8 offer symbolic visions, while chs. 10–12 speak allusively about the history of Israel's experience in the Greek Empire. Daniel 9 stands as the centerpiece. Alone in Daniel 7–12 its point of departure is a passage of Scripture.

In addition, George G. Nicol (1979: 501-505) points to seven correspondences between Dan. 7.1–10.16 and the report of Isaiah's vision in Isa. 6.1-10 that further guided the placement of materials within Daniel 7–12:

1.	The date formula	Isa. 6.1	//	Dan.	7.1
2.	The throne and its occupant	6.1	//		7.9
3.	The divine beings in attendance	6.2	//		7.10
4.	The confession	6.5	//		9.23
5.	The flight of a divine being	6.6	//		9.21
6.	The word about understanding	6.9-10	//		9.23
7.	The touching of the lips	6.7	//		10.16

(He notes that the seventh correspondence is followed in both cases by a long address from a divine being.) All but Dan. 7.9-10 derive from the hand the final redactor of Daniel, R3, who may well have seen in those two verses kinship to Isaiah 6 and built upon it.

The date of the writing of Daniel 7 can be calculated to within a couple of years. Critical scholars are agreed that the so-called 'little horn' of v. 8 is to be identified as Antiochus IV. His persecutions of Judeans during his attempt to Hellenize them are well, if at times fancifully, documented in 1 Macc. 1.20-64; 2 Macc. 4.4–10.9; and *4 Macc.* 4.15–14.20. Briefly stated, he raided the temple, plundered Jerusalem, killed some of its inhabitants, and built the Akra. Then he attempted to set up the cult of Baal Shamen, Lord of the Heavens. In doing so he prohibited worship at the temple, the observance of sabbaths and holy days, circumcision, and he forced Judeans to break the dietary laws. Finally, he had an altar erected in the temple and a pig sacrificed on it, but Daniel 7 does not mention those two actions. They were so offensive that the author of Daniel 7 cannot have omitted them if they had already occurred. Hence, one is safe to date this chapter after the attack on Jerusalem in 169, but before the infamous 'transgression that makes desolate' on the fifteenth day of Chislev (December 7) 167. Daniel 7 was the latest of the Aramaic chapters and was probably written for its place in the book by the redactor of Daniel 2–7 (R2).

The narrative is easily analyzed. Verse 1 provides the setting, vv. 2-14, 21-22 the dream, vv. 15-20, 23-27 the interpretation, and v. 28 the conclusion. Again, the framework in vv. 1 and 28 sets off the dream as a liminal experience. The various scenes in the dream are marked by formulae like 'as I watched', 'as I looked', and 'I saw in my vision'. The dream/vision involves the appearance of four animals (vv. 2-8), the trial of the beasts (vv. 9-14), a description of the antics of one of the horns of the fourth beast (vv. 19-22), in which vv. 21-22 add details to the dream. The interpretation begins with an explanation of the entire dream (vv. 15-18) and closes with more information about the fourth beast (vv. 23-27).

Given their position in the chapter, vv. 21-22 appear to many scholars (e.g. Hartman and Di Lella 1978: 210; Montgomery 1927: 309; Porteous 1965: 96; van der Woude 1986: 310), to be added. Those verses, however, are no more unnecessary than vv. 19 and 20, which merely repeat vv. 7-8. There is little reason to eliminate any of them (see the Introduction, p. 26). Separating the discussion of the last horn from the rest of the vision allowed the author to call attention to that horn (Antiochus IV), who was the object of his concern anyway.

THE SETTING (1)

The setting of this vision is **the first year of King Belshazzar**. In view of the report of his death in 5.30, Daniel 7 (and Daniel 8 as well) are to be construed as flashbacks. Since the overall chronology of the book of Daniel is from R3, this verse came from his hand, or was retouched by him. Miller (1994: 194) calls attention to the 'Verse Account of Nabonidus' (*ANET*: 313), which says that in the third year of Nabonidus he entrusted rulership to his son Belshazzar, while he departed to Teima. Nabonidus began to rule about 556, so the third year would be roughly 554/3.

Daniel had (literally, saw) **a dream and visions**. Daniel 2.1 used the plural for 'dreams'. As noted above, GKC §124 *o* cites 2.1 as an example of an indefinite singular noun. So is 7.1. Also, 2.1 makes it clear that Nebuchadnezzar was dreaming, but 7.1 says only that he **lay in bed**, not that he was asleep. It leaves the issue open (contra Smith-Christopher 1996: 100, who insists that Daniel was dreaming because he was lying on his bed). Daniel 7.1 employs the verb 'to see', which can be used either of dreams or visions. The MT adds: 'then he wrote the dream; the beginning of the words he said'. In other words, what follows in vv. 2-27 was the content of what he had seen. Verse 28 comprises the conclusion, so that vv. 1 and 28 provide a frame for the narration of the dream.

Verse 1 makes no distinction between dreams and visions, but the word 'dream' is not used again in the book of Daniel after 7.1. Daniel 7.13 and 15 simply call what he witnessed 'visions', and Daniel 8, 9 and 10 speak of Daniel's seeing a 'vision' in each case. The difference between dreams and visions is clear: dreams typically come while one is asleep, while visions come while one is in a state of altered consciousness. Lacocque (1988: 135) is more lyrical in his distinction: 'Dream is the writing on the "plaster" of the unconscious. Vision is the writing on the hidden face of history.' He suspects that the author of Daniel 7–12 wanted to avoid the criticism of dreams found in places like Deut. 13.1-5, 18.10-11; 2 Kgs 21.6; Isa. 8.20; Jer. 23.25-28, 32; 29.9-10; and Zech. 10.2. Daniel 10.1 describes a period of illness and dietary restrictions that led up to the vision in 10.2–12.4a, while 8.27 describes a period of sickness that followed the reception of a vision. In that light, 7.28 also functions as a report of the effect of this vision on his psyche.

Porteous (1965: 119) suggests that Daniel 7 is a report of a genuine ecstatic experience, while Daniel 8 is more contrived and planned. To what extent the use of visions is a literary device in Daniel 7, 8 and 10–12 is moot since the reports survived only in writing. Still, to be accepted by the Danielic community, they would have had to conform to the community's expectations.

It is possible to list a few features of Daniel 7–12 that look as if they may have been among those expectations. (1) The visions repeat key formulae that the community recognized, for example, 'I saw in my vision' or 'I lifted up my eyes', followed by 'and behold'. (2) The visions typically contain a description of Daniel's reception of the vision; for example, he was lying in his bed or fasting or praying. (3) The visions also report the effect of the visions upon Daniel; for example, he was terrified or ill. (4) The visions featured an angel who interpreted their meaning to Daniel. (5) Audiences probably expected consistency between themselves and the vision. In some way Daniel had to anticipate their situation; his vision had to describe a situation similar to their own; and the vision had to offer a solution clearly applicable to their situation (hence, the note that the vision was not for Daniel's time but for later days). (6) The visions had to pass the criteria for true prophecy articulated in Deut. 18.2, that is they must be spoken in the name of the Lord and they must come true. It is even possible they had to pass the text Jer. 28.8 added: that true prophets had to prophesy such things as war, famine, and pestilence.

DANIEL'S VISION OF FOUR BEASTS (2-14)

As in Zech. 1.7–6.15, Daniel's vision came at night. This first scene of his vision consisted of three parts: the rise of four beasts from the sea (vv. 2-7), the rise and actions of an eleventh horn of the fourth beast (v. 8), and the description of a trial (vv. 9-14). In the trial 'One Ancient of Days' appears as the judge (vv. 9-10), the fourth beast is destroyed and the other beasts lose their dominion (vv. 11-12), and 'one like a human being' receives dominion in place of the beats (vv. 13-14).

Verses 2-7. Daniel saw four beasts arising from the sea. What is the background for this vision? M. Delcor (1968: 290-312) suggests that the beasts were taken from signs of the Zodiac, a position refuted by J. Coppens (1969: 122-25). Thorne Wittstruck (1978: 100-102) argues instead that the sequence derives from the imagery of curse language, but J.A. Rimbach (1978: 565-66) refutes his position. The more obvious source for the vision is the Old Testament itself. For one thing Nebuchadnezzar dreamed of a statue made of four metals in Daniel 2. The notion of successive kingdoms or empires carries over to the four beasts in Daniel 7. Secondly, the types of animals in the vision seem to derive from Hos. 13.7-8, which mentions a lion, a leopard, and bear, and a fourth (unnamed) beast (cf. Jer. 5.6: lion, wolf, leopard).

What do these beasts represent? Most critical scholars agree that the four animals represent four empires: namely the Babylonian, Median, Persian and Greek Empires respectively. By contrast, traditional scholars (e.g. Baldwin 1978: 147; Miller 1994: 198-293; Walvoord 1971: 153-63) see the animals as the Babylonian, Medo-Persian, Greek, and Roman Empires. Since Rome appears as the Kittim in 11.30 and is named nowhere else in the book, the 'Roman interpretation' appears to be unjustified.

Verses 2-3. The four winds were **stirring up the sea**. The winds are the winds of heaven, coming from every direction as in Zech. 2.6 and 6.5 (see also Dan. 8.8 and 11.4). Smith-Christopher (1996: 101) notes that the LXX says that the winds 'attacked' the sea, implying warfare between the two. In the Old Testament the sea is often a symbol of antigodly forces or chaos that must be defeated, as in Gen. 1.1.

Hermann Gunkel (1895: 323-35) argued that the Akkadian creation myth, the *Enuma Elish*, was the source of the image of the chaos, as did Kvanvig (1981: 85-89). Occasionally scholars have suggested parallels to Iranian materials, but Collins (1993a: 283), who finds Zoroastrian parallels to Daniel 2, sees none for Daniel 7. The discovery of ancient Canaanite mythology, which portrays Baal doing battle with Yam (the sea god), led scholars to conclude that the chaos image was mediated instead from Canaan to Israel through royal and temple ideology (a conclusion contested by Ferch 1980: 85-86). The image of a battle against chaos shows up in various places in the Hebrew Bible, such as in God's defeat of the sea in Ps. 74.13-17 and God's defeat of Leviathan in Isa. 27.1.

P.G. Mosca (1986: 496-517) argues that the Canaanite mythology was mediated to Daniel 7 via Psalms 89 and 8. He points in the right direction. Whatever Daniel 7 might have borrowed from ancient mythology was mediated through the Hebrew Bible and shaped in light of Daniel 2.

Verse 4. The first beast was **like a lion**. The lion was feared for its power and ferocity. It is an oft-used symbol in the Hebrew Bible. In addition, the beast had **eagle's wings**. Technically, the bird may have been the griffon vulture (see Alon 1969: 220-21). Winged bulls with human faces were more frequent than winged lions in Mesopotamian art, and they decorated walls in both Nineveh and Babylon. Presumably a lion was thought to be more fierce than a bull and, thus, a more appropriate image for the Babylonian Empire. If so, this portrayal of Babylon is more violent and less admirable than that of the golden head in Daniel 2.

As Daniel watched, the beast had its wings plucked off and was made to stand upright like a man. The lion rampant was also a common image in Mesopotamian art. It might appear to be a softening of the image, as it becomes less bestial and more human. Scholars sometimes see here an allusion to the restitution of Nebuchadnezzar from his madness in 4.34-36. Alternatively, it might suggest a weakening of the empire over time. If so, the second beast was prepared to take advantage.

Verse 5. The second beast was a bear that **had three tusks in its mouth among its teeth**. The translation **tusks** is based on a slight but unnecessary emendation; the MT reads 'ribs'. Ginsberg (1948: 11-16), followed by Hartman and Di Lella (1978: 209-10), argued that the descriptions of the first two animals were switched in transmission. He thought that the tusks (or 'fangs' as he translated) properly belonged with the lion, while the bear, which can walk around well on its hind feet, was the animal made to stand erect and was given a human heart. The argument is plausible, but not necessarily correct, and it has no textual support. It is, however, the first step in Ginsberg's interpretation of the whole chapter (1948: 16-23). For him the three tusks symbolize the only three Babylonian kings known to the author of Daniel: namely, Nebuchadnezzar, Evil-Merodach (from 2 Kgs 25.27), and Belshazzar. In actuality, of course, the author of Daniel only spoke of two kings, Nebuchadnezzar and his 'son' Belshazzar, regardless of how many he might have known.

Returning to Ginsberg's theory, the Median Empire had only one head, signifying the one king of Media known to the author ('Darius the Mede'); the third beast, the Persian Empire, had four 'heads' (Cyrus, Ahasueras, Artaxerxes, and Darius I); and the fourth ten horns, which represented ten Greek kings, with Antiochus Epiphanes being the tenth. Ingenious as this view is, it is not convincing for the following reasons.

(1) It drastically alters vv. 4 and 5; (2) it treats 'fangs', 'heads', and 'horns' as equivalent symbols for kings; and (3) it treats as additions all references to the eleventh horn. Indeed, Ginsberg thinks, these additions were penned by a different author who did not even recognize what Ginsberg sees plainly, namely that the tenth horn was Antiochus IV, so there was no need to introduce an eleventh horn.

A better explanation lies at hand. Bears are presented in the Old Testament as fierce man-eaters (see 2 Kgs 2.24), and the brown Syrian bear may weigh five hundred pounds or more and has a voracious appetite (Baldwin 1978: 139). Gurney (1977: 43) thinks the three 'ribs' protruding from the mouth of the bear represent the nations of Ararat, Minni, and Ashkenaz, but conquering such small nations would hardly qualify as the ferocious deeds of a ravaging bear. It is more likely that they belonged to the 'man-like' figure the Babylonian Empire became. It is beside the point that Cyrus captured the city of Babylon peacefully; according to Dan. 5.30, Belshazzar was killed and 'Darius the Mede' succeeded him.

The detail that the bear was **raised up on one side** is simply enigmatic. Perhaps the best explanation is that of Noth (1984: 211) that oriental depictions of bears show them ready to attack with their front paws raised.

Verse 6. The third beast, a symbol for the Persian Empire, was a **leopard**. Bentzen (1952: 61) calls it a panther, which is a black leopard. The leopard is a swift and powerful predator. In v. 6, this animal too had wings, four in fact, and four heads as well. Traditional scholars see the heads as an allusion to the Didochi, the four generals who divided up Alexander's Empire upon his death. Other scholars often point to Dan. 11.2, which speaks of four kings of the Persian Empire, and suggest that the four heads represent four kings or the fact that Persia conquered in all four directions. Goldingay (1989: 163) speculates that the four heads could represent four kings of Persia or even Greece, but suggests the real point is that it could see in all four directions at once (cf. Baldwin 1978: 141). If four Persian kings are intended as Ginsberg claimed, they are nowhere named in the book of Daniel, which mentions only Cyrus, though Ezra 4.5-23 also knows of Darius I, Ahasueras (Xerxes), and Artaxerxes I. The book of Esther, of course, knows Ahasueras, and Neh. 2.1; 5.14; and 13.6 mention Artaxerxes I.

Verse 7. The most terrifying beast of them all, however, was the fourth, symbolizing the Greek Empire. It is compared with no other animal, making it seem more mysterious and, hence, more ominous. It is described as **terrifying and dreadful and exceedingly strong**. It chewed everything in its path with its **great iron teeth**, and it stamped anything remaining with its **feet**. Its most unusual characteristic was its **ten horns**, five times the normal two, bespeaking incredible power (so Baldwin 1978: 140). The horns are typically understood as kings.

Verse 8. As if ten horns were not enough, the beast grew an eleventh. That horn began small, but **three of the earlier horns were plucked up by the roots** like teeth **to make room for it** to grow. The identity of the horns has been—like everything else in this chapter—the subject of considerable debate. One suggestion is that the horns were kings of the Greek Empire. A.J. Sachs and D.J. Wiseman (1954: 202-11; cf. *ANET*: 566-67) published a king list from the Hellenistic period compiled in Babylon. The list began with Alexander and included nine more kings before Antiochus IV: Philip, Alexander IV, Seleucus I, Antiochus I, Antiochus II, Seleucus II, Seleucus III, Antiochus III and Seleucus IV.

One problem with this interpretation is uncertainty over the identity of the three horns uprooted by Antiochus IV. Caragounis (1987: 112-13) suggests Alexander the Great, Philip of Aridus and Alexander Aegus; or Philip of Aridus, Alexander Aegus and Seleucus IV. Smith-Christopher (1996: 102) prefers Seleucus IV and his sons Demetrius and Antiochus. Bentzen (1952: 65-66) thinks the three uprooted horns were Demetrius (whom Antiochus left as a hostage in Rome), Antiochus his brother, and Ptolemy Philometer, who was from the Seleucid line (cf. Owens 1971: 422).

A second line of interpretation sees the horns as ten independent states that comprised Alexander's former empire. By the end of the third century one may count Ptolemaic Egypt, Seleucia, Macedon, Pergamum, Pontus, Bithynia, Cappadocia, Armenia, Parthia and Bactria, though the overthrow of three of these kingdoms would fit better the actions of Antiochus III than Antiochus IV (Walton 1986: 32-33). Porphyry seems to have adopted this position, but with a difference: he named Ptolemy VI Philometer, Ptolemy VII Euergetes and Artaraxias of Armenia—kings whom Antiochus IV did defeat—as the three horns (Collins 1993a: 320).

A third interpretation, favored by some traditional scholars, is that Rome was the fourth beast. Jews during the Roman period offered this interpretation, and the Church followed it until the rise of modern scholarship. Walton (1986: 28) summarizes three variations. (1) The fourth empire and the ten horns all lie in the past, and the kingdom of God came in the Church. (2) The fourth kingdom is still in power through the abiding influence of the Roman Empire, but the ten-horn stage lies in the future. (3) The fourth kingdom is over, and people today live in a gap in time that will end when a ten-nation confederacy reconstitutes the Roman Empire. These interpretations make no effort to interpret the chapter within the context of the book of Daniel.

It should be clear that certainty on all these points is impossible, partly at least because the text itself is ambiguous. The interpretation in 7.17-18, 23-27 nowhere identifies a single one of the beasts, unlike Daniel 2 which identified the golden head as Nebuchadnezzar, and Daniel 8, which identifies its two beasts as the Medo-Persians and the Greeks. Consequently, a fourth view simply takes both 'ten' and 'three' as figurative numbers of Greek kings.

Nevertheless, some identifications do seem more plausible than others. The eleventh horn is Antiochus IV. Verse 8 says it had human eyes, which seems to indicate that it was a human being, not a kingdom. Verse 8 also speaks of his arrogance, which is not decisive. Verse 25, however, seems to describe the early efforts of Antiochus at restricting the practice of Judaism, though not the 'transgression that makes desolate'. If the eleventh horn was Antiochus IV, the ten horns would seem to have been Greek kings rather than independent 'kingdoms'. (Cf. *Sib. Or.* 3.381-400, which also interprets the horns as kings.) The suggestion that they began with Alexander and included Philip, Alexander IV, Seleucus I, Antiochus I, Antiochus II, Seleucus II, Seleucus III, Antiochus III and Seleucus IV seems best, as does the suggestion that Seleucus IV and his sons Demetrius and Antiochus were the three horns, though Bentzen's view might also be possible.

Indeed, it is difficult to be sure what the author meant to say about the horns. In v. 8 he holds Antiochus IV responsible for overthrowing three horns, presumably among his predecessors. In v. 20, he says simply that the horns fell out, which might imply the eleventh horn was not responsible for their demise. Then v. 24 says that the horn put down three kings, which does not seem to mandate that three horns were predecessors of the eleventh horn. Fortunately, it is not necessary to solve this problem completely in order to get the message of Daniel 7.

Verses 9-14. The second scene in the vision is that of a trial. One Ancient of Days takes his throne (vv. 9-10), destroys the fourth beast (11-12), and gives dominion to one like a son of a man (13-14). Verses

9-10 and 13-14 are poetic, as are vv. 23-27, where this part of the vision (along with vv. 21-22) is interpreted. Consequently, earlier critical scholars often divided the poetry from the prose and assumed the chapter was comprised of two, originally distinct traditions. More recent scholarship has denied that a switch from prose to poetry or vice versa necessarily implies different sources.

Once again scholars appeal to ancient mythology as the background for imagery in Daniel 7. Verse 9 speaks of 'One Ancient of Days', who took his throne to hear the case against the beasts. He is paired in the vision with 'one like a human being', who comes to the court borne on clouds. Morgenstern (1961: 65-77), on the basis of a reconstructed myth from Tyre, suggested that the two figures originally represented two phases of God, with the second phase reduced in status in Daniel 7. Bentzen (1952: 57) sees the One Ancient of Days as God and argues that vv. 9-11 and 14 are adapted from a coronation psalm. Heaton (1956: 178) takes that thinking further, arguing that the trial scene is based on Psalm 82, where God is enthroned, holds court, and passes judgment on false gods. The author of Daniel 7, Heaton thinks, drew upon the Babylonian creation myth for his depiction of God as One Ancient of Days, and he associated the one like a human being with the First Man and with kingship.

Despite such speculation, the issue of what the images in Daniel 7 might owe to such myths must remain open. The task here is to understand what Daniel 7 meant, not an unrelated issue to be sure, but not identical either.

Verses 9-10. First comes a description of One Ancient of Days, who clearly is God. He is depicted in terms reminiscent of the Canaanite god El, surrounded by light and fire. Smith-Christopher (1996: 103) notes, however, that such myths had long been taken over into Hebraic thinking and modified, so that the most pertinent background for vv. 9-10 is Ps. 97.2-4:

> Clouds and thick darkness are all around him;
>> righteousness and justice are the foundation of his throne.
> Fire goes before him,
>> and consumes his adversaries on every side.
> His lightnings light up the world;
>> the earth sees and trembles.

Verse 9a. Verse 9a only hints at the setting. Daniel saw thrones being set in place. Then an **Ancient One** (literally, 'One Ancient of Days'; cf.

1 En. 47.3) took his seat upon his throne. Nothing is said about occupants of the other **thrones**. They may have remained empty; or the writer may have employed a plural form though only one throne was intended; or the others may have been intended for the members of the divine council. Bentzen (1952: 57) is correct that the setting resembles a king coming to his throne room, but the purpose of his coming is unclear at this point in the chapter.

Verses 9b-10a. The description of the One Ancient of Days continues through v. 10a with two similes. (1) His clothing was **white as snow**, presumably symbolizing purity (cf. Isa. 1.18). (2) His hair was **like pure** [or clean] **wool**. Next, Daniel describes his throne in a metaphor: it was **fiery flames**; its wheels **were burning fire**. Two elements are combined here: fire and wheels. Fire is familiar from Exod. 3.2 as a medium of God's presence, and also familiar from Mal. 3.2 as a medium of God's cleansing of people from impurity. Wheels associated with God's throne are familiar from Ezekiel's vision of God (1.4–3.14, specifically 1.15-21; 3.13). Ezekiel 1.27 combines the two, comparing God to a circle of fire, and Dan. 7.10a speaks of fire issuing from his presence. Similar images can be found in *1 En.* 14.15-23. In both Ezekiel and *1 Enoch*, the setting of the visions is heaven, and that would appear to be the case here as well.

Innumerable angels surrounded the One Ancient of Days. Thousands of thousands of them **served** him. The Aramaic word for 'served' is from the root *šmš*, not the root *plḥ* (serve), which appears in vv. 14 and 27. **Ten thousand times ten thousand** angels stood around him. That so many beings attend the One Ancient of Days is an indication of his supreme worth and power.

Verse 10b. Verse 10b announces the purpose of the heavenly assembly: **the court sat in judgment**. The One Ancient of Days was the judge. Next, **the books were opened**. Books are associated with keeping records, and Mal. 3.16 speaks of the names of those who revered the Lord being written in a 'book of Remembrance'. Revelation 20.12 later spoke of books being open when God judges the dead. From these examples, one may conclude that the four beasts were to be judged by God based on records of their own foul deeds.

Verses 11-12. The One Ancient of Days obviously found the beasts guilty, a verdict so self-evident to the Danielic group the author did not bother to say it. In v. 11 the narrative switches from poetry back to prose. The scene switches to earth, where death and destruction immediately fall upon the fourth beast, while the others are simply stripped of dominion. The author gives few details, but like the original creation in Genesis 1, re-creation through defeating the beasts requires no great effort on God's part.

Verse 11. This verse picks up the thread from v. 8 that the eleventh horn was speaking arrogantly. What he said was noisy, but proved to be only braggadocio before the Judge. Verse 25 elaborates further on the noise he made: he spoke words against the Most High. In other words he committed blasphemy. That is not hard to believe about a person who called himself Theos Epiphanes, 'God Manifest'! The thoroughness of the defeat of the horn, and with him the fourth beast, is emphasized. He was put to death; then his body was destroyed by burning. This is not a literal prediction of how Antiochus would die. Rather, the point here was that the days of Antiochus IV were numbered, just like those of King Belshazzar (5.26), in the first year of whose reign Daniel saw this vision (7.1). Antiochus may have imagined himself as God on earth, but his mortality would prove otherwise.

Verse 12. The other beasts lost their dominion, but were allowed to live **for a season and a time**, that is, for a while. Scholars have seen in this phrase a reference to vestiges of the Babylonian, Median, and Persian Empires, but that seems unlikely since the Seleucids ruled those areas. It is more likely that the author meant that some nations would survive the destruction of Seleucid Empire. That is typical of postexilic, eschatological prophecy, where some of the nations or their remnants survive, though subordinate to Israel (cf. Fohrer 1960: 410-11).

Verses 13-14. The poetry resumes in v. 13, and the scene returns to heaven (Heaton 1956: 183). **One like a human being** appeared. While the New Testament makes a title of the phrase (i.e. Son of Man), Daniel 7 does not. In contrast with the beast-like figures from the sea in vv. 2-8, a human-like figure appears in vv. 13-14. If the beast-like figures held dominion over the world in vv. 2-8, the human-like figure receives dominion in v. 14. If they were opposed to God, the human-like figure received its dominion from God. His receiving dominion is the equivalent in Daniel 7 of the stone cut by no human hand that became the fifth (and last) kingdom in Dan. 2.44.

The scene has reminded scholars of the *Enuma Elish* or Canaanite mythology and a number of ancient rituals. Jeffery (1956: 461) mentions two possibilities: (1) that the author of Daniel 7 had in mind an old Semitic ritual, in which a new king, the 'son of God', would be announced to his people; or (2) that the author was thinking of an Achaemenid ceremonial in which the heir to a throne is led to the old king for his investiture. Hartman and Di Lella (1978: 88) mention others: the myth of the solar heavenly Man, Iranian rites of enthronement, the enthronement of Marduk, and a ancient solar rite from Tyre.

The more important question is the identity of the human-like figure. For traditional Christian scholars the answer is Jesus, but that case has been reduced to one basic point by Young (1949: 293-94): Jesus identified himself as the Son of Man, the heavenly figure of Daniel 7. Young ignores the fact here that v. 14 does not use the phrase 'a son of a man' as the technical title 'the Son of Man'. How Mk 13.26-27 (and parallel passages) used Dan. 7.14 is a matter of New Testament Christology that does not determine the meaning of the verse in Daniel.

Critical scholars have offered a number of alternative interpretations. A sampling must suffice. For Mosca (1986: 496-517) the figure is the Davidic king. For Lacocque (1979: 125-26; cf. 1988: 149-61) he was a priestly figure. Heaton (1956: 183, 187) thought in terms of a faithful subgroup within Israel. Louis-Fletcher (1997: 167-69) identifies him with the High Priest. For Bentzen (1952: 64) the figure represented Israel (cf. Baldwin 1978: 148-49; Delcor 1968: 294; and Mason 1988: 99). Beasley-Murray (1983: 55-56) agreed and further identified the representative as the Messiah (cf. Muilenburg 1961). Dequeker (1973: 185) identified him with the divine kingdom. Goldingay (1988: 495-97) suggested angels or glorified Israelites (cf. Black's deified saints in 1975: 99). Coppens (1964: 72-80) takes the human-like figure as a collective symbol for the angelic host, the saints of the Most High. Collins (1993a: 304-10) limited it to the archangel Michael, while Zevit (1968: 385-96) argues for Gabriel instead. (See further the discussion of the *Menschensohn* in Koch 1980: 216-34.)

The identification will hinge on what an exegete considers definitive. Three examples will illustrate. First, the phrase **like a human being** in v. 13 has engendered debate as to whether it typically designates a heavenly being, with Collins (1993a: 304-10) marshalling the evidence that it does and arguing that the holy ones in Daniel 7 were angels. Yet M.S. Smith (1983: 59-60) shows that the phrase could refer to a human being at Ugarit and cites Job 25.6 as well, and Collins (1993a: 305) himself mentions that 11QtgJob 9.9 and 26.2-3 use the phrase to mean 'human being'.

Secondly, v. 13 in the MT says that the human-like figure came **with the clouds of heaven**, while the LXX says he came 'upon the clouds'. The LXX is preferred by Miller (1994: 207), who argues that the human-like one descended from heaven; the MT was preferred by Heaton (1956: 183), who claims that he ascended to the One Ancient of Days from earth.

Thirdly, Lacocque (1979: 147-48) argues that the term *plḥ* used in v. 14 always refers to divine service. That statement is true as far as it goes. Outside of Dan. 7.14, 21, however, the word is used quite sparingly, namely, in Ezra 7.24 and Dan. 3.12, 14, 17, 28; 6.17, 21; in all of which it refers to serving God. That it can *only* refer to the service of a god is a claim that goes beyond the evidence available (Anderson 1984: 86).

It would seem better to take the interpretation of the dream given in vv. 17-18, 23-27 as definitive for the meaning of the figures in the vision. The important figures numbered three: the eleventh horn, the One Ancient of Days, and the human-like figure. Of the three, only the last remains to be identified. In v. 14 the human-like figure receives the kingdom from God, the One Ancient of Days. In v. 27 kingship and dominion are given to **the people of the holy ones of the Most High**. In the interpretation, then, the human-like one is identified as the one who will rule in the coming kingdom.

Collins (1993a: 322) takes the phrase 'the people of the holy ones of the Most High' as a genitive of possession and translates it 'the people pertaining to or under the protection of the holy ones'. The shorter phrase **the holy ones of the Most High,** which Collins thinks applies only to angels, appears in 7.25. There, however, the holy ones are given over to Antiochus. Hartman and Di Lella (1978: 95) are correct that it seems implausible that Daniel 7 portrayed an attack on angels by Antiochus, who controlled them for three and a half years and changed their laws, though Collins (1993a: 320) argues that is precisely what v. 25 means. It seems better to understand the 'holy ones' in vv. 25 and 27 as Israel, or perhaps a righteous subgroup within Israel. Also, the phrase 'the people of the holy ones of the Most High' should be taken, not as a genitive of possession, but as an appositional construct phrase, to be translated 'the people, i.e. the holy ones of the Most High' (Hartman and Di Lella 1978: 95). (Also see the discussion on 'Die Heiligen (des) Höchsten' in Koch 1980: 234-39.)

Verse 13. The one like a human being ascended to God **with the clouds of heaven**. Montgomery's translation is lyrical: '...wafted in the upper atmosphere with a nimbus of a cloud...' The clouds of heaven stand in contrast with the chaos out of which the beasts arose (Montgomery 1927: 303). The one like a human came to the One Ancient of Days and **was presented before him** as a loyal subject to a sovereign. The Judge had found the beasts guilty and sentenced them; the one like a human now stood before him as their replacement.

Verse 14. The Judge gave **dominion and glory and kingship** to the human-like figure. The word translated 'kingship' can also mean 'royalty', 'reign', 'royal authority', or 'realm'. The three terms together emphasize that he would replace the beasts as the dominant empire on the earth. Further, unlike the temporal reign of the beasts and even the eleventh horn, **His dominion is an everlasting dominion that shall not pass away**, again like the fifth kingdom in Dan. 2.44.

THE INTERPRETATION OF THE VISION (15-18)

Daniel was mystified by what he had seen, and asked an angel what the vision meant (cf. Zech. 1.9, 19; 2.3; 4.1; 5.5; and 6.4). Interpreting angels are typical in apocalyptic literature, but seem jarring at this point in the book of Daniel, since Daniel had interpreted dream/visions and mysterious handwriting in the previous narratives.

The interpretation of the vision is presented in two parts, separated by further details of the vision. In the first part (vv. 15-18), the angel speaks of the fall of the beasts and the elevation of the 'holy ones of the Most High'. In the second part (vv. 23-27), the angel says more about the fourth beast and the holy ones.

THE ANGEL'S INTERPRETATION OF THE FOUR BEATS AND THEIR DESTRUCTION (15-18)

Verses 15-16. The narrative returns to prose once more for a brief explanation of the vision. In vv. 15-16 Daniel confessed that **his spirit was troubled** within him. The statement is not an indication of a tripartite anthropology of body, soul, and spirit; it simply means that he was moved deeply or was greatly disturbed. More specifically, his vision scared him, partly, no doubt, because he did not understand it. Hence, Daniel asked one of the angels attending the One Ancient of Days to interpret it for him.

Verse 17. The angel interpreted vv. 2-8 to mean that four great **kings** shall arise. As in Daniel 2, 'kings' here stand for the kingdoms they rule. They would rise from the **earth**, not the sea, as in the vision. The sea represented their opposition to God; earth was where they would rule.

Verse 18. The angel interpreted vv. 13-14 to mean that holy ones of the Most High (who would include the 'wise' responsible for the book of Daniel, the Israelites who followed them [11.33-35], and perhaps others) would receive the kingdom. The duration of their reign was said to be **forever—forever and ever**. The Aramaic word *'ālam*, like the Hebrew word *'ôlam*, refers to the indefinite past or future. Repetition of the word was an attempt to emphasize extreme duration. Hence, the clause probably meant that God's kingdom on earth would last and last and last.

THE REPORT OF THE VISION CONTINUED:
THE ADDITIONAL HORN (19-22)

The first explanation left Daniel unsatisfied; it was too brief. In vv. 19-22 he requested further information. Verses 19-20 essentially repeat vv. 7 and 8, while vv. 21-22 add new details to the vision, which are interpreted in vv. 24-26. R2 was ready to speak of his own time, so he set the stage to announce God's judgment on the eleventh horn.

Verses 19-20. These verses add a few details to the previous description of the beast and its horns. Verse 19 says the beast had **claws of bronze**, but that detail is not mentioned in the interpretation that follows in vv. 23-27. Verse 20 says that the three horns **fell out**, a milder statement than v. 8, which says they were **plucked up by the roots**. It is also different from v. 24, which says the eleventh horn **put down** three kings. Nothing is said there about the kings' being among his predecessors.

Also, while v. 8 called him a 'little' horn, v. 20 says that the eleventh horn was larger than the others. Hartman and Di Lella (1978: 207) translate the phrase literally: 'and its visibility was greater than that of its fellows'. The point seems to be that it was stronger than the other horns. Some scholars suggest that the horn was little as it was coming in and became great as it grew. It is also possible that the adjective 'little' was read back from 8.9 either by R3 or a scribe to make sure the reader identified the two horns.

Verse 21. The eleventh horn **made war with the holy ones and was**

prevailing over them. This is a reference to the early persecutions of Antiochus, during which a number of Judeans were killed (see 1 Macc. 1.31).

Verse 22. His success ended abruptly when the Judge took his seat for the trial. Again, Daniel reports no battle. God rendered judgment on behalf of the 'holy ones', and the time of the new kingdom began.

THE INTERPRETATION OF THE FOURTH BEAST AND ITS DEMISE (23-27)

Like vv. 9-10 and 13-14, these verses are poetry; indeed, Montgomery (1927: 311) calls them 'a poetic rhapsody'. Since Daniel had asked specifically about the fourth beast, the angel told him it would be different from the other three in its destruction of other kingdoms. Further, the eleventh horn of that beast would be the one upon whom judgment would fall.

Verses 23-24. The angel again interpreted the fourth beast as a kingdom that devoured the earth, the ten horns as its kings, and the eleventh horn as one who put down three kings, but here nothing is said to indicate the ten kings were his predecessors.

Verse 25. The actions of the eleventh horn were threefold. First, he spoke words against the Most High. In other words, he committed blasphemy. Secondly, he wore out the holy ones, presumably with his warfare against them (cf. v. 21: he **was prevailing over them**). Thirdly, he attempted **to change the sacred seasons and the law**. The sacred seasons were the sabbaths and the annual festivals. The mention of the law was possibly a reference to Antiochus's efforts to abolish customs like circumcision.

The community of the book of Daniel could recognize its own situation in this description. Their question must have been the question of apocalypticists of every age: 'How long, O Lord, will these conditions continue?' Verse 25 offers an encouraging answer that must have meant 'not long'. The faithful would be under the control of Antiochus **for a time, two times, and half** (cf. 12.7). The word for 'time' (*'idān*) can mean time in general or a point of time. It is often understood here to mean 'year', based largely on the calculations of time in 8.14; 9.27; and 12.11, 12, but the word is less precise than *šᵉnâ* (year).

Verses 26-27. The demise of the arrogant, eleventh horn comes as quickly in the interpretation as it did in the vision. No sooner will the court sit in judgment than his dominion will be taken from him and

given to the people of the holy ones of the Most High. Unlike the kingdom of the eleventh horn, **their kingdom shall be an everlasting kingdom** (cf. vv. 14 and 18). What is more, as seen in v. 14, the other kingdoms will **serve and obey them**.

THE CONCLUSION (28)

Daniel 7 is a framed story, with vv. 1 and 28 providing the framework for the narration of Daniel's vision. Verse 28 opens simply: **Here the account ends**. What follows is a brief description of the psychological and physiological effects the vision had on Daniel. He was so terrified his face turned pale. Indeed, he was too terrified to forget what he had seen, but kept it in his mind.

THE THEOLOGY OF DANIEL 7

If the point of Genesis 1 was 'In the beginning God...', the point of Daniel 7 was 'In the end God...', and the author used motifs from various mythologies filtered through Hebraic thought to make that point. Such thinking was no small achievement. In a context where Antiochus IV could insult God and exercise hegemony over God's people, the author of Daniel 7 believed that God could and would defeat the forces of evil and establish God's kingdom on earth through the faithful ones in Israel.

Secondly, Stephen D. O'Leary (1994: 198-99) notes that in apocalypticism, time must have an end, and soon. This motif stands front and center in Daniel 7. World events and the history of Israel seemed to point to the evil of humanity and a delay in God's dealing with the various world empires (Steck 1980: 78). This delay, however, was not due to failure on God's part. Rather, he had revealed those very events to Daniel, which meant to the redactor's community that God was actually in control of them all, appearances to the contrary notwithstanding. The 'visions of the future' were actually a reading of history, a looking back from the proper perspective. That reading, moreover, was fine-tuned in the following chapters, as one vision after another unfolded.

O'Leary points out that apocalypticists may find themselves caught in a dilemma. On the one hand, the need of their audience to know precisely 'how long' (i.e. how much longer?) they must endure may lead apocalypticists to set a specific date or period when this age will end and the next will begin. On the other hand, the setting of dates for future events is risky business, because if the date passes without the foreseen divine inbreak the message may be compromised. Daniel 7.25 may be read as an attempt to give a less than specific answer to the question of the time of the end, while 12.5-12 gives a specific answer, with 9.24-27 standing somewhere in between. R. Stahl (1993: 493) notes, however, that even though the calculations of the date were wrong, the author was still correct that the space-time world is limited by God's world, which breaks into it.

Finally, Daniel and his readers learned that despite the depiction of Nebuchadnezzar as the golden head of the image, no human government was a suitable object for Judeans to trust. A fundamental mistrust of earthly kingdoms was beginning to set in; and it should have in the light of the Seleucid persecution.

DANIEL'S VISION OF A RAM AND A GOAT
(8.1-27)

In Chapter 8 the book of Daniel returns to Hebrew, the language with which it began. That transition is attested also in 4QDan[a]. The change of language probably signals changes in the community's self-understanding, not the least of which is a reversion from Aramaic, the language of captivity, to Hebrew, the ancient language of the homeland. The literary quality of the Hebrew is so poor that scholars (e.g. Ginsberg 1948: 41; Hartman and Di Lella 1978: 228) have often argued that it is a translation from Aramaic. It seems better, however, to assume that Daniel 8 was composed in Hebrew, even though its author was more at home in Aramaic (cf. Porteous 1965: 120). Despite the poor quality of the Hebrew, the text can be read practically without emendation (cf. Schindele 1994: 1-16).

Reverting to Hebrew would have been one manifestation of a larger pattern of behavior in which a subgroup within the Judean community reacted to the measures of Antiochus IV by deliberately adopting older values, beliefs, and behaviors. Such a reversion is called nativism and is not unusual among societies under intense stress. Clearly, circumstances in and around Jerusalem had worsened since the writing of Daniel 7. Specifically, 8.11-12 indicates that the 'transgression that makes desolate' had occurred. To many of the faithful, it was the most abhorrent act of Antiochus in his efforts to Hellenize the members of the Judean community.

On the other hand, Daniel 8 continues enough of the concerns of Daniel 7 for Goldingay (1989: 219-22) to suggest that it forms a commentary on the previous vision. If the point of Daniel 7 was that God had the future under control, proved by his disclosing it to Daniel, the point of Daniel 8 is to answer more clearly the question raised in Daniel 7, namely 'How long will these conditions last?' (Cf. Bader 1994: 49)

Scholars sometimes argue that vv. 13-14 are secondary, since vv. 15-19 continue without reference to them, but v. 26 does refer to them, so there is no reason to consider them secondary. Quite the contrary is

true, in fact. It is v. 13 that raises the central question 'How long?'
Also, vv. 18-19 appear to repeat v. 17, but they add that the end time
was a time of wrath. It may be that the writer was somewhat repetitious
here, but that is insufficient reason to excise any of the three verses.

Daniel 8 is an apocalyptic narrative. It opens with a brief setting
(v. 1), continues with the vision (vv. 2-26), and concludes (v. 27) with
Daniel's return to his normal state (Bucher-Gillmayr 1994: 59-67), setting off the vision again as a liminal experience. Verses 2-14 report
Daniel's vision, and vv. 20-26 record Gabriel's interpretation. The transition piece (vv. 15-19) introduces the interpreting angel Gabriel.

THE SETTING (1)

The date for Daniel's vision is **the third year of the reign of King
Belshazzar**. If his first year was 554/3 (see comments on 7.1), his third
year would be roughly 552/1, though Hasel (1977: 153-68) argues for
548/7. The setting, which establishes a connection with Daniel 7, rever-
berates with the situation under Antiochus IV. If Belshazzar was the
worst ruler of the Babylonians, Antiochus was the most infamous ruler
of the Seleucids. The connection between the two chapters also raises
the possibility that the date included a coded but intentional reference to
the date of the writing of Daniel 8, namely two years after Daniel 7
(Lacocque 1979: 159). If the date of Daniel 7 was somewhere between
169 and 167, the date of Daniel 8 was somewhere between 167 and
165. That time frame is probably valid, whether the author intended to
signal the date or not.

THE REPORT OF DANIEL'S VISION (2-14)

Introduction to the Vision (2)
Daniel suddenly saw himself in **Susa the capital**. Susa was one of three
capitals of the Persian Empire during and after the reign of Darius I.
According to Xenophon (*Cyropedia* 8.6.22), the Persian rulers spent the
winter in Babylon, the spring in Susa, and the summer in Ecbatana. The
word *bîrâ*, translated **capital** (cf. Neh. 1.1; Est. 1.2; 3.15; and 8.15),
usually referred to a palace or a fortress, and perhaps implied that the
city was heavily fortified. Susa was located in Southwest Iran in the
Persian province of Elam (modern Khuzistan), about 220 miles east of
Babylon and about 150 miles north of the Persian Gulf. It had been one
of three capitals of the former Neo-Elamite kingdom, until Asshurbani-

pal razed it in 646. It was restored on a much more modest scale c. 625.
Cyrus captured it in 539, on the eve of his victory over Babylon, and
Darius I rebuilt it.

Porteous (1965: 121) notes that one can not tell from the MT whether
Daniel's presence in Susa was meant to be understood literally or as the
result of a visionary journey. The obvious dependence of Daniel 8 on
Ezekiel suggests the latter. Ezekiel claimed to have been transported to
Jerusalem in a vision (Ezek. 8.3), and Dan. 8.2 may well mean to say
that Daniel was transported to Susa, as both the Peshita and Vulgate say.

Daniel says that the vision appeared to him while he was **by the river
Ulai**. The Ulai was a canal that connected the rivers Choaspers and
Coprates and that ran by Susa (Montgomery 1927: 327). The word
'Ulai' in Hebrew meant 'perhaps', and was 'an expression of hope,
prayer and dread' according to KB. The river Chebar, a canal in Babylonia, was the setting for Ezekiel's call vision (Ezek. 1.1), which was
probably the pattern for Dan. 8.2. The word translated **river** (*'ûbal*) is
taken to be the equivalent of the word *yûbal*. Arabic and Akkadian cog-
nates mean 'conduit' (Slotki 1951: 64). An alternative translation of the
word is 'gate' (cf. NRSV footnote).

Daniel's Vision of Two Animals (3-14)
Daniel saw a vision of a ram and a goat, which are domestic, not wild
animals, emerging from a primordial chaos. Even so, the behavior
detailed in the vision is, if anything, more savage than the behavior of
the beasts of Daniel 7. Also, the portrayal of the action is more transparent; Lacocque (1979: 161) calls it an allegory of the struggle
between Persia and Greece. In addition, the angelic interpretation is
uncharacteristically specific.

Verses 3-4. First, Daniel saw a 'a two-horned ram butting towards
three points of the compass...' (Montgomery 1927: 324). No other beast
could withstand its charge. It **did as it pleased and became strong**.

The interpreting angel Gabriel identified the horns as **the kings of
Media and Persia** (v. 20). Reference to the Medes and Persians
together like this appeared earlier in 6.8, 13, 15, in connection with
'Darius the Mede'. The next king mentioned (in 6.28) was Cyrus. While
it is not explicitly said that Cyrus succeeded 'Darius the Mede', no
intervening king is mentioned in the book. Presumably these are the
two kings in view here. Since 'Darius the Mede' is unknown in extra-
biblical sources and is probably a composite of several kings, nothing

more can be said about him. Besides, the description of the ram fits the career of Cyrus, who defeated the Medes in 550 and marched west as far as Lydia in Asia Minor before turning back east to Elam and Babylon in 539. At its height the Persian Empire stretched east to the border of India, south to Egypt, and north to the Caspian Sea. In 480, Xerxes I moved through Macedonia, defeated the Spartans at Thermopylae, and captured Athens, but he lost a third of his fleet at the Greek island of Salamis and returned to Asia.

Verse 3. As the vision began, the first thing Daniel noticed was a ram standing beside the river. It grew two long horns, first one and then the other, and the second was longer than the first. The length of the horns was probably an indication of the military prowess of each king, with Cyrus getting the nod as the more powerful.

Collins (1993a: 330) cites a fragmentary text from Babylon that contains a list of the signs of the Zodiac, with a country identified with each sign. Aries the ram is identified with Persia. Presumably, that identification would have been clear to the reader of Daniel 8. The ram is also used in *1 Enoch* 89–90, part of the 'Animal Apocalypse' from 165–61 BCE. In 89.42-48 rams represent Kings Saul, David and Solomon, and in 90.13 a ram represents Judas Maccabee. The rams defeated their enemies all around, so the notion that the ram would be invincible was probably well known too.

Verse 4. Since the Persians ultimately reached India in their conquest, it is not clear why the vision did not speak of the ram's charging toward the east. Perhaps the author did not know how far east the Persian Empire had stretched, or perhaps he considered the territory east of Persia part of the Persian homeland.

Verses 5-7. Next, Daniel saw a male goat, coming from the west. Verse 21 identifies it as the king of Greece, obviously Alexander the Great. When the ram charged toward the west, it could not defeat the goat, try as it might. Then it was the goat's turn to charge. First under Philip of Macedon (ruled 359–36) and then under his son Alexander the Great (336–23), the Greeks proved militarily superior to the Persians. Alexander himself crossed the Hellespont in 334 and marched all the way to India by 326. Then he was forced to retreat to Babylon, where he died in 323 at the age of 33. Alexander was the great horn of v. 8 (v. 21) and his four generals (Ptolemy Lagus, Lysimachus, Cassander and Seleucus Nicator) who divided up his empire after his death were the four new horns (v. 22).

Verse 5. As the male goat approached from the west, it traveled **without touching the ground**. That detail is unclear, but it might mean that it traveled rapidly or that it flew like the lion and the leopard in 7.4, 6. The second option seems unlikely, since the verse mentions no wings.

Verses 6-7. The goat attacked the ram. Its savage force and its rage are emphasized, certainly not a flattering portrait of Alexander. It broke the two horns of the ram. One should not press that detail to demand that the two kings the horns represented were still alive in the time of Alexander. Rather, the same fluidity between king and kingdom that obtained in Daniel 7 is present in Daniel 8 also.

Verse 8. The goat (the Greek Empire) grew exceedingly strong, but at the height of its power its great horn Alexander broke off. In its place grew four other **prominent horns**, the four generals of Alexander. They vied for control of the empire after his death. In that struggle, which lasted from 323 to 301, Ptolemy I Soter won control of Egypt and Seleucus I Nicator gained Babylon and Palestine. Ptolemy I then took Palestine, and his successors retained it until Antiochus III won it back in 198. (The details of the struggles between the Ptolemies and the Seleucids is the subject matter of Daniel 11.)

Verse 9. A 'little horn' grew out of one of the four prominent horns. It symbolized Antiochus IV, an identification not made in the text, but crystal clear nevertheless. Josephus (*Ant.* 10.11.7 §276) spoke of Antiochus in his discussion of Daniel 8, and the identification holds even among traditional scholars today (e.g. Baldwin 1978: 159; Miller 1994: 225; Walvoord 1971: 185). A reference to this title appears in Dan. 7.8, where the eleventh horn is referred to as a **little one**. The deeds of the eleventh horn of Daniel 7 and the 'little horn' of Daniel 8 correspond well, except that the 'transgression that makes desolate' ends the list of his sins in 8.13.

The 'little horn' **grew exceedingly great**, that is, it became powerful and waged war. It attacked the **south** (Antiochus successfully invaded Egypt in 169, but was forced by Rome to withdraw from his attack in 168), the **east** (he attacked Parthia in 165), and **the beautiful land** (when he returned from Egypt in 169 he plundered the temple, and in 167 he dispatched Apollonius, who butchered inhabitants of Jerusalem, looted and partially destroyed the city, and built the Akra and stationed soldiers there).

Verses 10-12. The text of vv. 10-12 is obscure and may have suffered in transmission. Indeed, Heaton (1956: 191) calls vv. 11-12 the most puzzling of the entire book of Daniel. Hence, it will be useful to hazard an annotated translation of vv. 10-12 before discussing each of the verses individually.

10. And it[1] became great as far as[2] the host of heaven; and it[1] cast down earthward some of the host and some of the stars, and it[1] trampled them.
11. And even to the degree of[2] the prince of the host he[3] did great things; and from him [i e., the prince of the host] the daily sacrifice was abolished[4] and the place of his sanctuary was brought low.
12. And [][5] it set itself[6] above the daily sacrifice in rebellion; and it[1] threw down truth earthward; and it[1] worked[7] and it[1] prospered[7].

[1] The verbs are third feminine singular, agreeing with 'horn', a feminine singular noun.

[2] In v. 10 'ad carries a spatial meaning, i.e., 'as far as'; in v. 11 'ad carries a comparative meaning, i.e., 'to the degree of'.

[3] Although the subject is still Antiochus, the 'little horn', the verb here is a third masculine singular, perhaps partly under the influence of the other third masculine singular verbs in the second half of v. 11. Moreover, the verb higdîl is a hiphil perfect, third masculine singular, used earlier in 8.4, 8 of the he-goat. Verse 10 employed the third feminine singular niphal of the same verb, which might have been expected here.

[4] It is best to read this verb as a pual, following the qere.

[5] Following the LXX, the word for 'host' has been omitted. The omission also preserves the meter all the way through vv. 10-12. NRSV retains 'host' as the subject of the verb, but 'host' is masculine and the verb is feminine. C.G. Ozanne (JTS 16 [1965], p. 446) suggests redividing wsb' tntn as wsb't ntn and translating 'and hosts he delivered up', which in and of itself is attractive, but the solution causes additional problems.

[6] The verb is a niphal imperfect, third feminine singular, translated here with a reflexive meaning. It, like the other verbs in vv. 10 and 12, refers to the 'horn' in v. 8.

[7] These verbs are perfects instead of imperfects, but 'horn' in v. 8 is still the ruling noun.

Verse 10. The little horn's power was unmatched on earth; it stretched up to heaven. It cast down some of the **host** and some of the **stars**. 'Host' and 'stars' are sometimes synonyms and might be used that way here (cf. Deut. 17.3; Zeph. 1.5). Isaiah 24.21 used 'host' in parallelism with 'kings'. It is also possible that 'host' refers to angels in Dan. 8.10 (cf. 1 Kgs 22.19; 2 Chron. 18.18; 1 En. 104.2, 4, 6).

However one understands the reference, the verse can not be taken literally. The fulfillment would be much more mundane: Antiochus's

army attacked people in Jerusalem. The passage itself is based on Isa.
14.12-15, which applies an image from Canaanite mythology to the
predicted fall of the king of Babylon. In a poetic and mythic description, the writer of Daniel 8 spoke of Antiochus's raiding the skies and
throwing down and stomping the 'host' and the stars (cf. 2 Macc. 9.10,
which speaks of Antiochus's early years when 'he thought that he could
touch the stars of heaven').

Verse 11. The 'little horn' rivaled the **Prince of the host** in his
might. The reference to the **daily sacrifice** (see Exod. 29.38-42; Num.
28-29; Ezra 3.5; Neh. 10.34; and Ezek. 46.1-5) and to his **sanctuary**
(the temple) make it clear that the 'Prince' is God (cf. the title 'Prince
of princes' in the interpretation in v. 25). Scholars of quite different
persuasions (e.g. Baldwin 1978: 157; Collins 1993a: 333; Lacocque
1979: 162; Miller 1994: 226; Montgomery 1927: 335; Smith-Christopher 1996: 113) agree on that identification.

The statement that Antiochus attempted to rival God seems quite in
character for the man. On the fifteenth of Chislev (early December)
167, he instituted a pagan festival to the sun and had an altar to Zeus
erected on the altar in front of the temple. On the twenty-fifth he had a
sacrifice offered to Zeus and commanded that a sacrifice be offered on
the twenty-fifth of every month as part of the celebration of his birth-
day.

Verse 12. As reconstructed above, v. 12 extends the thought of v. 11.
Antiochus seemed to set himself above the daily sacrifice with his
demand that Zeus be worshipped on the twenty-fifth of each month. In
addition, Antiochus **cast the truth** [Torah] **to the ground** and met with
success in everything he did. According to Gerhard Langer (1994: 91)
this verse portrays royal misuse of power at its height.

Verse 13. In light of the success of Antiochus, one 'holy one' asked
another the perennial apocalyptic question: how long? The question
carried with it the implication that things had been going badly too long
already and underscored the urgency of God's setting things right.

The context makes clear that *qādôš* (**holy one**) here means 'angel'.
The meaning of the vision was so mysterious that one angel had to
explain it to another! Without such help mortals like Daniel had no
chance of understanding why God had allowed such things to happen
and how long they would last. These are issues of theodicy, which
sooner or later raises its head in apocalyptic thinking. Hence, Daniel 9
dealt with the question of 'Why?' Daniel 8, however, dealt with the

question of 'How long?' That is, how long would it be until the works of Antiochus were undone, the sanctuary was restored, and the daily sacrifice was offered again upon the altar to God.

Verse 14. The second angel responded that it would be **two thousand three hundred evenings and mornings** until the restoration of the sanctuary, measured from the time of the abomination. Under the influence of Dan. 9.27 which interprets 'a time, times, and half' of 7.25 as the last half of the last seven weeks of years, this verse is typically understood to mean 1150 evenings plus the same number of mornings (cf. Bentzen 1952: 71; Lacocque 1979: 163; Porteous 1965: 126-27; Shedl 1964: 101-105). Gese (1991: 410) concurs, but argues that the figure is a rounded number. On the other hand, Walvoord (1971: 190), Goldingay (1989: 213), Miller (1994: 228-30) and S.J. Schwantes (1978: 375-85) accept the full number 2300 and relate it to the last week in Dan. 9.27 (i.e. the years 171–164). Suffice it to say that the number was sufficiently vague that it could designate anywhere from just over three to about seven years.

THE TRANSITION TO THE VISION (15-19)

Having seen the vision, Daniel attempted to understand it. He was assisted by Gabriel, who told him that the vision was for a later time, not the period of the exile.

Verse 15. While Daniel was pondering the meaning of the vision, someone with **the appearance of a man** suddenly appeared before him. He was not a human being, but resembled one in some ways. The word for 'man' used here is neither *'ādām*, nor *'ᵉnôš*, but *geber*. It is a term that distinguishes a male from 'women, children, and non-combatants whom he is to defend' (BDB: 150). It comes from the same root as *gibôr* (mighty man).

Verse 16. The 'man' is identified in v. 16 as Gabriel, whose name included the root *gbr* plus a suffix and the word El, or God. The word *geber* in v. 15, therefore, anticipated the name Gabriel. In view of the fighting activity of Michael and Gabriel, who appeared to Daniel in 10.5 and 13, he was well named. Gabriel was the first angel named in Bible, and along with Michael, Uriel and Raphael was thought of as an archangel in later Judaism.

Daniel reports that he heard a **human voice** (literally, 'the voice of a man') directing Gabriel to explain the vision to Daniel. The speaker, either God or one of the two holy ones in v. 13, apparently was standing

by the Ulai. The NRSV translates the preposition *bên* with the word 'by', which it can mean. When it does, it normally takes the inseparable preposition *l* (lacking here) on the following noun. BDB (p. 107) suggests: 'between the Ulai, i.e. between its banks'.

Verse 17. The short introduction to Gabriel's interpretation appears in v. 17. He came near Daniel, with a frightening effect upon the seer, who fell prostrate before him. The angel addressed Daniel **O mortal** (literally, 'son of Man'). The phrase is the same as the one used to address Ezekiel (cf. 2.1, 6, 8; 3.1, 3, 4, 10, 17, 22; and often elsewhere). Daniel was not identified here as the 'one like a human being' in 7.14; rather he was simply a mortal like Ezekiel.

Verse 18. According to v. 17, Daniel was already lying prostrate before Gabriel. Verse 18 adds that while the angel was speaking to him, Daniel **fell into a trance, face to the ground**. Though the NRSV translation is interpretive here, it is probably correct. The Hebrew verb *rādam* means 'to be in, or fall into, heavy sleep' (BDB: 922). In Ps. 76.7 it is used of the sleep of death. So, how is it used in v. 18? Is this sleep or a trance? It is probably the latter since it designates the effect of awe upon a man who had been wide awake and scared.

Gabriel then **touched** Daniel and lifted him to his feet. Lacocque (p. 169) calls this a 'miraculous' touch, which occurs again in Dan. 10.10, 16, and 18 (of which the latter two seem similar to this verse). Its model is found in Isa. 6.7; Jer. 1.9; or Ezra 1.1, 5. The point is either that he brought Daniel out of his trance, or that he simply stood Daniel on his feet to hear what Gabriel had to say.

Verse 19. The reason for Daniel's perplexity now becomes clear. The vision was not for his own time, but a later time, **the appointed time of the end**. The end of what? Of history? No. Daniel 8 does not deal with the end of history. Rather, it deals with the end of the domination of the empires over Judah. It looks toward a day when God intervenes within history and makes things right, that is, establishes the kingdom of God in which Israel, or a righteous subgroup within it, will be pre-eminent. Verse 19 (and v. 17 as well) refers to vv. 13-14. What the angel asked in vv. 13-14 was when the time of the temple's defilement would end. That is the 'end' in question in v. 19 as well.

THE INTERPRETATION OF THE VISION (20-26)

The angel interpreted the vision for Daniel quite specifically. Unlike Daniel 2 (which only interpreted the head specifically) and Daniel 7 (which did not identify any of the animals), Daniel 8 equates both animals with specific kingdoms. The book of Ezekiel also interpreted animal symbols in 17.11-21. This way of treating a text also appears in the commentaries at Qumran For example, in 1QpHab 2.12, 14 the Chaldeans in Hab. 1.5 are identified with the Kittim or Romans.

Verses 20-21. The two horns of the ram represented the kings of Media and Persia (see above on vv. 3-4), while the he-goat represented Greece and its horn the first great Greek king. It is these two verses, along with the identification of Nebuchadnezzar of Babylon as the golden head in 2.37-38 that provide the internal evidence for understanding the symbols of the various kingdoms in the book of Daniel. Critical scholars understand the four metals of Daniel 2 and the four animals of Daniel 7 to be the Babylonian, Median, Persian, and Greek Empires respectively. The following chart represents those interpretations visually.

Kingdom	Daniel 2	Daniel 7	Daniel 8
Babylonian	Golden Head	Winged Lion	———
Median	Silver Chest	Bear	Ram's Horn 1
Persian	Bronze Middle	Leopard	Ram's Horn 2
Greece	Iron legs	Fourth Beast	He-goat

Chart of Daniel 2, 7, and 8 for Critical Scholars

Traditional scholars typically differ on one crucial detail. They take the ram of 8.3 as a single entity: a Medo-Persian Empire. They equate it with the silver chest of the image and with the bear. Then they identify the he-goat with the bronze middle and thighs and the leopard. That leaves the legs of iron and the fourth beast unidentified. They see it as the Roman Empire. In that way they are able to interpret the 'one like a human being' as Jesus the Son of Man in Daniel 7.

Kingdom	Daniel 2	Daniel 7	Daniel 8
Babylonian	Golden Head	Winged Lion	———
Medo-Persian	Silver Chest	Bear	Ram
Greek	Bronze Middle	Leopard	Goat
Roman	Iron Legs	Fourth Beast	———

Chart of Daniel 2, 7, and 8 for Traditional Scholars

The most obvious problem with this second schema is that the 'little horn' in Daniel 8, widely recognized by traditional scholars as Antiochus IV, is interpreted as a different individual from the 'little horn' of Daniel 7. This is so despite the obvious parallels in the descriptions in the two chapters. Daniel 7.21 says that he made war against the saints, and v. 25 adds that he blasphemed God, 'wore out' the saints, and changed seasons of worship and the Torah. At the height of his power, God will judge him and turn over his kingdom to the 'people of the saints of the Most High' (v. 27). This change in kingdoms would occur in a 'time, two times, and half'. Daniel 8.10-12 says that he made war against the host and trampled on them, rebelled against God, took away the daily offering, and defiled the sanctuary by committing the 'transgression that makes desolate'. In 2300 nights and days, his hegemony would end (v. 14). The lists are remarkably similar, except that Daniel 8 refers to the 'transgression'.

Since that 'transgression' and the specific identification of the animals nails down the historical references in Daniel 8, traditional scholars are forced to defend their contention that Daniel 7 looks ahead to different people. They handle the difficulty in a variety of ways, so one example must suffice. Walvoord (1971: 198) does so by giving the 'little horn' a double referent in Daniel 8. He sees Antiochus IV as the first but not the final fulfillment of Dan. 8.23-26, a conclusion he defends by distinguishing the meaning of the vision itself from the interpretation given by the angel.

> [T]he principal problem of the passage when interpreted as prophecy fulfilled completely in Antiochus is the allusions to the end of the age. These are hard to understand as relating to Antiochus in view of the larger picture of Daniel 7 which concludes with the second advent of Christ... If the vision itself of the little horn can be fulfilled in Antiochus Epiphanes, the interpretation given by the angel seems to go beyond Antiochus to the final world rulers.

This quotation appears to say what Walvoord clearly did not mean, namely that God revealed one thing to Daniel in a dream, but when Daniel could not understand it God sent an angel to interpret the dream to mean something different. The problem with Walvoord's interpretation, if indeed this is a problem, is that he reads Daniel 7 through the bifocals of the Synoptic Apocalypse and then wants to try to find the same meaning in Daniel 8. If, as Walvoord and others have to admit, Daniel 8 is about Antiochus IV, primarily or entirely, so is Daniel 7. The New Testament writers were free to apply Daniel 7 to the Roman period because of similarities they saw between Antiochus's attack on the temple and that of the Romans, but their applications do not control the meaning of the earlier Scriptures.

Nor does the difference between critical and traditional scholars stop here. The interpretation of the kingdoms in Daniel 7 and 8 will carry forward into Daniel 9 and 11 as well, with critical scholars contending that the time frame of the book of Daniel never advances beyond the Greek period and traditional scholars claiming that it looks forward not merely to the Roman period but to the end of the world as well.

Verse 22. Alexander's four generals succeeded him, but could not match his power. See comments on v. 8.

Verses 23-25. These verses interpret the reference to the 'little horn'. Roughly speaking, v. 23 interprets v. 9, v. 24 interprets v. 10, and v. 24 interprets vv. 11-12. The angel said that Antiochus would grow strong, cause destruction, and rise up against the Prince of Princes (God). Verse 25 adds a note drawn from Dan. 2.34 and 45, namely that **he shall be broken, and not by human hands**.

Verse 26. The interpreting angel assured Daniel that the vision about **the evenings and the mornings** is true. Then he commanded Daniel to seal up the vision. A seal implies a written document. Daniel 7.1 specifically said that he wrote down the first vision; Daniel 8.26 implies the same for this vision. Why were such provisions for the care of the vision necessary? The vision was not for the exilic period, the ostensible time of the writing, but for the Maccabean period, the actual time of the writing.

THE CONCLUSION (27)

Daniel reported the psychological and physiological effects of receiving the vision. It had not come easy; it rendered him **dismayed** and **sick** for days. His last words were that he did not understand what he had written. His readers, however, for whose time it was written, could understand easily what was so baffling to Daniel.

THE THEOLOGY OF DANIEL 8

Porteous (1965: 124) points out that the Judean resistance to Hellenism meant that there were other values than those expounded by Hellenism worth defending and following. Those values were taught in the Torah: belief in and worship of God, living and worshipping according to a divinely ordained calendar, the observance of practices associated with the covenant with God such as circumcision and dietary regulations, and the observance of rules of morality and charity.

Daniel 8 addresses three of the themes O'Leary considers typical of apocalyptic rhetoric: spiritual authority, theodicy, and time. First was the issue of spiritual authority in Daniel 8. As just noted, vv. 26 and 27 emphasize that the vision came directly from God. Far from being a creation of Daniel's imagination, these verses claim it came to him as a message from outside. It was incomprehensible, even after the angel interpreted it to him, and the reception of the message made him ill. All of those details seek to establish that Daniel wrote under the authority of God.

Secondly, Daniel 8 dealt with the issue of theodicy in the form of the question 'Why do the godless rule?' The answer, of course, was that the godless were not really the world's rulers, God was. No matter how dreadful the situation had become, it was still not beyond God's control. The proof of that control was that God had divulged in advance to Daniel the terrible 'transgression that makes desolate'. Awful as it was, it would not bring about the death of God.

Thirdly, Daniel 8 dealt with the issue of time. God had even told Daniel how long the days of persecution would last: a mere 2300 evenings and mornings. To be sure, Daniel 8 was mistaken that the death of Antiochus would usher in the kingdom of God, but it was not wrong in its prediction of the end of the hegemony of Antiochus. Perhaps others in Jerusalem were saying the same thing, and certainly the Maccabees took action to end Seleucid control of Jerusalem and its sanctuary. Neither of those things detracts at all, however, from the fact that at what seemed to be Israel's darkest hour the author had the faith to proclaim that Antiochus was on the brink of destruction by God.

DANIEL'S PRAYER AND GABRIEL'S REVELATION OF THE 70 WEEKS (9.1-27)

The structure of the book of Daniel takes another turn at ch. 9. In the court narratives of chs. 2, 4 and 5, Daniel was the interpreter of dreams (or visions) and mysterious writing. In chs. 7 and 8 he saw visions himself, but needed an interpreting angel to offer explanations, which in the case of ch. 8 he still did not understand. In Daniel 9 an angel appeared to Daniel to interpret Scripture. The angel was Gabriel, whose appearance in Daniel 9 forms an immediate link with Daniel 8. Links with other chapters are found in 9.27b, which presupposes 7.25, 8.14, and anticipates 12.7 (Lacocque 1979: 178). Also, the arrangement of the narratives in Daniel 7–12 probably drew upon the pattern of the man-thological anthology. (See the discussion in the introduction to Daniel 7.) Daniel 9 stands as the centerpiece of Daniel 7–12 and takes as its point of departure Jer. 25.11-12 and/or Jer. 29.10 (see below).

In Daniel 9 God dispatched Gabriel to Daniel as soon as Daniel turned to God in fervent prayer. That prayer appears in 9.4b-19. It distinguishes itself from the rest of the chapter in several ways. (1) The transitions from the narrative to the prayer and back again in vv. 4a and 20 are rough and obvious, while the connection between vv. 3 and 21 is quite smooth. (2) The inquiry into the remaining number of years of Jerusalem's devastation is not obviously addressed by the prayer. (3) The prayer uses the divine name Yahweh six times (all between vv. 4 and 14); the transition verses 4a and 20 each use the name Yahweh once, and v. 2 uses it in the formula **according to the word of the Lord**. Outside of those verses the name does not appear in the book of Daniel. (4) The Hebrew of 4b-19 is better than that of the rest of the chapter or the rest of Daniel 8 and 10–12 and is free from Aramaisms. (5) In fact, the prayer is more like prayers elsewhere in the Bible than anything else in Daniel. A chart taken from Smith-Christopher (1996: 127, fig. 1 and modified slightly) will illustrate that point by comparing this prayer with a prayer of confession by Ezra over the practice of mixed marriages offered at the time of the evening sacrifice, Solomon's prayer at the dedication of the temple, and the penitential prayer of Baruch to the Exiles at the time of the fall of Jerusalem.

Penitential Prayer in Daniel 9.4-19 Compared with Ezra 9.6-15,
1 Kings 8.23-53, and Baruch 1.15–3.8

A.   The prayers open with a confession of guilt.
        We have sinned, committed iniquity, wickedness, rebellion.
        Ezra 9.6-7   1 Kgs 8.47   Bar. 2.12   Dan. 9.5a, 9
        We have turned from the commandments and from justice/ordinances.
        Ezra 9.10   1 Kgs 8.58   Bar. 1.18   Dan. 9.5b, 10
        We have not listened to 'your servants the prophets'.
        Ezra 9.11   ——   Bar. 1.21   Dan. 9.6, 10
        We are all guilty.
        Ezra 9.7   1 Kgs 8.46   Bar. 1.15   Dan. 9.7a, 11
        We are (will be) driven into foreign lands as you threatened.
        Ezra 9.9   1 Kgs 8.46   Bar. 2.1-2a   Dan. 9.7b, [12-13]
        We know of you through Moses, the 'servant of God'.
        ——   1 Kgs 8.53   ——   Dan. 9.13
        We sinned, so you were right to punish us.
        Ezra 9.13   ——   Bar. 1.15   Dan. 9.14
B.   The prayers usually turn on the phrase 'and now' to request deliverance.
        (1)   Remember that you brought us from Egypt.
              ——   1 Kgs 8.51   Bar. 2.11   Dan. 9.15
        (2)   Turn aside your righteous anger.
              Ezra 9.15   ——   Bar. 2.13   Dan. 9.16
        (3)   Preserve Jerusalem and the temple (Holy Mountain).
              Ezra 9.9(?)   ——   Bar. 2.26   Dan. 9.16
        (4)   Notice our disgrace among the neighbors.
              Ezra 9.7   N/A   Bar. 3.8   Dan. 9.16
        (5)   Listen, for your sake.
              Ezra 9.14   1 Kgs 8.28   Bar. 3.2   Dan. 9.17, 19
        (6)   Look on our situation (open eyes, ears, etc.).
              ——   1 Kgs 8.29a   Bar. 3.4-5   Dan. 9.18
        (7)   Forgive us.
              Ezra 9.14   1 Kgs 8.30   ——   Dan. 9.19
        (8)   Act for *your name's sake*, and your people, and your city.
              Ezra 9.14   1 Kgs 8.29a   Bar. 2.15   Dan. 9.19

Scholars have long debated whether the prayer is original to the chapter. On the one hand, the factors listed above seem to prove conclusively that it was written by someone other than the author of the rest of Daniel 9; consequently Benzten (1952: 75), for example, calls vv. 4-19 an addition. (See also Ginsberg 1948: 33, 41; and Hartman and

Di Lella 1978: 245-46; but see Jones 1968: 488-93 for a defense of its authenticity.) On the other hand, some recent scholars (e.g. Collins 1993a: 347-48; Lacocque 1979: 178) have declined to call the prayer an addition. They prefer to say that the author incorporated a previously existing prayer into his narrative.

If, as seems likely, that is so, the next task is to say why he did it. The prayer proposes an answer to a question not formulated in this chapter, but crucial to its second-century readers nevertheless: if 70 years were required to atone for the sins of Judah and Jerusalem, why were Judah's conditions still so bad in the second century?

The answer was that Judah had continued to sin. The author worked with the exilic Danielic material, but expressed through that the author's assessment of his own time. G.H. Wilson (1990: 96) calls attention to Daniel's confession that Israel had not heeded the words of the prophets (vv. 6, 10-11). The charge in v. 5, however, was that they had 'sinned and done wrong, acted wickedly and rebelled', and turned aside from God's commandments. It was not simply the case that the sins of the ancestors still had not been atoned for; rather new generations had perpetuated their sins. Postexilic Judeans had not kept God's commandments, and some, perhaps many, second-century Judeans had followed Antiochus's plan of Hellenization and sin. That is why full atonement did not come to Jerusalem after 70 years, but would require 70 weeks of years.

Before atonement could come, God's people must repent, confess their sins, and obey God, even in the face of persecution by Antiochus IV. As Wilson (1990: 97) saw, the prayer in vv. 4-19 was an attempt to have Daniel do what Jeremiah 29 said Israel had to do in order to be restored (cf. Lacocque 1979: 177-78). So Daniel 9 agreed with what Daniel 2, 7, and 8 had already said: the Exile did not end with the Babylonian Empire, but extended through the Median, Persian, and Greek Empires as well. Daniel 9 as a whole showed what Israel must do to end the anti-godly power of the world empires.

The prayer is framed by a short narrative (1-3, 21-27). The setting for Daniel 9 (v. 1) is the first year of 'Darius the Mede', that is, the first year after the fall of Babylon in the chronology of the book. It is plausible that exiles in Babylon would have raised precisely the question the author places on Daniel's mind: is it now time to go home and to rebuild Jerusalem? Historically speaking, Cyrus the Great issued his edict in 539 (2 Chron. 36.22-23, Ezra 1.1-3a), which was followed by a succession of groups returning to Jerusalem, including but probably not limited to those under Sheshbazzar in 538, under Zerubbabel and Jeshua in 522, under Ezra in 458, and under Nehemiah in 445.

For the author of Daniel 9, however, those efforts did not end the Exile. He lived and worked among a group that itself had come from Babylon to Jerusalem even later, shortly after the Seleucids had wrested control of Judah away from the Ptolemies. What they found was anything but the utopia described in such passages as the book of consolation in Jeremiah (30.1–31.40), the song to the barren wife Jerusalem in Second Isaiah (54.1-17), or the final vision of the book of Ezekiel (40.1–48.35). The books of Haggai, Zechariah, and Malachi, as well as Ezra and Nehemiah—all probably known to the author of Daniel 9— made clear on the one hand that Jerusalem was making a comeback, but on the other hand that problems still remained. Probably nothing, however, had prepared them for the reversals Jerusalem experienced under Antiochus IV. The author of Daniel 9 could not, therefore, accept the conditions under which he and his community lived as a fulfillment of the promises of God. Something better had to be in store for Jerusalem and the temple. (This idea was taken from Wilson 1992).

Seen in this light, perhaps 9.1-3 reflects the situation of the author of Daniel 9 more than one might suppose. It reports a meditation upon Jer. 25.11-12 (which speaks of 70 years of Babylonian hegemony over Judah and its neighbors) and/or Jer. 29.10 (which speaks of God's returning the exiles to Judah after Babylon's 70 years). Perhaps those verses were among many whose meaning the transplanted community of scribes had begun to ponder. If so, their answer must have been the answer of the postexilic prophets before them: God had not yet restored the city because of the sins and failures of its people (cf., Isa. 57.4-13; Hag. 1.2-10; Zech. 13.1-9; Mal. 1.6–2.17). The problem in second-century Judah was not just the obvious sins of Antiochus but also the not-so-obvious sins of God's people, from which sins the author repents through the exilic figure of Daniel.

In Dan. 9.21-27 the author returns to the topic in 9.1-3 of when the devastation of Jerusalem would be over. The angel Gabriel appeared to give exilic Daniel a timetable for the 'future' down to the restoration of the temple after Antiochus IV desecrated it. The timetable employs the typical apocalyptic device of a periodization of history. The 70 years of Jeremiah became 70 weeks of years or 490 years, seven times the judgment Jeremiah had in mind. Four hundred and ninety years, however, is both 70 sabbath years and ten jubilee years. According to Lev. 25.1-7, farm land should be allowed to observe its sabbath by lying fallow every seventh year. According to Lev. 25.8-17 the seventh sabbath year was a jubilee year in which land not only rested but was returned to the family that traditionally owned it if it had changed hands. Leviticus 26.34-39 interprets the exile in terms of sabbaths, and 2 Chron. 36.21 interpreted the 70 years of Jeremiah as ten sabbaths, giving the author of Daniel 9 his cue for reading the 70 years as 70 sabbaths.

Stripped to its essence, Gabriel's timetable envisioned seven weeks of years (seven sabbath years or one jubilee) between the time the call went out to rebuild Jerusalem and the coming of an 'anointed one', 62 weeks of years or sabbath years until an 'anointed one' would be cut off, and one last week of years, during which a 'prince to come' would make the sacrifices cease and set up the 'abomination that desolates' during the first half-week. At the end of the week, the desolator himself would meet his end. By implication, so would the devastation of the temple. While a full discussion of this timetable will follow, it is clear that the desolator was Antiochus and that the timetable in Daniel 9 ends with his demise, which was the same place as in Daniel 2, 7, and 8.

Daniel 9 alone among the surveys of time in Daniel presents itself as the interpretation and application of a text. In terms of its genre, it may be classified as an apocalyptic narrative utilizing the form of midrashic exegesis. The conversation with Gabriel in vv. 21-27 was a vision, though the text does not call it that. The brief narrative in vv. 1-3, 21-27 is overwhelmed, however, by the lengthy prayer in vv. 4-20. The relative disparity in their lengths is cited sometimes as evidence that the prayer is authentic, on the apparent assumption that no one would write a narrative of only ten verses. The assumption appears to be without merit.

THE SETTING (1)

The setting of Daniel 9 is the court of 'Darius the Mede' in the first year of his reign, the first year after the fall of Babylon. (Historically, one can not pinpoint that date because of the problems associated with 'Darius the Mede'.) Introduced in 5.31 and 6.1 (MT 6.1-2) as the successor of Belshazzar, Darius is furnished with a genealogy here. He is said to be the son of Ahasueras, usually the name for Xerxes I (Ezra 4.6; Est. 1.1). As shown in the Introduction (pp. 32-33) and the comments on 5.31, the author of Dan. 9.1 seems to have worked with the tradition that appears as well in Tob. 14.15 that Nebuchadnezzar and Ahasueras together captured and destroyed Nineveh. If the author of Daniel 9 thought the two kings were contemporaries, then it would make sense for him to suppose that a son of Ahasueras captured Babylon and succeeded Belshazzar the son of Nebuchadnezzar after a short reign.

DANIEL'S MEDITATION ON A PROPHECY OF JEREMIAH (2-3)

Daniel is pictured meditating on the number of years Jerusalem must lie in ruins according to the prophet Jeremiah, namely 70. He turned to God for the answer to the implied question of whether the capture of Babylon by 'Darius the Mede' meant that the devastation of Jerusalem was nearing its end.

Verse 2. The date of the setting is repeated: **in the first year of his reign** (i.e., the reign of 'Darius the Mede'). Theodotian omits this phrase, but there is no reason to strike it. Baldwin (1978: 26-27) suggests that the repetition might imply that Cyrus used the name Darius his first year only, but her identification of 'Darius' with Cyrus remains unsubstantiated.

Daniel **perceived in the books**. Baldwin (1978: 164) suggests that the use of the word $s^e p \bar{a} r \hat{i} m$ (**books**) shows that the prophetic books were considered Scripture (cf. Hartman and Di Lella 1978: 241). One would have to agree at least that the word seems to be functioning as a technical term. If she is correct, she would still want to exclude at least the postexilic prophets Haggai, Zechariah and Malachi since she holds to the authenticity of the book of Daniel. G.H. Wilson (1990: 93) makes a better suggestion, namely that the word refers to the two letters in Jeremiah 29, the first of which was explicitly called a $s\bar{e}per$. Jeremiah 29.10 is one of the passages, along with 25.11-12, which mentions the 70 years.

The books contained **the word of the Lord to the prophet Jeremiah**. Here for the first time in the book of Daniel the divine name Yahweh appears. It is used in a phrase similar to Jer. 29.30.

Verse 3. To gain understanding of the 70 years, Daniel turned to God (facing Jerusalem? cf. 6.11) in prayer and supplication. Daniel also mentions **fasting**. Individuals might fast to prepare themselves for worship, to acknowledge public disaster, to express grief or contrition, or to develop moral discipline. The wearing of **sackcloth** and the covering of the head with **ashes** expressed mourning or self-abnegation (Jon. 3.6; Est. 4.1-4). These actions would have been appropriate for Daniel as a means of preparation to receive a revelation (cf. Exod. 34.28; Deut. 9.9; Est. 4.6; Dan. 10.13; 2 Esd. 5.13, 20; *2 Bar.* 20.5-6). The fact that they were appropriate also as acts of contrition gave the author the opportunity to insert the prayer of contrition and lamentation that follows.

DANIEL'S PRAYER OF CONFESSION AND PETITION (4-20)

The prayer the author inserts at this point gives the entire narrative the flavor of repentance. The author makes his transition to the prayer in v. 4a. In 4b-6 Daniel confesses the guilt of his people. The subject changes in vv. 7-14, as Daniel exonerates God from any blame for the delay of the restitution of the temple, while vv. 15-19 beg God to hear the prayer, forgive the sins of the people, and restore the fortunes of the sanctuary.

Verse 4a. Having mentioned prayer, the author now introduces the prayer he will place on Daniel's lips. Daniel prays to **Yahweh my God**, thus counting himself within the confessing community (cf. v. 20). In vv. 9, 10, 13, 14, and 15, he prays on behalf of the people to 'Adonai/Yahweh our God', thus assuming the role of the prophet as intercessor.

Verses 4b-6. Confession is the acknowledgment of sins. As intercessor, Daniel confesses the sins of the people, but always in the first person plural, thereby including himself. In v. 20 the author has Daniel say explicitly that he was confessing his sins and the sins of the people. In vv. 4b-6 he enumerates those sins by employing five verbs, which form the skeleton of the confession.

Verse 4b. Daniel begins the prayer, however, on a note of praise. He invokes God by the name **Yahweh**. Then he proclaims that Adonai (the **Lord**) is **great and awesome**. 'Awesome' is a niphal participle from *yr'*, denoting that which is fearful and dreadful, or which inspires reverence and godly fear (BDB: 431). The invocation continues with the phrase **keeping covenant and steadfast love with those who love you and keep your commandments**. The entire verse is taken almost word for word from Neh. 1.5, which in turn put together the title for God from Deut. 7.21 and a phrase from Exod. 34.8. It is clear from the opening words that the prayer is a concatenation of scriptural verses.

Verse 5. Daniel began his confession in v. 5, employing five verbs signifying sinful behavior. He confessed that he and the people had

sinned, using the root *ḥṭ'*, a very common term for missing one's goal or way, going wrong or sinning. Next, he confessed that they had **done wrong**, employing the denominative verb *'āwâ* from a noun denoting iniquity or guilt. Thirdly, they had **acted wickedly** (*ršʿ*, a word associated with criminal behavior). These first three verbs appear in confessions in 1 Kgs 8.47 and in Ps. 106.6. Daniel also confessed that they had **rebelled** (*mrd*). The fifth verb makes clear the nature of their rebellion: they **turned away** from God's commandments and ordinances. While these verbs do not make explicit what the sins were, they do carry ethical connotations.

Verse 6. God had sent his servants the prophets (cf. Jer. 25.6; Ezra 9.11; Zech. 1.6) to warn the people about the consequences of their behavior, but they had ignored the prophets. The exilic Daniel could have pointed to the great pre-exilic prophets as the persons he had in mind. Their words and the words of the postexilic prophets also had been collected by the time of the Maccabean author. The larger corpus left him and his audience more, not less, guilty.

Verses 7-14. Daniel's prayer also exonerated God from any blame for what was happening. Because the people had kept sinning, it was their fault that shame fell upon them. By contrast, God was wholly righteous, merciful and forgiving. God had warned the people that calamity would befall them if they sinned, but they rebelled anyway. They had no one to blame but themselves for their circumstances.

Verse 7. This verse draws a contrast between God and the people. God is righteous, but they are shame-faced. (No Hebrew word corresponds to the word **falls** in the NRSV.) A second contrast also surfaces in this verse, which contrast betrays the place of origin of this prayer. The phrase **to us** stands in apposition to the list of people that follows. Within that list, however, the prayer distinguishes those who are **near** (i.e., those who live in Judah, Jerusalem, and Israel) from those who are **far away** (i.e., those who live **in all the lands to which you have driven them**...) It is clear from this distinction that the prayer was compiled by and for people living in Palestine for use in the temple. The prayer also confesses the **treachery** of those who had gone into exile, confirming an exilic or postexilic time of origin for the prayer.

Verse 8. The prayer invokes **Yahweh** once more, and again confesses the **open shame** (literally, 'shame of faces', cf. 'shame-faced' in the comments on v. 7) of God's people. The list includes those offering the prayer: **us, our kings, our officials, and our ancestors**. Though it is not immediately clear, this verse too makes a distinction, that between those of the generation of the ones praying ('us'), and those of the past generations with their kings, officials and ancestors. Even if one adopts the traditional position that exilic Daniel was offering the prayer, the setting was the first year of 'Darius the Mede'. There was no (Judean) king in Daniel's time any more than in the Maccabean period.

Verses 9-10. These verses essentially repeat vv. 4b-6 and present another contrast between God and God's people. **Mercy and forgiveness** belonged to God, while the people rebelled and refused to obey God's commandments.

Verse 11. No one could claim innocence; **all Israel** had **transgressed** God's law by refusing to obey God's words. Consequently, God was justified in pouring out **curses and the oath written in the law of Moses** upon them. Verse 11 alludes to the curses in Deut. 27.11-26 and 28.15-68, and to 29.20, passages that put predictions of the exile on the lips of Moses, but which actually were written after the fact, just like Daniel. Also in view here is Lev. 26.14-45, which includes the interpretation of the Exile as sabbath rest for the land of Israel (vv. 34-39, 43).

Verses 12-13. In destroying the temple and sending people into exile, God was simply carrying out the threats made in Leviticus 26 and Deuteronomy 28 and 29 (cf. Lam. 2.17a). The claim that the devastation on Jerusalem surpassed anything ever seen on the face of the earth may be understood as hyperbole. Yet, despite all that God had done, the people did not **entreat the favor of the Lord** (Yahweh) their God. Nor had they repented from their sins or reflected on God's truthfulness.

Verse 14. Daniel defended the actions of God in sending the people into exile in two ways. (1) Yahweh postponed punishing the people, giving them every opportunity to repent, but ultimately sending the punishment on them they deserved. (2) Yahweh was righteous; that is, God was justified in punishing the people (cf. Lam. 1.18a).

A PRAYER OF PETITION (15-19)

With the words **and now**, the prayer turns into a petition. Daniel begs God to turn from wrath against Jerusalem and the temple, to forgive the people, and to act on their behalf. The request, however, was not based on the righteousness of the people, but on the nature of God.

Verse 15. God is invoked by the name Adonai (Lord) six times in vv. 15-19, once each in vv. 15, 16 and 17, and three times in v. 19. The prayer acknowledges God's great act of rescuing Israel at the exodus.

This deed, and others that followed, made God's name renowned **even to this day**. In contrast with God's faithfulness to Israel, therefore, Israel's infidelity to God stood out. Hence, Daniel confessed once more the collective guilt of the people.

While no one would have questioned God's great acts in the past, the claim that God was still renowned among the people (or among the nations) would have stood in conflict with the ostensible setting of exilic Daniel and the actual setting of the second-century author. Even so, in the timetable with which this chapter ended, Gabriel promised Daniel God would act once again.

Verse 16. Next, Daniel appeals to God's nature as the basis for an appeal for forgiveness. God's past great acts are referred to now as God's righteousness. The NRSV translates **righteous acts**, which catches the relationship with v. 15. The word also underscores God's truthfulness and ethical correctness. It also denotes justice, but the appeal here is not that past or present generations deserve God's blessing. They had become a disgrace among the surrounding neighbors (cf. Ps. 44.13-16). The request, rather, was for God to turn the divine anger and wrath from Jerusalem and bless the city with mercy.

Verse 17. Such a response would be for God's sake. This appeal appears in other penitential prayers as well (cf. Pss. 25.11; 44.26; 109.21), and was given as the basis for God's rescuing Israel from Egypt in Ps. 106.8. The thinking seems to have been that other nations would consider God a weakling if God could not save and protect the people of Israel (cf. Moses' intercession in Exod. 32.11-12).

The prayer continues: **let your face shine on your desolated sanctuary**. The request echoes the Aaronic Benediction of Num. 6.25, which invokes God's face to shine upon the Israelites. Here, instead, the request was to bless the desolated sanctuary. In Daniel's time, the temple lay in ruins; in Maccabean times it lay under the ignominy of the 'abomination that desolates' (v. 27).

Verse 18. The petition moves to its climax in vv. 18-19. In v. 18 Daniel implores God to harken to his prayer (cf. 1 Kgs 8.28) and to look at both the human and physical desolation in Jerusalem. Again, the appeal is made, not on the basis of justice, but of God's **great mercies**. The noun $rah^am\hat{i}m$ (mercies) is the plural form of the noun for 'womb'. It connotes 'motherly' love and the protection afforded the infant safely inside the womb.

Verse 19. This verse opens with three requests delivered in staccato-like fashion: *O Lord, listen;*
       O Lord, forgive;
       O Lord, listen and act and do not delay.
Daniel had offered the prayer of confession requisite to God's forgiving Israel; now he asked God to act. The second-century reader would know that God had not acted yet, or had not acted completely. That reader, no less than an exile, would have wanted God to act without delay. Hence, the prayer leads ultimately to the question posed by Daniel: how much longer will it be before God chooses to act?

The prayer sounds the note that such action would be for God's own sake, because the temple was God's dwelling in Jerusalem. In that case, it would be God's own reputation, not simply the well-being of the people, that would motivate God's acting to restore the city and the temple.

Verse 20. This verse makes the transition back to the narrative. It simply sums up the past 16 verses; then it anticipates the action of vv. 21-27. Daniel begins: **While I was speaking and was praying...on behalf of the holy mountain of my God**.

THE APPEARANCE OF GABRIEL (21-23)

Verse 21 repeats the essence of v. 20: **while I was speaking in prayer...**, and adds that the 'man' Gabriel was already winging his way to Daniel. Verse 23 makes clear that God dispatched Gabriel the moment Daniel began praying. Gabriel approached Daniel with the news (v. 22) that he had come to answer Daniel's question about the 70 years for the devastation of Jerusalem. Verses 21-23 thus reach back to v. 3; one could omit vv. 4-20 and never miss them.

Verse 21. Verse 3 says Daniel was praying; v. 21 specifies that his prayer took place **at the time of the evening sacrifice**, which would have been about twilight. In response to his prayer, Gabriel comes to him **in swift flight**. The phrase in the MT means something like 'wearied with weariness', a strange comment to make about an angel. Hence, some scholars have preferred to read it as a comment about Daniel's condition when he saw Gabriel, whom he recognized because he had seen him **before in a vision** (8.17-18). However, 8.17-18 emphasizes that Daniel was terrified, not that he was weary, despite his falling into a trance. The NRSV, therefore, followed several versions in emending the text of 9.21 to read the root *'wp*, which meant 'fly' (cf. note b in *BHS*).

Verse 22. Again the NRSV emends the text. It reads: **He came and said to me**, reading *wyb'* (the word for 'come' or 'go'; cf. the suggestion in *BHS*). The MT reads instead: 'He caused me to understand and he spoke to me.' Either way, Gabriel promised to answer Daniel's question.

Verse 23. As soon as Daniel had begun his prayer, **a word went out**. The word obviously was the answer to Daniel's question, and the source of the word was God. The answer, and hence the proper interpretation of the troublesome passages in the book of Jeremiah, went from God to Daniel via Gabriel. The readers could accept it as valid.

GABRIEL'S ANNOUNCEMENT OF THE 70 WEEKS OF YEARS (24-27).

Gabriel announced that it would take 70 weeks of years, rather than 70 years, to atone for the sins of Jerusalem. That was so, not because pre-exilic Israel deserved seven times more punishment than Jeremiah had thought, but because exilic (and postexilic) Israel had continued to sin. The author's generation no less than Daniel's needed to repent before God restored the temple.

Scholars have disagreed over the interpretation of vv. 24-27 no less than over Daniel 2, 7, and 8. Traditional Christian interpreters have typically taken the 490 years more or less literally and have seen the second 'anointed one' as Jesus. So, for example, Walvoord (p. 210) begins the years with the mission of Nehemiah in 445, the year the word went out to rebuild Jerusalem (Neh. 2.1-6). He continues that it would take a generation (or the first 49 years) to clear out the debris and get the city functioning. Another 62 weeks of years would bring the timetable down to 30–32 CE, that is, the time Walvoord accepts as the time of the death of Jesus (p. 210). (Even so, his math is suspect; the years total 475 or 477, not 483 [69 × 7]). Finally, Walvoord interjects a gap in time before the 70 week at the second coming of Jesus.

Other scholars differ on certain details, but not the christological thrust. Payne (1978: 101) begins with the mission of Ezra in 458, but still brings the 69 weeks of years down to 26 CE, the time he thinks Jesus died. He then claims that the vision looks ahead to the destruction of Herod's Temple in 70, which makes a total of 528 years. Miller (1994: 262-73) agrees that the timetable begins in 458 and looks forward to the first coming of Christ and his death. The final seven years will occur at the time of his second coming. Baldwin (1978: 171), recognizing that the numbers do not fit, says that the numbers are figurative and not literal, but still sees Jesus as the slain 'anointed one' and says the 70 years include the second coming (pp. 176-77).

By contrast, critical scholars find the end of the 70 weeks of years in the Maccabean period. Heaton (1956: 203-204) may be taken as typical. He begins with the fall of Jerusalem in 586. The first 49 years more or less cover the exile, and Cyrus is the first 'anointed one' (see Isa. 45.1, where God calls Cyrus his 'anointed'). The next 62 weeks should end at 104/3 BCE, but no known messianic figure appeared then. As is typical, Heaton identifies Onias III with God's 'anointed' and his execution at the hands of the Seleucids in 171 with the end of that period (cf. 2 Macc. 4.23-28) and does not worry about the math. The last week of years would run from 171 to 164.

Variations on this dating system include Lacocque's idea that the second period begins with 605 (1979: 178), the date of the oracle in Jeremiah 25. Sixty-two weeks of years later would be 171. Interestingly, Lacocque also stipulates that the first period of 49 years covered the period from the beginning of the Exile to the enthronement of Jeshua as high priest, which he dates in 538. It is not clear why the eighth week of years would begin 67 years earlier, earlier even than the first one. Goldingay (1989: 257) offers a slight improvement. He notes that it was 49 years from the time of Jeremiah's message in 605 (based on Jer. 25.1) to the rise of Cyrus in 556, and 434 years from 605 to the death of Onias in 171, but ultimately concludes (p. 258) that the 70 weeks of years are not amenable to any literal interpretation. Grabbe (1987: 72) even suggests that the difficulties are so great in making the numbers match known history that the author must have simply borrowed a previously existing interpretation of Jer. 25.11-12 and 29.10 and incorporated it into his later message.

The disagreement over details should warn interpreters that the numbers are not precise. In fact, as mentioned above, the numbers constitute a periodization of history built around sabbath and jubilee years. Verse 24 begins by saying 'Seventy sevens are decreed', and the passage marks time in terms of 'sevens': seven 'sevens', 62 'sevens', and one 'seven'. The first division of time, seven 'sevens', is a jubilee, and the whole period is ten jubilees. If 2 Chron. 36.21 interpreted Jeremiah to mean that the sins of the pre-exilic period would require 10 sabbath years of rest for atonement, Dan. 9.24-27 interpreted that verse to mean the sins of the pre-exilic and postexilic periods would require ten jubilee years of rest for full atonement.

Nor is Daniel 9 alone in dividing history into jubilees. In the book of *Jubilees* a period of seven years was called a 'week of years', and the time between Adam and the Exodus was calculated at 2401 years or 49 jubilees. Also 11QMelch 6-8 speaks of ten jubilees or 490 years until the final judgment. These passages suggest that Daniel takes up the idea of jubilees as a way of thinking about time, but does not invent it (cf. Goldingay 1989: 232, who nevertheless denies jubilee thinking in Daniel 9). (As will be shown later, 12.11-12 employs a solar calendar, as in the book of *Jubilees*.)

If the 490 years constitute a periodization of history, the keys to interpreting the timetable are the identities of the two 'anointed ones' in vv. 25-26 and the reference to 'an abomination that desolates' in v. 27 (cf. 11.31 and 12.11). The surest key is the last. The 'abomination' referred to near the close of the 70 weeks of years is the same act as the 'transgression that makes desolate' of 8.13, that is the desecration of the temple by Antiochus IV. The second anointed one, who dies at the end of the 62 weeks is most likely the priest Onias III. His death in the early years of the reign of Antiochus IV was now set in its eschatological context: it inaugurated the last sabbath of years, the last week of the tenth jubilee.

The identity of the first anointed one, who is also called a prince, is more difficult to determine. Nominees include Cyrus, who is called God's anointed in Isa. 45.1; Zerubbabel, the descendant of David called 'governor of Judah' in Hag. 1.1; and Jeshua, called the high priest in Zech. 3.1, who together with Zerubbabel is credited with the rebuilding of the temple in Ezra 3.8, 5.2; Hag.1.1, 12; 2.2 (but see Zech. 4.9). At first glance Cyrus or Zerubbabel would seem to deserve the nod, but a reader could hardly be expected to think of Cyrus simply from the title 'anointed one' in Isa. 45.1 and the fleeting references to him in Dan. 1.21, 6.28, and 10.1. Nor was the title 'anointed one' confined to kings and princes; priests were anointed too.

Zerubbabel certainly had connections with the temple and might well be considered a prince, but so could Jeshua. The word *nāgîd* (prince) is used of Saul (1 Sam. 9.16), David (2 Sam. 5.2), and Solomon (1 Kgs 1.35) in the Deuteronomistic History and of the ruler of Tyre in Ezek. 28.2, but also of a priest in Neh. 11.11 and of Onias III in Dan. 11.22. Based on Dan. 11.22 and comments made about Jeshua in Zech. 6.12-

14, he might be the better choice. If so, the two 'anointed ones' were the priests Jeshua and Onias III, but certainty is not possible.

Verse 24. Thus, 70 weeks of years would be required to atone for Jerusalem and the people. The author uses six phrases to describe what would happen to them. The first three are concerned with the sins enumerated in the prayer in v. 5, further evidence that the author of Daniel 9 himself and not some later editor employed the prayer. (1) The first phrase is **finish the transgression**. The Hebrew word for transgression in v. 24 is *peša'*, from the root *pš'*, which means 'rebel' or 'transgress', while v. 5 uses a verbal form of the root *mrb*, which means 'to rebel'. The word translated 'to finish' is *l*^e*kalê'*, listed in BDB as the piel infinitive construct of *klh* ('to bring to an end') (BDB: 478). Alternatively, it could be from the verb *kl'* and mean 'to shut up' or 'to withhold'. Either way, the idea seems to be that the people had to stop their sinning.

The second phrase is **to put an end to sin**, a repetition of the first idea in synonymous terms. The noun for sin in v. 24 is derived from the root for sin *ht'* in v. 5; it is a general term for wrongdoing. The verb in the MT *lah*^e*tôm* actually means 'to seal up', but modern translations adopt the *qere*, a similar verb *l*^e*hātēm* 'to end' instead. The third phrase **To atone for iniquity** makes the same point.

The last three phrases deal with the fulfillment of God's righteous purposes. God will **bring in everlasting righteousness**, a phrase which echoes v. 7: 'Righteousness is on your side, O Lord...' The word for 'seal' appears here: **to seal both vision and prophet**. The phrase constitutes a word-play on the phrase 'Seal the vision' (Lacocque 1979: 193). The idea is that God will bring to fruition all that God promised Daniel in his visions and Jeremiah in 29.11-12. When a king or someone sealed a document, he was signing it, so to speak, or validating the contents. Such a seal by God would connote 'guarantee'. Finally, God would **anoint a most holy place**. Contra Lacocque (1979: 194), the reference is to the Holy of Holies, not to a holy people (cf. Hartman and Di Lella 1978: 244).

Verse 25. In v. 25 Gabriel announces the first jubilee and the next 62 sabbaths, the end of each marked by an 'anointed one'. Enough has been said already about Jeshua and Onias III, but a few smaller details need further attention. First, it is not yet clear when the 70 weeks of years began. Verse 25 simply reads: **from the time the word went out to restore and rebuild Jerusalem**. When was that? No verse in the

Hebrew Bible, let alone the book of Daniel, places exactly that command on the lips of any one, God or king. However, since Daniel 9 was largely a midrashic interpretation of hope passages in Jeremiah, the command may well have been that of God in Jer. 30.18 and 31.18. Since these verses probably came from late in the career of Jeremiah (that is, at or about the time of the fall of Jerusalem) or from an exilic editor, the first period, lasting one jubilee, can reasonably be said to have been roughly the time of the Exile, ending with the coming of Jeshua and the rebuilding of the temple. The precise dates are beside the point, and were probably unknown to the author of Daniel 9. The next period of time, 62 weeks of sabbaths, would last until the death of the second 'anointed one' Onias. Again the exact number of years was irrelevant, but the time of death of Onias III (in 171) would have been well-known to the Danielic group in the next decade. The final period of Jerusalem's punishment would last one sabbath of years, at which time Antiochus would fall and the temple would be restored.

The other point needing clarification in v. 25 is the mention of Jerusalem's being **built again with streets and moat**... The word for 'streets' was $r^e\hat{h}\hat{o}b$, which designates the broad space or plaza just inside city gates. The word for 'moat' appears only here in biblical Hebrew with such a meaning, but it was found in the Copper Scroll at Qumran (3Q15 5.8), where it means 'conduit'. Montgomery (1927: 380) suggested that the two terms signified the whole of the city, with 'plaza' denoting the city's interior and 'moat' denoting its exterior. In other words, Jerusalem would be built again 'inside and out'.

Verse 26. The identification of the second 'anointed one' as Onias III has been made above. Another person appears in this verse: **the prince who is to come**. His **troops** (literally, 'people') will destroy the city and the sanctuary. He can only be Antiochus IV. The NRSV next translates **Its end shall come with a flood**. In the context of the fate of the city, that translation makes sense. In the MT, however, the previous sentence is inverted (object, verb, subject), so that the immediate antecedent for this masculine singular verb is 'prince'. Hence, the NRSV gives 'his end' as an alternate translation, which is to be preferred. Gabriel was not speaking of the end of Jerusalem or the temple. Rather, the overall subject was the end of the devastation of Jerusalem, which was tied up with the end of Antiochus. Although there would be war and desolations to the end, Antiochus would be swept away.

Verse 27. Antiochus would make a **strong covenant with many** for the last week. The word for 'many' is *rabbîm*, literally 'the great ones'. They were the leaders in the Judean community who sympathized with the Hellenizing efforts of Antiochus. Many of them held high status.

The first half-week of years of Antiochus's reign would culminate with the 'abomination that desolates'. The symbolism here is subtle. Seven, of course is the divine number. Half of seven is three and a half, a broken number, which Gese (1991: 406) calls an unlucky number (*Unglückszahl*). Its brokenness might suggest that is was a number for 'godlessness', comparable to 666 in the book of Revelation. Three and a half weeks also could be taken more or less literally, so for the community of Daniel 9, living in the last half week of Antiochus, the message that the desolation of the temple would not last much longer would have been encouraging.

THE THEOLOGY OF DANIEL 9

Daniel 9 portrays a world in the grips of foreign, pagan kings, running uninterruptedly from 'Darius the Mede' through Antiochus IV. No less than the previous chapters, Daniel 9 also points to God's control of that time. It began with God's command in Jer. 30.18 and 31.38 to rebuild Jerusalem, a command probably understood to follow close on the heels of the fall of Jerusalem. It was marked by the coming of two 'anointed ones', and included the death of the second one, and then the desecration of the temple. Even so, nothing that happened could thwart God's ultimate goal of restoration.

Something new in Daniel 9 is the outright acknowledgment of the author that God's own people had sinned. It was not punishment for the sins of the people of Jeremiah's time that was still being inflicted on the people; traitors among God's people had formed a covenant with Antiochus and sinned along with him. Hence, in his prayer Daniel confesses their sins and his own in an attempt to fulfill the conditions necessary to bring about the restoration of Jerusalem and the temple. The problem of theodicy had led the author of Daniel 9 to pursue the issue of sin to a deeper level and give this chapter an ethical overtone. His prayer exonerates God for the hegemony of the Greeks and the spoiling of the temple. Daniel's actions were a model for others to follow, and hope for the future liberation of city and temple was the motivation for the readers of Daniel 9 to do likewise.

Also the chapter links together faith and understanding (which is the comprehension of the mysteries or signs of God's working; Lacocque

1979: 184). It was precisely at the moment Daniel turned to God in prayer that God dispatched Gabriel to answer Daniel's questions. Daniel knows of no abstract truth, no theory of all things, that explains what has happened. Rather, the explanation of the mysteries of the history lies in the confession of sins and meditation on God and God's word sent through Moses and the prophets. Reason is neither suppressed, nor given free reign, but provided answers in the context of obedience.

Porteous (1965: 134) comments that in finding the relevance of this passage for today, modern readers 'must allow [them]selves to be guided by the witness of this man to the availability of God in every crisis in history'. At the same time, Porteous warns, modern readers must not follow the author of Daniel 19 in his mistake of supposing that one can calculate in advance when God would act.

Because modern readers know how close Antiochus's death came to being seven years exactly after the death of Onias III, they may overlook the nature of the presentation as a periodization of history and see more precision here than was meant. That does not mean, of course, that the author expected the end to delay a decade or more, but it does mean that the author of Daniel 9 was not trying to pinpoint an exact date.

GABRIEL'S REVELATION OF CONFLICT
AMONG THE NATIONS
(10.1–12.4)

This is the last of the apocalyptic narratives and the longest vision in the book of Daniel. Lacocque (1979: 201) and Montgomery (1927: 404) combine it with Dan. 12.5-13 and analyze it as follows: prologue (10.1–11.2a), revelation (11.2b–12.4), and epilogue (12.5-13). Here too one uncovers the structure of the rite of passage, in which Daniel moves into a different mode of consciousness (the prologue), learns secret information (11.2b–12.3, 5-12), and returns to normal life (in 12.4, 13).

The prologue describes an epiphany to Daniel and its effects on him. It resembles a report of a call vision (Anderson 1984: 119; Smith-Christopher 1996: 138), and scholars debate whether the details of the psychological impact of the vision are genuine (Smith-Christopher 1996: 137; cf. Stone 1974: 47-56) or literary (Bentzen 1952: 77). It concludes with transition verses to the revelation (10.21–11.2a). The revelation (11.2b–12.4a) includes a journey through time from the Persian Empire to the predicted fall of the Seleucids and 'the time of the end'. The epilogue (12.5-13) calculates for the last time in the book the date of the end. It will be treated separately in this commentary because (except for v. 13) it is an addition to the vision.

The secondary nature of 12.5-12 is clear from the following considerations. The statement in 12.9 that the words are to remain sealed suggests time had passed since the command to Daniel to seal them in 12.4. Also, in 12.4 Gabriel told Daniel to seal the words of a book containing the names of God's people, but in 12.9 it is the meaning of the words 'time, times, and a half' that is to remain sealed. Thirdly, 12.10 blurs the distinction between the 'many' and the 'wise' in 11.33. Fourthly, vv. 5-12 do not simply conclude 10.1–12.4, but tie up loose ends from elsewhere in the book. The most notable example is the calculation of the time of the end. The book includes several calculations: a time, times, and a half (7.25); 2300 days and nights (8.14); and 70 weeks of years (9.24-27). Daniel 12.7 chooses the phrase 'a time, times, and a half' in answer to the question of when the end would come, and vv. 11 and 12 offer a recalculation of how long that will be. (For a further discussion of this last point, see the introductory comments below on 12.5-13, pp. 198-99.)

Baldwin (1978: 178) notes that Daniel 9 would have served poorly as the conclusion of the book; it needed some more positive assurance for its readers, which appears in 11.40–12.4 in its prediction of the death of Antiochus and the resurrection of the righteous. At that point, however, the reader would be left to wonder about Daniel, whose ultimate reward for his fidelity is not promised until the very last verse in the book, 12.13. Hence, that verse belongs with 10.1–12.4 rather than 12.5-12.

This last conclusion leads one to observe how the figure of Daniel is treated in the last half of the book. In 7.21 Daniel confesses that his vision terrified him, and in 8.27 he confesses that he has not understood the vision of the ram and the goat even after the angel explained it. His failure to understand would have stood in marked contrast with the situation of the readers, who would have understood it perfectly. Moreover, his failure sets up this final vision in Daniel 10–12. Here too, Daniel confesses three times (10.8-9, 11, and 15-17) his helplessness and fear, and he must be strengthened to receive God's message. In 11.2b–12.4 Daniel does not reveal the message; an angel does. By that point the readers, the community of the 'wise', are equipped to assume for themselves Daniel's role, to hear the messenger, and to lead the Judean community in the last days.

A source-critical analysis of Daniel 10.1–12.4, 13 reveals that the author combined a primary narrative about Daniel's receiving a vision with a second narrative about the relationship between the Seleucids and Ptolemies. The primary narrative was 10.(1)2-20 + 12.1-4a, 13 (cf. Jepsen 1961: 389-90). The connection between 10.20 and 12.1 is smooth. The mention of Gabriel's leaving Daniel to fight against the 'princes' of Persia and Greece in 10.20 was originally followed by the appearance of Michael to help in 12.1. As the text now stands, after Gabriel said he was leaving, v. 21 introduces Michael, who plays no role until 12.1. Then, 11.1 adds a new historical superscription, connecting Daniel 10–12 to Daniel 9 with the mention of 'Darius the Mede' (as does 10.2-4). Thus, 10.21–11.1 is clearly redactional.

Gabriel still does not depart, however, but delivers the second narrative, recast as a message 44 verses in length. That message, introduced by the redactional transition in 10.21–11.1, was reported in 11.2-45.

Daniel 12.1-4a follows nicely on 10.1-20, while v. 4b seems anti-climactic but might have been original. Then v. 13 brings the vision narrative to its proper conclusion.

The message added in 11.2-45 was a review of the dealings of the Seleucids and the Ptolemies with each other and with Judah. It is unique in extant Israelite literature from the period; hence, scholars often suggest that it was borrowed (see Redditt 1998: 470-71). The author did not simply insert the historical review as he found it; rather he commented on and supplemented it. Verses 3-20 relate the wars between the Ptolemies and the Seleucids, but v. 8 calls the images of Seleucid gods 'idols', and vv. 14b and 16b look like redactional notes or comments. In addition, the titles 'king of the south' and 'king of the north' probably betray the author's locus between Egypt and Mesopotamia. Verses 21-45 deal with Antiochus, but the hand of the author of Daniel 11 is much heavier here. In places, particularly vv. 25-26, the borrowed material resembles the narrative in vv. 3-20, so one may conclude that it came down into the reign of Antiochus IV. That material would have included vv. 3-20 + 25-26, and perhaps more, with even 3-20 having undergone discernable modification.

DANIEL'S ENCOUNTER WITH GABRIEL (10.1-20)

The basic vision narrative opens with an editorial introduction (v. 1) written in the third person, and continues in the first person singular with the setting (in which Daniel's mourning is described in vv. 2-4), the appearance of a mysterious 'man' (vv. 5-6), a description of the effects of the vision upon Daniel (vv. 7-10), the 'man's' first speech (vv. 11-14), Daniel's reaction to that speech (vv. 15-17), the 'man's' touch, which reassured Daniel at last (vv. 18-20a), and the announce-ment of the 'man's' intention to depart (v. 20b). The narrative resem-bles a prophetic call vision with an epiphany, except that no one com-missions Daniel to speak.

Editorial Introduction (10.1)
Verse 1 constitutes an editorial introduction. It gives the date of this vision as **the third year of King Cyrus**. One might assume the date intended was 535, but the historical problem of the person and date of 'Darius the Mede' makes precise dating impossible. Earlier commenta-tors often saw this date as a contradiction of 1.21, which says that Daniel 'continued' in Babylon until the first year of King Cyrus. It does

not say that Daniel died in that year; it says only that he remained at the Babylonian court until the rise of the Persian Empire. Thus, 1.21 and 10.1 do not necessarily contradict each other.

The author mentions Daniel's Babylonian name **Belteshazzar** from the first half of the book, and reports that **a word was revealed to Daniel**. Further, v. 1 reports that he **understood the word**, a feature of the court narratives, but not of Daniel 8 and 9. Also, the phrase might be said to fit the lengthy message of Daniel 11 better than Daniel 10 (where no audition is reported), but that would ignore the rather broad meaning associated with 'word' in prophetic literature generally. The choice of the term is one more evidence that this vision stands closer to the prophetic tradition than some others do. Also, one should note with Goldingay (1989: 282) that the vision in Daniel 10 prepares Daniel for the message which follows in Daniel 11.

The word translated **conflict** in the NRSV normally refers to warfare or an army. The word does not, therefore, foreshadow the inner turmoil the appearance of the 'man' in vv. 5-6 would produce in Daniel, but indicates the basic thrust of the message itself: much warfare was on the way. In Daniel 10.20 and 12.1 that warfare was celestial, but in Daniel 11 it concerned Judah and the kings to her north and south.

The Setting (10.2-4)
The setting for the vision appears in vv. 2-4. On the one hand, the verses continue the theme of Daniel's mourning from Daniel 9. His sorrow prompted Gabriel to depart at once to come to him (v. 12), though opposition from the 'prince of the kingdom of Persia' delayed his arrival (v. 13). On the other hand, vv. 2-4 detail the preparations Daniel made before he received the vision.

The debate over the genuineness of the portrayal of such preparations needs mentioning once more. Daniel 10 is not reporting the activities of exilic Daniel, so as it stands the account is literary (cf. the conclusion of Bentzen 1952: 77). Thus it is neither necessary nor proven that Daniel 10 relates the actual experience of its author. On the other hand, such details were most likely included to authenticate the message that follows. Hence, the verses would almost certainly describe the kind of preparations and experiences expected and recognized by the Danielic group. (See also the comments on 7.1.)

Verse 2. In v. 2 the narrative switches to the first person singular. Daniel reports that he had been **mourning for three weeks**, presumably over Jerusalem as in Daniel 9. Verse 4 adds that the vision did not come until the **twenty-fourth day of the first month**. According to Lev. 23.5, the Feast of Passover/Unleavened Bread was to be observed from the fourteenth to the twenty-first of the first month. Hence, Daniel's mourning lasted right through the festival.

Verse 3. Instead of feasting, he also fasted. His fast is reminiscent of the diet of Daniel and his friends in 1.8-17 (both from the hand of R3), except that there is no mention of his eating seeds ('vegetables' in the NRSV) as in 1.12 and 16. Nor had Daniel anointed himself during his period of mourning.

Verse 4. Daniel reports that he was standing on the bank of **the great river**, normally the name for the Euphrates. That meaning would be appropriate for an exile in Babylon. However, R3 identified the river as the Tigris. The change was deliberate, probably an allusion to the Seleucid capital of Seleucia built in 312 BCE on the Tigris. If the group responsible for Daniel had lived there before moving to Palestine, the change would also identify the group with Daniel's experience.

The Vision of the 'Man' (10.5-6)
The identity of the 'man' Daniel sees in vv. 5-6 has prompted considerable debate. (1) Some traditional Christian scholars have identified the 'man' as Jesus in one way or another. Young (1949: 222-23), for example, identifies him as 'a preincarnate appearance of the eternal son', and early Christians saw him as the Messiah. (2) Since there is no warrant in Daniel for either reading, scholars both traditional and critical often see the 'man' as God (e.g. Lacocque 1979: 206; Miller 1994: 282). This identification is based on the similarities between the description of the 'man' and the description of God in Ezekiel's vision (see below, p. 172) and the fact that Daniel is badly scared by the sight, whereas he allegedly showed no such fright when he met Gabriel earlier (but see 8.17-18, where Daniel describes his terror at meeting Gabriel). (3) Probably the majority interpret the 'man' as an angel, either left unnamed (e.g. Collins 1993a: 373; Goldingay 1989: 291) or identified with some angel, usually Gabriel (e.g. Bentzen 1952: 78-79; Porteous 1965: 151). Anderson (1984: 122-23) concluded that the 'man' was neither Gabriel, nor Michael, nor God, but a 'theophany-like experience' in which Daniel was 'made to feel as though he has come close to seeing God' (cf. Bampfylde 1983: 129-31, who called him 'the supreme archangel').

In arriving at a conclusion, the first thing to notice is the use of previous Scripture. Bauer (1996: 193-94) creates a table to show the dependence of Dan. 10.4-6 on Ezekiel 1 and 9:

Daniel	Ezekiel
date of the vision (4)	date of the vision (1.1)
I stood on the bank of the great river, the Tigris (4)	as I was among the exiles by the river Chebar (1.1)
a man clothed in linen (5)	a man clothed in linen (9.2)
with a belt of gold from Uphaz around his waist (5)	upward from what appeared like the loins I saw something like gleaming amber (1.27)
his body was like beryl (6)	their appearance was like the gleaming of beryl (1.16)
his face like lightning, and his eyes like flaming torches (6)	something like torches moving to and fro among the living creatures (1.13)

Of these verses from Ezekiel, the only one speaking about God is 1.27, hardly convincing proof that the model for the 'man' in Dan. 10.5-6 was God.

Nor is Daniel's extreme fright at the vision (vv. 8-9, 15, 17) proof that the figure was God. Rather, it is the same kind of response reported in 7.28 to the vision of the four animals: 'As for me, Daniel, my thoughts greatly terrified me, and my face turned pale' (NRSV). Likewise, Daniel described his reaction to the vision of the ram and the goat as follows (8.27): 'So I, Daniel, was overcome and lay sick for some days;... But I was dismayed by the vision and did not understand it' (NRSV).

In addition, Daniel's fright in 10.8-9 is directly connected to speechlessness in vv. 15 and 17. A concentration on speech (Exod. 4.1-16), the mouth (Isa. 6.5, 7; Jer. 1.6-9), and receiving God's message (Ezek. 3.1-3; cf. Jer. 15.16) are regular features of call visions, which is what Dan. 10.1-20 most resembles. Hence, the genre of the literature itself is sufficient to account for many of the details adduced to prove that Daniel was quaking before God instead of an angel. Besides, Daniel's companions are afraid also, and they did not see the vision (v. 7).

To be sure in the other call visions mentioned above it is God who speaks, but God's identity is made quite clear in those visions. By contrast, here the word 'man' had been used a scant 11 verses earlier in 9.21 to introduce Gabriel, and in 10.13-14 a speaker identifies himself as one who had come to help Daniel understand his new vision, precisely the role of Gabriel in Daniel 8 and 9. Further, 10.16 and 18 speak of one in human form, presumably the same as the 'man' in v. 5. It seems best, therefore, to identify the 'man' in v. 5, the speaker in vv. 13-14, and the one in human form in vv. 16 and 18 as Gabriel.

Verse 5. One feature in the description of Gabriel is the phrase **gold from Uphaz** (found elsewhere only in Jer. 10.9). The word for 'gold' here is *ketem*, a word for a purer form of gold than *zāhāb*. The location of 'Uphaz' is unknown, but is identified in ancient translations with Ophir, a region in extreme southwest Arabia known for its gold.

Verse 6. The description of Gabriel continues with phrases drawn from Ezekiel 1 and 9. (See the examples cited above, p. 171). His voice is said to have been **like the roar of a multitude**. His volume signifies his importance and helps account for Daniel's fear.

The Effect of the Vision on Daniel and his Companions (10.7-10)
The narrator builds the suspense of the scene by discussing the effect of the vision on Daniel and his companions. All were afraid, whether they saw the vision or not, suggesting that it was not simply the appearance of Gabriel that induced the reaction, but the auspiciousness of the event as well.

Verse 7. Daniel says that he alone saw the vision, a feature sometimes taken as evidence of the authenticity of Daniel's experience (see Stone 1974: 47-56). As mentioned above, however, all one can really say is that the report of the experience conformed to the community's expectations. Daniel's companions, not previously mentioned, did not see the vision. Had they mourned and fasted too, or were they unprepared to receive it? The very fact that the text leaves open that question heightens the drama in the narrative. Either way, the occasion was so auspicious that the companions trembled and fled.

Verse 8. Daniel next describes the impact of the vision on himself. Twice he mentions a loss of strength and once a change in his complexion to a **deathly pale**. The description is that of a person's being 'scared to death'. Such fear is perhaps beyond what one ordinarily finds in a call vision, but a severe reaction is quite customary. Isaiah cried out (Isa. 6.5): 'Woe is me I am lost, for I am a man of unclean lips...' When Ezekiel saw a vision of God, he fell on his face until he was revived by a spirit (Ezek. 1.28–2.1).

Verses 9-10. Daniel's fear at the sight of the vision was attended by his falling into a trance, face to the ground, at the sound of Gabriel's voice. Then **a hand** touched Daniel and roused him to his hands and knees. The hand here is the instrument that corresponds to the 'spirit' in Ezek. 1.2. It belonged to Gabriel, who speaks in Dan. 10.11, commanding Daniel to stand up (cf. Ezek. 2.1), which he does.

Gabriel's First Speech (10.11-14)

The narrative continues with Gabriel speaking to Daniel. He explains that he has come to help Daniel understand what would happen to Israel at the end of days. As in ch. 9, Gabriel had begun his journey to aid Daniel the minute Daniel first humbled himself (10.12), but he was delayed 21 days by the **prince of the kingdom of Persia**. Scholars are generally agreed that the **prince** is not King Cyrus or some other earthly figure, but a patron angel for Persia. (For the opposite view see Shea 1983a: 235.) Israel also had a protecting angel, identified in 12.1 as Michael. Appropriately enough, Michael came to do battle with the patron angel of the Persians (10.13), thus freeing Gabriel to visit Daniel. Even so, after relating the vision for the future, Gabriel would return to the battle against the patron of the Persians and then against the patron of the Greeks (10.20).

The relationship between Gabriel and Michael seems fuzzy. Michael is clearly identified as the 'protector' of Israel (12.1), an identification made elsewhere in Israelite literature. Collins (1993a: 375) cites the following examples: *1 En.* 9.1; 10.1; and 20.5, where Michael is one of the chief angels; 1QM 9.15-16, where he is one of four archangels; and 1QM 17.6-7, where he is given authority among the *'elōhîm*. It is also possible that he was identified with the prince of light and with Melchizedek in 11QMelch (so Davies 1985: 113). On the other hand, Gabriel had functioned in Daniel 8 and 9 simply as an interpreting angel. Apparently, then, Daniel 10–12 mixes the roles of interpreting angel and patron angel together in connection with Gabriel, or else reflects a situation in which the two roles were not conceived of as mutually exclusive.

Verse 11. Gabriel calls Daniel **greatly beloved**. This phrase explains what v. 7 had left open, namely why Daniel but not his companions saw Gabriel: God loved Daniel greatly. As in Ezek. 2.1, so here also the hero is told to stand to his feet. He is also admonished to pay attention to the words Gabriel was about to speak. Despite the assurance, Daniel was still **trembling** when he stood up.

Verse 12. Hence, Gabriel's first words were **Do not fear, Daniel.** In the prophetic literature, the admonition 'Fear not' characterized the priestly salvation oracle, which predicted God's imminent intervention and the reasons for that intervention. Here, however, the phrase was simply part of the angel's attempt to calm down Daniel. Gabriel mentioned a second feature of Daniel's prayer: **you set your mind to gain understanding.** That was true also of Daniel 9, but there the emphasis on confession outweighed the motif of wisdom. Here gaining wisdom is mentioned first.

Verse 13. Next comes the explanation for why Daniel had to wait 21 days for Gabriel to arrive: the patron angel of Persia had opposed him. So stout was his resistance that Michael had to come to Gabriel's aid to free Gabriel to come to Daniel.

It is not clear what this warfare signified. It is often interpreted as celestial warfare which preceded and determined the outcome of terrestrial warfare. In that case, however, the conclusion to draw would seem to be that Israel would defeat the Persian Empire in battle. Clearly no such defeat happened, nor does the book of Daniel even hint at such an outcome. Rather, Greece would defeat Persia, and God would defeat Greece. Gabriel's battle against the patron angel of Persia would appear to signify something else, perhaps something like a struggle over the severity of Persia's hegemony over Israel. In other words, the thinking might have been similar to that in the court narratives, where God acted to improve Israel's lot within its servitude, not to end it. If so, Gabriel's opposition to the prince of Greece should be understood the same way. When it came to overthrowing Antiochus, that would be God's job.

Verse 14. Gabriel tells Daniel that he has a vision for **the end of days.** That message comes in 12.1-4a, 13. It would begin with a time of anguish, from which Daniel's people would be rescued, and continue with a limited resurrection (including Daniel's) and the reign of the wise over the kingdom of God. The intervening message in 11.2-45 deals with events occurring between the exile and the end.

Daniel's Further Reaction to Gabriel (10.15-20a)
Verses 15-20a do not advance the plot of the narrative, or the reader's information about the end, but they do raise the readers' anticipation for what will follow. Verse 16 also validates the authority of the message.

Verse 15. Daniel reported that he fell face forward on the ground and was speechless. Speechlessness was a characteristic of the call vision.

Verse 16. The next act also was typical of a call vision: Gabriel touched Daniel's lips. Only then did Daniel speak, complaining of the pain and exhaustion caused by the receiving the vision. The mention of such features is sometimes characteristic of reports of ecstatic prophets and other such seers. The author of Daniel 10 is building his case that the appearance of Gabriel to Daniel was genuine and, thus, his message was reliable.

Verse 17. Daniel asks how Gabriel (an angel, a representative of the Lord) can speak with him (a mere human). The question is phrased in deferential language that may seem confusing to the modern reader. The title **My lord** refers to Gabriel, and **my lord's servant** is Daniel himself. In plain English, Daniel is simply asking: 'How can you speak with me?' Then he speaks again of his shaken, breathless condition.

Verses 18-20a. Gabriel assured Daniel that he was in no personal danger. This time, Daniel was strengthened and grew confident enough to ask Gabriel to divulge his message. Gabriel asked if Daniel did not know why Gabriel had come to him, almost as if the angel were surprised. He had just told Daniel that his message was about the end of time (v. 14). The implication may be that what the angel was about to say (12.1-4a) should have been self evident.

Gabriel's Departure Announced (10.20b)

One more time the author postpones divulging the message by having Gabriel inform Daniel that he had to return to the battle against the prince of Persia, which would be followed by warfare against the prince of Greece. That information also served the purpose in the original narrative of covering the time from the exile to the end, with which 12.1 began. The insertion of the historical narrative (11.2-45), which covered in great detail the same time frame, made this sentence superfluous.

THE REPORT OF THE FUTURE (10.21–11.45)

The second major section of 10.1–12.4 (+13) is 10.21–11.45. It differs from the previous vision in that it is a historical review of the experience of Israel under foreign hegemony presented in coded language. Two verses (10.21–11.1) provide the transition between the two sections, while 44 (11.2-45) recount events from the Persian Empire to the time of Antiochus IV. Delcor (1993: 365-86) notes that the chapter is historically reliable in general and that the further the narrative goes (i.e. the nearer it comes to the lifetime of the second-century author), the fuller the exposition becomes. It deals with the Medes and the Persians in one verse (v. 2) and the Greek Empire from 332 to 175 in 18 verses (vv. 3-20), but it devotes 25 verses (vv. 21-45) to the reign of Antiochus IV.

The argument was made above (pp. 167-69) that the report of the future in 11.2-45 was added to the original vision 10.1-20 + 12.1-4a + 12.13. The addition is unique in extant Israelite literature for its detailed presentation of the relationship between the Ptolemies (called 'the kings of the south') and the Seleucids (called 'the kings of the north'). That fact, coupled with the coded names, suggests that a group of scribes at one point associated with the Seleucids was responsible for 11.2-45 (cf. Redditt 1998: 463-74). Their contribution to those verses was 14b, 16b, 21-24, 27-28, 30b-45; the titles 'king of the south' and 'king of the north'; and retouching vv. 8a and 29-30a.

Introduction to the Report (10.21–11.1)
The introduction to the report of the future consists of two verses. The first (10.21) picks up the motif of the fight against the patron angels of Persia and Greece from 10.20 and the motif of a book from 12.2. In 10.21, however, Gabriel speaks of an authoritative book, the contents of which he will divulge directly to Daniel. These observations offer further evidence that 11.2-45 employs a previously existing document. Calling it 'the book of truth' also anticipates 11.2, where Gabriel promises to announce the truth to Daniel. The second verse (11.1) appears to back up in time from the third year of King Cyrus (537) to the first year of the putative 'Darius the Mede' and states that Gabriel had aided him. How Gabriel aided 'Darius' is not said. Perhaps he is advancing the claim that he was the one from whom 'Darius' received Belshazzar's throne (5.31, MT 6.1).

Verse 10.21. In v. 21a Gabriel tells Daniel that he will inform Daniel of the contents of **the book of truth**. Since Gabriel is an angel, he is a messenger of God. The book, therefore, would have been understood as a true book about what God was going to do at the time of the end. Verse 21b simply connects the addition to the original narrative by repeating information from v. 20.

Verse 11.1. The next verse, 11.1, refers to 'Darius the Mede' and claims that Gabriel had **stood up to support and strengthen him**. The verse has the effect of tying Daniel 11 to Daniel 9, also set in the reign of 'Darius'. It might also imply that the reason Darius was so much more solicitous of Daniel (cf. 6.14, 28) than Nebuchadnezzar was that Gabriel was already at work on Daniel's behalf even then.

The Persian Empire (11.2)

Gabriel says that he will announce the truth to Daniel, an announcement anticipated by 10.21. He foresees **three more kings** of the Persian Empire, followed by a fourth of great riches, who would stir up **all** (i.e., other nations) against **the kingdom of Greece**. The author of Daniel apparently knew the names of few of the kings of Persia. The Bible mentions only Cyrus, Darius (I), Xerxes (known as Ahasueras), and Artaxerxes (I). (There were three Persian Emperors by the name of Artaxerxes, but the Bible simply uses the name Artaxerxes without any numbers or further designations.) One problem with this view that the third of those kings, Xerxes, was wealthy and had immensely more success against in battle against the Greeks than did the fourth, Artaxerxes I. On the other hand, Artaxerxes II was wealthy enough to bribe Greeks to war against other Greeks until they had exhausted each other. If the author did know that there was more than one king Artaxerxes, it may have been Artaxerxes II that he intended.

The Greek Empire before Antiochus IV (11.3-20)

The next 18 verses highlight the rise of the Greek Empire and the ensuing stormy relationship between the Ptolemies and the Seleucids after the death of Alexander. The characters and events are easily identifiable.

Verses 3-4. The warrior king to arise is Alexander the Great, who died in 323. His half-brother Philip of Aridus became nominal king for seven years, with Alexander's generals serving as military satraps. Then the generals divided the empire among themselves, eventually reducing the number of rulers to four by 301. These four were Seleucus in Babylon and Phrygia, Ptolemy in Egypt, Lysimachus in Thrace and Bithynia, and Cassander in Greece and Macedonia. Of the four, the two of importance in the book of Daniel are Seleucus and Ptolemy.

Verse 5. Ptolemy I (governor from 322 to 305 and king from 305 to 285) was the first 'king of the south'. In 301 he extended his control over Palestine, control the Ptolemies held until 198. The reference to one of his officers who grew strong may have been to Seleucus Nicator (ruled 312–280), who was for a time a companion of Ptolemy and who disputed Ptolemy's claim to Syria and Palestine. Ultimately, Seleucus did indeed rule a larger area than did Ptolemy.

Verse 6. The phrase **after some years** moves the chronicle forward to the reigns of Ptolemy II (285–46) and Antiochus II (261–47). About the year 250 Ptolemy II sought peace with Antiochus II, and ratified the agreement by giving his daughter Bernice to Antiochus II as his second wife.

Verse 6b is harder to understand. The NRSV reads: **but she shall not retain her power**. That clause presumably meant Bernice would not be able to maintain her position in the Seleucid court, which she did not after the death of Antiochus II, who died, allegedly, by poisoning at the hand of his first wife Laodice. The NRSV next makes a slight emendation (based on Theodotian and Symmachus) to read *zr'* (seed, offspring) for *zrw'* (arm), and translates **and his offspring shall not endure**. If the emendation is accepted, the reference is probably to Laodice's murder of his infant son by Bernice. That action opened the way for Antiochus's son by Laodice (Seleucus II) to succeed his father.

The next sentence is difficult as well. The MT reads simply: 'she shall be given'. Something appears to have fallen out of the sentence. One possibility is that suggested by Jeffery (1956: 515): 'to death'. The NRSV simply translates **she shall be given up**, and adds a plausible translation of the next phrase: **and her attendants** (literally, 'those who brought her'), that is Egyptian attendants.

The NRSV emends the vowels of the next Hebrew word to read it as a masculine singular noun with a third feminine singular pronominal suffix and translates it **her child**, thus completing the thought of the previous phrase. As pointed in the MT (a qal active participle with a third feminine singular pronominal suffix), however, it meant 'he who begot her'. Her father, Ptolemy II, did die about then, but not at the hands of Laodice or other Seleucids as that reading would imply. Hence, the NRSV is probably correct. The **one who supported her** also might have been her father, but more likely was her husband Antiochus II, whose death slightly preceded hers. This whole phrase (**she shall be given up, she and her attendants and her child and the one who supported her**, i.e., her husband) seems to summarize the events surrounding Bernice's death and that of her son. The last word in v. 6 translated **In those times** belongs with v. 7.

Verse 7. The **branch from her roots** was her brother Ptolemy II (ruled 246–21) who avenged the murder of his sister. He campaigned against the army of Seleucus II Callinicus, son of Laodice. He captured **the fortress of the king of the north**, that is, Seleucia.

Verse 8a. Verse 8a notes that Ptolemy II carried home as booty the images of the gods (explicitly called **idols**) and their vessels. The use of the word 'idols' as well as the parallel to Nebuchadnezzar's taking vessels from Jerusalem (2 Kgs 25.13-17) suggests that R3 touched up this verse. Also, if there were any doubt about the identity of 'the king of the south', the explicit mention of Egypt in this verse would remove it.

Verses 8b-9. The NRSV plausibly construes v. 8b to mean **For some years he shall refrain from attacking the king of the north.** A description of warfare resumes in v. 9 with the mention of an attack by the king of the north, no doubt that of Seleucus II in 242, which ended with his army so severely reduced in number that he returned to Antioch in 240.

Verse 10. A new chapter in the ongoing war began with the rise of Antiochus III the Great, who succeeded his brother Seleucus III Ceraunus in 223. Antiochus III eventually wrested control of Palestine from Egypt. Verses 10-19 discuss his career. According to v. 10, he raised a large army to invade Egypt. The invasion began in 219 and went well at first. He was able to **carry the war as far as his fortress**. The fortress in question belonged to Ptolemy IV Philopater, but which of his fortresses was meant is unclear. Suggestions include Gaza, Raphia, and Pelusium.

Verses 11-12. Ptolemy IV fought back, and at the battle of Raphia (in 217) defeated the Seleucid invaders (the **great multitude** mentioned in v. 11). Nevertheless, Ptolemy IV did not press his advantage against Antiochus III, but settled for occupying Coele-Syria and making peace with him.

Verse 13. Antiochus III rebuilt his strength with successful raids in Persia and Asia Minor. The death of Ptolemy IV in 205, leaving an infant son Ptolemy V as his successor, provided Antiochus III his opportunity to attack again **after some years**. Literally the phrase reads 'and at the end of the times years', but it is so awkward scholars emend it by dropping the word for 'times' (cf. NRSV) or the word for 'years'.

Verse 14. The rebellions referred to in v. 14a were the insurrections in Egypt during the reign of the infant king. **The lawless among your own people**, however, appear to be Judeans who aligned themselves with the Seleucids. Verse 14b seems to address Daniel himself, and the readers through Daniel, thus showing itself to be an addition.

Verse 15. This verse returns to the subject of the battle between the

Seleucids and the Ptolemies. The Egyptian army under a general named Scopas was crushed at Sidon and surrendered in 198.

Verse 16. Verse 16a notes that no one could defeat Antiochus. Verse 16b, which again appears to be an insertion, draws the implication of the defeat of the Egyptian army for Judah: it ended Ptolemaic control over Palestine and left Antiochus III in charge.

Verse 17. Antiochus imposed **terms of peace** on them. Actually, the MT at this point is quite difficult. It may be translated: 'And he set his face to go with strength [into] all the kingdoms, and righteous ones with him, and he did [so].' The last clause in the LXX reads 'and covenants with him shall he make'. That reading makes more sense and apparently stands behind the NRSV translation.

The Hebrew of v. 17b is even more confusing. It may be translated as follows: 'and the daughter of the women he [Antiochus] shall give to him to destroy her, and she shall not stand, and it shall not be for him'. The phrase 'the daughter of the women' means something like 'the most remarkable woman of all'. The woman in question was Cleopatra, the daughter of Antiochus III. (The description of her may constitute another piece of evidence that the borrowed narrative was Seleucid in origin.) Cleopatra went to Egypt in 194/193 as the wife of Ptolemy V Epiphanes. It is doubtful that the author meant to say that Antiochus sent his daughter to Egypt to destroy her. Alternatively, the feminine pronoun ['her'] may have referred to the kingdom of Egypt. A better reading is found in 4QDan^c, which has a masculine singular suffix on the verb 'destroy'. It would mean that Antiochus sent Cleopatra to Egypt to destroy 'him', that is, her new husband Ptolemy V. Hence, the NRSV renders this whole sentence: **he shall give him a woman in marriage, but it shall not succeed or be to his advantage.**

Verse 18. Antiochus turned his attention to the **coastlands** of the Mediterranean, against which he campaigned from 196 to 191. Eventually, he landed in Greece, where he was defeated by the Romans, first at the battle of Thermopylae in 191 and then at Magnesia in 190. The phrase **indeed he shall turn his insolence back upon him** translates an uncertain phrase. C.G. Ozanne (1965: 448) suggests emending *lô biltî* ('indeed') of the MT to read *l^{e}ballōtô* and translating the resulting verb: 'so as to wear him out'.

Verses 19-20. Defeated, Antiochus III returned home, where he died in 187. He was succeeded by his son Seleucus IV, who ruled from 187 to 175. Due to financial difficulties, Seleucus sent Heliodorus to exact duty from Jerusalem (2 Macc. 3.1-40), earning the wrath of many Judeans. Eventually, Heliodorus assassinated Seleucus IV.

The Rise and Fall of Antiochus IV (11.21-45)
The real interest of the author of Daniel 11, however, was the career of Antiochus IV (174–63) and its end at the hands of God. Hence, the author devotes 25 verses to his career, more than to the previous years of the Greek Empire put together.

Verses 21-24. The first four verses deal with Antiochus's accession and early years. After the battle of Magnesia in 190, Antiochus lived in Rome as a hostage. In 175 he was released through the intervention of his brother Seleucus IV, who substituted his own son Demetrius I. Antiochus was in Athens when Heliodorus murdered Seleucus IV. He returned to Antioch and usurped the throne from the sons of Seleucus IV, Demetrius and his infant brother. Almost his first act in Jerusalem was to replace the high priest Onias III. From the perspective of the author of Daniel 11, the career of Antiochus was off to a horrible start and went nowhere but downhill.

Verse 21. The opening verse calls Antiochus a **contemptible person**. The second-century reader would need no help in understanding why. In Daniel 7 and 8 he was the arrogant 'little horn' (cf. the 'sinful root' of 1 Macc. 1.10) who thought of himself as 'God Manifest'. He had set up 'the transgression that makes desolate' and made other attempts to subvert Judaism (8.11-13). In Daniel 9 he was the 'prince who is to come' who destroyed Jerusalem and its sanctuary, and the end of whose reign would end the devastation of the city. He needed no introduction in Daniel 11; the readers knew him first hand.

Nor had **royal majesty** been conferred upon him. As seen above, he seized his throne from his nephew, **without warning** according to v. 21. Literally, the word meant 'quietness' or 'ease', and with the preposition *b* 'at a time of ease'. So he struck when the companions of his nephew were 'at ease', that is, when they were being careless or not on guard. He also obtained the kingdom **through intrigue**. The basic meaning of that word was 'smoothness', 'fine promises', or 'flattery'. Differently put, this verse accused Antiochus of lying and flattering his way into office.

Verse 22. The next comment, namely that **Armies shall be utterly swept away** (literally, 'the arms of the flood shall be swept before him'), was a general comment about his military successes. He also met defeat, but that was not the author's point here. Part of his exercise of power was his murder of the high priest Onias III, **the prince of the covenant**, in about 171, fcllowed by his appointing Jason, the brother of Onias, who had offered money for the office (cf. Dan. 9.26 and 2 Macc. 4.7-10).

Verse 23. Antiochus made **an alliance**. Collins (1993a: 382) thinks the alliance was one with Pergamum, which allowed Antiochus to gain control of the Seleucid Empire with only a small force. Heaton (1956: 233) interpreted the alliance as that with Jason. Antiochus quickly acted deceitfully toward Jason by accepting a larger bribe from Menelaus, and named him high priest (2 Macc. 4.23-28). Since the word translated 'alliance' was a hiphil plural participle (literally, 'joining themselves together'), the author may have had both of those alliances and others as well in mind. Perhaps the point really was that *whenever* someone made an alliance with him, Antiochus eventually double crossed him.

Verse 24. Antiochus is said to have acted **without warning**, entering **the richest parts of the province**. Older commentators often thought this verse referred to Egypt, but some recent commentators think it referred to richer inhabitants of Palestine. Collins (1993a: 382) understands v. 24 instead as a statement about his typical behavior. The phrase **lavishing plunder, spoil, and wealth on them** does correspond to what Polybius 26.10 says of him: 'in the sacrifices he furnished to cities and in the honors he paid to the gods he far surpassed all his predecessors'.

Still, that understanding of v. 24 seems at variance with the way the verse begins: 'without warning'. In light of vv. 21-23, one would expect to read here about another instance when Antiochus fell upon someone as he did his nephews, not about his generosity, unless that generosity were at the expense of Israel at large or (more likely) some part of Israel that included the author's group. Indeed, the clause about booty begins in Hebrew with the words 'plunder, spoil, and wealth' and reports that they will be scattered (or distributed) **among them**. Whom did the author have in mind? Smith-Christopher (1996: 142) seems correct in arguing that the recipients of the booty are the Judean Hellenizers who aligned themselves with Antiochus, and the victims of the despoiling were those who opposed him, including the Danielic group.

The verse concludes with the statement that Antiochus would devise plans against **strongholds**, but only for a time. While this sentence too is a generalization, it probably was intended to foreshadow the ultimate failure of Antiochus. Bleak as things no doubt looked for Jerusalem while Antiochus and his cohorts were in control, that state of affairs would not last indefinitely.

Verses 25-26. These verses resemble the kind of report encountered in vv. 3-20. These verses, and the two that follow, deal with Antiochus's first campaign against Egypt. They are the first verses to do so definitely, distinguishing them from the generalizations in vv. 21-24.

In 169, the courtiers Eulaeus and Lenaeus led Egyptian forces in attacking Palestine. Antiochus responded, leading his army against the forces of his nephew Ptolemy VI and capturing the frontier fortresses Pelusium and Memphis (cf. 1 Macc. 1.16-19). The last clause in v. 25 continues into v. 26 and reads: **But he shall not succeed, for plots shall be devised against him by those who eat of the royal rations**. The problem is that one can not tell for sure who did not succeed. Grammatically speaking, the antecedent was the king of the south, even though the person who had been under discussion had been Antiochus. So many commentators, following Polybius 28.21, argue that the verse meant it was Ptolemy VI who did not succeed because of the actions of Eulaeus and Lenaeus. Indeed, Antiochus took his nephew Ptolemy into custody.

Continuing that line of interpretation, one would understand v. 26b to mean that **they**, the soldiers of Antiochus, defeated **him**, Ptolemy VI. The phrase **his army shall be swept away** also refers to Ptolemy VI, but the translation involves the repointing of the verb *štp* from an active verb (a qal imperfect) to a passive one (a niphal imperfect).

Verses 27-28. The background for vv. 27-28 is the attempt by envoys from Greece to arrange for peace between the two parties. The verses have been cast from the perspective of the Israelite author. First, he calls both kings liars. Secondly, he thinks their efforts at peace were doomed because it was not yet time for God's kingdom to come (Dan. 7 and 8) and put an end to the desolation of Jerusalem (Dan. 9).

Verse 27. The statement that both parties **shall sit at one table and exchange lies** expresses the opinion of a third, interested party. The fact that Antiochus was in charge of Palestine infused the meeting with significance for the author, as v. 28 shows. Both Antiochus and Ptolemy VI traveled to Memphis for the talks.

Verse 28. This verse says only that Antiochus IV returned home with great wealth, implying that the negotiations went his way. Historically, they may have been more of a draw, but Antiochus left a garrison in Pelusium and added the title 'Conqueror' to his coins. Of more interest to the narrator, however, were his policies toward Israel. To that subject he turns with the comment that **his heart shall be set against the holy covenant**. That, apparently, was a reference to his raid on the temple in 169 (1 Macc. 1.20-23), where he stripped the temple of its gold and silver vessels. Scholars usually explain that he needed money, which is no doubt true. Warfare has always been expensive.

Verses 29-30a. These verses deal with Antiochus's next campaign in Egypt, his second. Something like those verses perhaps stood in the borrowed document, but if so they were retouched by the author of Daniel 11. Nothing later than these verses concerns itself with the relationships between the Ptolemies and the Seleucids, so perhaps the borrowed document ended here.

The term **at the appointed time** (one word in Hebrew) perhaps indicated that the author thought the time was decreed by God (Heaton 1956: 235). Alternatively, it could mean that the meeting was held by prior arrangement.

Regardless, the reference is to the second campaign of Antiochus into Egypt. His nephews, Ptolemy Philometer and Physcon, had patched up their differences and recruited the Romans as allies against him. Antiochus besieged Alexandria, but was confronted by a contingent of Romans and forced to withdraw. The Romans are called the **Kittim**. The name was taken from Num. 24.24, which says that ships from the shores of Kittim (Cyprus) would bring soldiers to attack Assyria. The term 'Kittim' had come to include the islands and coasts of the Mediterranean (cf. Josephus, *Ant.* 1.6.1 §128), and here was extended to mean Rome (cf. 1QpHab 2.12, 14; 3.4, 9; 4.10).

Verses 30b-35. The author turns his attention now to the aftermath of Antiochus's second Egyptian campaign and summarizes his attempts to Hellenize the larger Judean population between 167 and 164. A nucleus of well-placed Judeans had already joined forces with him, constituting a 'fifth column' that led the city to give up without a fight (cf. Josephus, *Ant.* 12.5.3 §246). The author wanted to encourage the Danielic group to stand fast in their version of the faith.

Verse 30b. The author attributes Antiochus's actions to rage at his humiliation by the Romans. In his rage he struck out at **the holy covenant**. The 'covenant' would be the Sinai covenant in particular, but it would include all of Scripture and the practices of Judaism as understood by the author of Daniel 11. The verse concludes by saying that Antiochus paid special heed **to those who forsook** that covenant, clearly the Judeans who had collaborated with Antiochus.

Verse 31. This verse alludes to several of Antiochus's actions against the covenant. (1) In 167 he sent soldiers under Apollonius to capture Jerusalem and establish a garrison of Gentile soldiers south of the temple hill (1 Macc. 1.29-35). In the process they **occupied and profaned** the temple. (2) They stopped the daily offering. (3) In December of 167, they **set up the abomination that makes desolate**. This term, used earlier in 9.27, is a technical term mentioned also in 1 Macc. 1.54. It involved erecting something on the altar of the temple. Josephus (*Ant.* 12.5.4 §253) says that Antiochus had an altar to a foreign God erected on the temple altar and sacrificed a pig on it. Jerome explained instead that Antiochus erected an image of Jupiter Olympius (so Collins 1993a: 358), but the older explanation by Josephus is probably to be preferred.

Verse 32. This verse distinguishes those Antiochus seduced from those who remained loyal to Judaism (cf. Collins 1975: 603). Such black-and-white distinctions are typical of crisis literature, where an 'us vs. them' mentality is beneficial to the survival of a group. Verse 32 also says the faithful **will take action**, an allusion to people like those who continued to obey laws about circumcision and diet (cf. 1 Macc. 1.62-63).

Verse 33. Another way the 'wise' (the Danielic group itself) will take action is to instruct people (literally, 'the many') in their faith. Many among the faithful (presumably including but not limited to the 'wise') would **fall by sword and flame**, that is, be killed, and/or **suffer captivity and plunder** (see 1 Macc. 1.57-61).

Verse 34. In the struggle, they (either the 'wise' or the faithful at large) received **a little help**. Typically, the phrase is taken as a reference to the Maccabees, who revolted against Antiochus, and that may be correct. If so, the phrase would express the author's lack of confidence in and/or agreement with their military action. The fact that he never calls believers to arms is probably proof of his pacifism.

Another possible interpretation is to drop the indefinite article from the translation. That would change the force of the comment. To say that they received 'little help' is even bleaker than to say they received 'a little help'. That distinction is probably not possible in Hebrew, however. In some ways the best interpretation is a third one, namely to take the last phrase in the verse (**and many shall join them insincerely**) as the author's explanation of what he meant by 'little help'. Their insincerity would not be apparent at first, of course, but would become apparent only after time passed and they did not remain faithful.

Verse 35. The admission that some of the 'wise' themselves had died in the turmoil might raise in the mind of a reader the question of whether God could and should have saved them. The author's explanation is that they died in order that they might be **refined, purified and cleansed**. Heaton argues that their death would serve to 'refine, sift, and cleanse the whole body of the nation during the short period remaining before the time appointed by God for the coming of his Kingdom' (1956: 238). That is a worthy sentiment, and it may be what the author meant, but it is more likely that the 'wise' were purifying themselves. In the struggle against Antiochus, death was to be preferred to surrender, and even some of the 'wise' had to die less they succumb to sin.

Verses 36-39. In vv. 36-39 the author turned once again to discuss the behavior of Antiochus IV. He portrayed Antiochus as a man who thought of himself as answerable to no one. Lebram (1975: 769) suggests that the author took these verses from a Ptolemaic polemic against Antiochus. That suggestion is possible though not necessary to account for the tone of the passage. The author of Daniel 11 was as anti-Antiochene as anyone in Egypt. Even if correct, however, the suggestion is compatible with the view advocated in this commentary that the Danielic group was comprised of scribes once employed by the Seleucids.

Verse 36. This verse makes a number of charges against Antiochus. (1) He acts as he pleases. He is autonomous, that is, a law unto himself. (2) He considers himself greater than any god. (3) He speaks horrendous things against the God of gods; he attempts to dissuade people from following Judaism.

What is more, **He shall prosper until the period of wrath is completed**... It might seem to the second-century reader that things had gotten beyond God's control, but that was not true. For the time being God would allow Antiochus to hold sway, but only temporarily. The visions of the book of Daniel consistently indicated that God would end tyranny, and end it soon. God's control of the eventual outcome was to override any concern about the time leading up to the end.

This thinking does not explain the more basic question: why should tyrants prevail in the first place? The author would surely think that the problem lay within the character of the tyrants themselves, the whole line of them, not in some failure or insufficiency on God's part, and certainly not in some grand design of God in which God predetermined that certain people would be tyrants and others their victims. In other words, the so-called determinism of Daniel really only holds that God would at the appointed time straighten things out. Meanwhile, tyrants were free to be tyrants and believers to believe.

An apocalypticist always faces the pressing problem of survival or deprivation. Theoretical questions like 'Why?' had to wait, as important as those questions might be. The answers to those questions are never the answers that help people survive, and they tend not to be answered in apocalyptic discourse.

Verse 37. Not only did Antiochus blaspheme against the God of Israel, he paid **no respect to the gods of his ancestors**. Whose would those gods have been? Greek gods? Babylonian gods? He is also said to pay no respect to the god **beloved by women**. That was the dying and rising god of Egypt and the Middle East, Tammuz Adonis. These two sentences seem strange in light of what is known about Antiochus. Polybius reports the presence of images to innumerable gods at Daphne in 166 (Collins 1993a: 387). If anything, Antiochus seems to have been guilty of respecting too many gods. The author of Daniel 11, however, was making the polemical point that Antiochus could not have properly worshiped any god since he considered himself superior to them all.

Verse 38. The next accusation was that he worshipped the **god of the fortress** (literally, 'of strongholds') and honored him with gifts of gold and silver. Collins (1993a: 388) understands the title as a derisive epithet aimed at Zeus Olympius, the only god whose cult Antiochus is said to have imposed on Jerusalem (2 Macc. 6.2). The title also contains an allusion to the citadel erected by Antiochus in Jerusalem.

Logically, of course, this verse somewhat contradicts the previous one, which claimed that Antiochus worshiped no god because he worshiped himself. Neither logic nor divinity is the real point here, however; fortifications are. Antiochus built fortifications in Jerusalem, including a tower that overlooked the temple and gave him power over what went on inside (1 Macc. 1.33-36). This tower perhaps stood north of the temple where a Persian tower may have stood in the days of Nehemiah (see Goldstein 1976: 214-19; but see the view that the fifth-century 'tower' was the temple itself in Schwartz 1996: 30-31). Wherever it stood, it was a source of irritation to pious Judeans.

Verse 39. Antiochus also overpowered other fortifications with the help of **a foreign god**, surely the 'god of fortifications' mentioned in v. 38. The author actually was having a little fun at the expense of Antiochus. The man who called himself 'God Manifest' paid homage in the form of gold and silver to the 'god of strongholds' and overthrew foreign strongholds with the aid (he supposed) of that false god.

Verse 39b adds a new charge to the list against Antiochus. He honored people who acknowledged his rulership and made them **more wealthy**. Among the people who sided with Antiochus were people of wealth who had much to lose if they offended the new ruler. Among the means Antiochus had to reward them were positions within his government (including perhaps some offices the Danielic group might have wanted to hold) and the opportunity to buy land, perhaps land he had confiscated from people who refused to acknowledge him.

Verses 40-45. At v. 40, Daniel 11 makes a decisive change. Verses 3-35 had looked to the author's past, and vv. 36-39 looked at his own time, but vv. 40-45 attempted to look ahead. These verses contained the message the group longed to hear: the time of the end was near, and the demise of Antiochus IV would be its precursor. To be sure the death of Antiochus did not come about exactly as predicted here, but it did come about and it did so quickly.

Verse 40. The author switches to the future with the phrase **At the time of the end**. What follows is his idea of events that would lead up to that time. His method is to read the past and make projections from the past into the future: **the king of the south shall attack; the king of the north shall rush upon him**; [h]e **shall...pass through like a flood**. These phrases had appeared before in describing the battles between the Seleucids and the Ptolemies. They had fought for years; the author predicted they would do so in the future.

Verse 41. Nor had Antiochus spared Judah in the past, so the author projected a future campaign: **He shall come into the beautiful land**. In previous attacks he had slain loyal Judeans (Dan. 11.33; 1 Macc. 1.30; Josephus, *Ant.* 12.5.3 §247) and taken many captive, Josephus says about 10,000 (*Ant.* 12.5.4 §251). In the future **tens of thousands shall fall victim**. Broshi (1978: 12-13) calculated the population of the city of Jerusalem at about 30,000 to 35,000 in the Hasmonean period. The population of Judah is more difficult to estimate, but there were no other significant Judean cities (Safrai 1996: 66). Hence, the prediction that tens of thousands would be harmed would include a sizeable percentage of the population.

On the other hand, **Edom and Moab and the main part of the Ammonites shall escape from his power**. These three nations were traditional enemies often threatened with punishment by other prophets. If they were to be around for God to deal with, the author presumably concluded, Antiochus would have to leave them alone.

Verses 42-43. Egypt in particular would not escape Antiochus's attention. As he had in the past, he would become the **ruler** of the **gold**, the **silver**, and the **riches of evil**. In his last attack, however, he would do even more: he would extend his hegemony over Egypt's neighbors **the Libyans and the Ethiopians**.

Verses 44-45. In the past Antiochus III had returned home after defeating the Egyptians, only to die (Dan. 11.18-19). So it would be in the future with Antiochus IV. At the height of his victory in the south, rumors from the north and the east would cause him to leave Egypt with his army and crush his opposition. Antiochus would camp **between the sea and the beautiful holy mountain**. There, somewhere on the coastal route along the Mediterranean Sea, **he shall come to his end, with no one to help him**. Actually, Antiochus died in Persia in the year 164, the cause of his death the object of diverse speculation in Polybius, *History* 31.9-11; 1 Macc. 6.1-17; and 2 Macc. 9.1-29. Even so, the author of Daniel 11 correctly predicted his coming demise.

Concluding note on Daniel 11.21-45

Baldwin (1978: 201-202) notes that some of the data here do not mesh with the known events of history during the Maccabean period. Hence, she concludes that Rome is also in view, as well as the end of time. She does not specify which details pertain to the Romans or to later times. Rather she invokes the image of an observer looking through a telescope. Things at a distance will look much closer together than they actually are. Hence, she says, texts like Dan. 11.40-45 and the Synoptic Apocalypse 'telescope' the future so that only in retrospect can the reader see what was really meant (cf. Miller 1994: 305-13; and Walvoord 1971: 274-79). With regard to the Synoptic Apocalypse, only after the events of 70 CE could one see which details applied to that event and which to the end of time. So it was also, she says, with Daniel 11. Only after the events of 165 could one see which predictions pertained to Antiochus and which to later times.

This device, however, explains less than Baldwin claims. Since she wants to hold to the exilic Daniel as the author, her explanation amounts to saying that neither the original exilic audience nor the second century readers of the book could have understood the vision properly! Only after the Romans came would ancient readers any more than modern readers know what the text actually meant. If she is correct, second-century readers would have had a text which Baldwin admits (1978: 41) deals with Antiochus: '...there can be no doubt about the primary reference of the chapter: it has to do with the confrontation between the mighty Antiochus IV...and the struggling people of God...' Yet they would not have had her perspective that other events happened centuries later that fulfilled some of the details of the chapter. What would such readers have assumed? Surely that Daniel was wrong. Under Baldwin's apparent assumption that every detail of 'prophecy' has to be absolutely correct before ancient or modern readers can accept it as Scripture, they would quite likely have repudiated the book of Daniel.

Actually, of course, believers in difficult situations do not make anything like such stringent demands on their seers. Groups inside and outside the Church have continued to believe their 'vision' of the future even after its details prove less than literally true. What matters is that new programs for the future address the real needs of the readers: for example, the need to know that God rules; virtue will be rewarded; a new day will dawn (if not now, sooner or later); and they are on the right track. The book of Daniel as a whole and in its individual narratives meets just those needs, and this last vision is no exception. In its concluding vision, the book also looked ahead to the fall of Antiochus while he was at the height of his power. That was no small achievement; it got the essence of the future correct (cf. Smith-Christopher 1996: 149). As Goldingay put it (1989: 305): vv. 40-45 presented 'an imaginative scenario of the *kind*' of result that had to come from the events the faithful were enduring.

THE CONCLUSION TO GABRIEL'S REPORT (12.1-4)

Daniel 12.1-4a, along with 12.13, concluded the original narrative in Daniel 10–12. If Daniel 11 spoke of events leading up to the end of time, 12.1-4a + 13 speak of the end itself, the subject that Gabriel originally announced to Daniel (10.14).

The most important concept introduced in these verse is that of resurrection. It was an idea whose time had finally come. In the early books of the Old Testament, punishment was corporate and this-worldly. If people sinned, or perhaps if a large enough group within a people sinned, God punished the people as a whole. Jeremiah 31 and Ezekiel 18 both attacked that view, and proposed individual retribution, but the book of Job pointed to the obvious truth that God does not always punish sinners and reward righteous people in their lifetime.

If, however, God is just, but retribution does not always come in one's lifetime, then it must come after death. Job 14.13-14 considers the possibility that Job would be vindicated in the grave. Daniel 12.2, however, offers the more satisfying suggestion that individuals would receive just retribution beyond the grave, with many of the dead being raised to everlasting life and others to everlasting contempt.

Scholars divide over the identity of those who will be raised. Typically, scholars understand resurrection in Daniel to be exceptional, applying only to people who did not get their just deserts in their lifetime (cf. Collins 1993a: 395). Some argue that the word 'many' in Hebrew may mean 'all', and interpret the verse to anticipate a universal resurrection (so Baldwin 1978: 204; cf. Miller 1994: 318). Davies (1985: 117) objects that the word appears between two restrictives, so that a general resurrection is not intended. Goldingay (1989: 307) even contends that only a revival of the nation was in view here (cf. Ezek. 37.1-14), but he goes too far. This much is clear: 12.13 includes Daniel among those who will be raised. Also, the word 'many' in 11.14, 33 and 39 probably refers to ordinary members of the community behind Daniel (cf. Péter-Contesse and Ellington 1993: 292, 324), so the resurrection is not limited to the heroes and villains of the Maccabean period. It includes dead members of the community of the book. It was they whom the author and his readers were most interested in.

Verse 1. The mention of Michael would follow naturally upon 10.20, but seems out of place in 12.1. Gabriel tells or reminds Daniel that Michael was Israel's **great prince, the protector of** [Daniel's] **great people**. As Israel's patron angel, Michael would do battle against the patron angel of Greece (10.20). Israel would face persecution from them more severe than that any other nation had ever suffered, an allusion to the Maccabean persecutions.

Daniel's people would be delivered, however. This deliverance was not attributed to Michael, whose function seemed only to be as their 'protector'. The author instead means that God would deliver the people. And who were God's people? They were **everyone who is found written in the book**. Such a book is mentioned occasionally elsewhere in the Old Testament. God himself recorded the names of people in a book in Exod. 19.5; Pss. 69.29; and 87.6. The phrase is even more reminiscent of Mal. 3.16, where names were inscribed in a book in the presence of God. In Mal. 3.17, God promised to spare them when he acted to punish the wicked. Daniel 12.1 applied that kind of thinking to the author's community.

Verse 2. In addition to those who would be delivered by God, some dead believers would be raised to join with them, including their hero Daniel. This is neither a national nor a general resurrection, but a resurrection of select individuals in the community (and in Israel's past, unless Daniel is an exception). The resurrection also would include individuals deserving punishment, which is not said to be hell, but **everlasting contempt**. It is possible, of course, that the author meant something like 'hell' or the 'lake of fire' mentioned in Rev. 20.10, but he does not say so. Nor was there a Hebraic precedent for such an idea. Perhaps he envisioned something more along the lines of ongoing mockery by the redeemed community. It is usually assumed that he had in mind the 'little horn' Antiochus IV, the most contemptible person in the book of Daniel, and others who aided him. It is just possible, however, that he thought their death (11.45) would be sufficient punishment, and that those deserving of contempt included (or were limited to) members of the larger Judean community who had collaborated too much with the Hellenists.

Verse 3. The heroes of the future are described as **the wise** and as **those who lead many to righteousness**. These characteristics constitute the heart of the community's self-understanding. That scribes would style themselves as 'wise' is not surprising. All along the group had portrayed as heroes scribes attempting to succeed by wits and piety in the court of foreign kings. The function of leading others to righteousness, however, appears to be a more recent task they assigned themselves vis-à-vis the Hellenist sympathizers in Jerusalem and its environs. It implies a teaching role, which might suggest these people included priests, but more probably it reflects the prophetic emphasis noted by Wilson (1981: 92). If so, Mal. 3.5-6 [MT 3.23-24] might have been in view. It predicts that God would send Elijah before the great and terrible day of the Lord came, and he would come to turn the hearts of parents and children (literally, 'fathers and sons') to each other.

The 'wise' **shall shine like the brightness of the sky** and **like the stars forever and ever**. The Hebrew language does not really have a word meaning 'forever' (or 'everlasting' in v. 2), so the meaning of this phrase was that the 'wise' would experience their reward an indefinitely long time, as would those raised to 'everlasting life'. The word 'brightness' is used elsewhere of the sun (Hab. 3.4, where it is compared to God), the moon (Isa. 60.9), the dawn (Isa. 60.3), lightning (Ezek. 1.4), and God (Ezek. 8.2; 10.4). In combination with the word 'stars', the phrase 'the brightness of the sky' probably refers to the sun or the moon. The 'brightness' of the 'wise' contrasts with the 'contempt' which would be the lot of some of the dead who would be raised and suggests a future high status in God's kingdom. Put differently, one could say that the 'wise' would be the 'stars' of that kingdom.

Verse 4a. Gabriel next commands Daniel to **keep the words** of the vision **secret** and the book sealed **until the time of the end**. Hutter-Graz (1984: 14-18) points to the similar instructions in 2 Esd. 12.35-39 to put that book in a hidden place as evidence of the use of an apocalyptic phrase in Dan. 12.4a. Of course, the fact that the second-century reader had access to that vision meant that 'the time of the end' was near. That assurance was always part of the message of the apocalypticist.

Verse 4b. Transition to the Epilogue. Meanwhile, **[m]any shall be running back and forth**. Presumably that phrase meant that many members of the larger Judean community would be vacillating back and forth between their traditional faith and Hellenism. (On this issue, see Cohen 1990: 204-23; and Hyldahl 1990: 188-203.) The inevitable result would be that **evil shall increase**. Only the inbreak of God's kingdom would reverse that condition. The RSV and older translations generally rendered the noun (*d't*) in the MT as 'knowledge'. Thomas (1955: 226) argues that the noun was derived from a second root for *yd'* that meant 'become still', and suggests the meaning 'humiliation' for the noun form. The NRSV has emended the text to read *r't* or *r'h* (to be evil) instead.

As mentioned above, v. 4b probably belongs with the epilogue, since it shifts attention from the time of the end back to the Maccabean period and makes a smoother transition to v. 5 than would 4a. Verse 13, however, would follow v. 4a even better than it does v. 4b.

THE THEOLOGY OF DANIEL 10.1–12.4

Daniel 10.1–12.4 offers perspectives on four theological issues that deserve a final mention. First, it is not deterministic in the sense that

God determines every detail of human life. Hence, tyrants might rule and saints might die, but not because God had foreordained such things. Such events were the result of choices by people with the opportunity to exercise moral judgment. On the other hand, such events were predictable and would not prevent or even postpone God's intervention into world events to straighten things out. That would happen precisely when God decided it would, because God would do it. What was predetermined, if that is the correct word here, was what God would do and when.

That means, of course, that human beings were free within certain limits to make their own choices, but that idea is not unique to the book of Daniel. There is no such thing as absolute freedom. The word 'freedom' is best used to designate the ability and opportunity to choose between or among more or less equivalent alternatives. The price tag for freedom is always responsibility. Consequently, in Daniel people who make wrong choices will reap what they have sown. Moreover, these choices seem to deal with the major issues of the community: for example, whether to remain faithful to God and God's covenant, to observe dietary regulations, to circumcize the sons of the family, and to offer sacrifices.

The author of Daniel clearly thought God set limits to human behavior and just as clearly thought Antiochus exceeded those limits. Differently stated, he portrayed Antiochus's behavior as blasphemy. What Antiochus did in calling himself **Theos Epiphanes** may have been 'politics as usual' in the Greek world and even among his supporters in Jerusalem, but it was blasphemy to the Danielic group. What he did in seeking to spread Hellenism may have seemed rational and even civilized to him, a necessary correction to a local cult, but it seemed like a threat to the lifestyle and faith of loyal Judeans.

Finally, the most important achievement of this vision may well have been to interject the idea of the resurrection once and for all into biblical thinking. It articulated an idea whose time had come. Pharisees and Sadducees might disagree about it later, but no one could ignore it any longer. There were precursors (see Alfrink 1959: 14-18) and later authors who developed the doctrine more fully, but Dan. 12.2 established it within biblical religion, both Jewish and Christian.

EPILOGUE: CALCULATIONS OF THE END
(12.5-13)

Verses 5-13 serve both as an ending to the narrative in 10.1–12.4 and as an epilogue to the whole book. As the conclusion to 10.1–12.4a, it continues that narrative by introducing new characters and reinvestigating the time of the end mentioned in 10.14; 11.40; and 12.1-4a. Even so, the epilogue is not a unity. As shown in the introductory comments to 10.1–12.4, 12.13 originally followed 12.4 or 12.4a and concluded that vision. Verses 5-12, then, constitute an addition to 10.1–12.4, 13 and share its genre: apocalyptic narrative.

Verses 5-12 draw upon the language of 10.1–12.4, 13. The setting (v. 5) returns to that described in 10.4, but it introduces two new characters, one of whom speaks to Gabriel. Verse 9 repeats from 12.4 the motifs of secrecy and sealing with respect to the words of the vision. It also anticipates the reference in v. 13 to the end of the days and the command to Daniel to go his way. Verse 10 repeats the phrase 'refined, purified, and cleansed' spoken about the 'wise' in 11.35, though in a slightly different order. It also employs the word 'understand' in connection with the 'wise', as did 11.34.

As the conclusion for the book as a whole, on the other hand, vv. 5-12 attempt to tie up loose ends from various chapters. The most obvious example is its own calculation of the time of the 'end'. In previous chapters, the book had offered three basic calculations of the end: a time, times, and a half (7.25); 2300 nights and days (8.14); and 70 weeks of years (9.24-27). All three pointed to the duration of the reign of Antiochus IV and his policies, after which God would intervene and set up God's own kingdom (2.44-45; 7.27). The epilogue offers a fourth calculation of time. Daniel 12.7 repeats the phrase 'a time, times, and a half'. Then vv. 11 and 12 give the numbers 1290 and 1335 days, which amount to three and a half years.

Verses 11-12 are widely viewed as a addition, or even as two additions, and they present special problems of interpretation. What did they mean, and why might they have been added? The simplest solution is that of Gunkel (1895: 269), who suggested that the 1290 and 1335 days were successive reinterpretations of the 1150 days in 8.14. The reinterpretations became necessary when the end did not come within that time frame. Collins (1990: 96) basically agrees, suggesting that 'the end' in vv. 11-12 was the resurrection.

Another solution is that of Shedl (1964: 101-105), which is based on his understanding of the numbers 1290 and 1335. He argues that the 'time' was a lunar year of 352 days plus an intercalary month needed to realign the lunar calendar with the solar, for a total of 384 days. The 'times' were two regular years or 708 days, and the 'half' was half a year with an intercalary month, plus one week, for a total of 198 days. It would end with the Festival of Weeks in 163. He thinks v. 12 begins with the seventh day of Ab, the traditional day for observing the destruction of Jerusalem by the Babylonians, but in the year 164 (July 31). The 1335 days would then conclude with the entry of Judas Maccabee into Jerusalem in March of 160.

Several calculations are based on the assumption that the author of these verses was using a solar calendar. Some scholars point to the 1260 days in Rev. 11.3 and 12.6, and suggest that the figure 1290 is really three solar years plus an intercalary month. The problem with this view is that one did not need extra months with a solar calendar. J. van Goudoever (1993: 538) argues that 1335 is really the sum of two numbers: 1260 and 75. The 1260 days were three and a half solar years. Seventy-five days would bring one to the Festival of Weeks. Van Goudoever concludes that v. 12 looks to the celebration of the Festival of Weeks in the restored temple.

P.-M. Bogaert (1986: 207-11) begins his calculations with the date of Daniel's vision found in 10.4, namely the twenty-fourth day of the first month, instead of 'the time that the regular burnt offering is taken away' as v. 11 explicitly says. Then he assumes that the year to reckon from is 167, the year of the desecration of the temple (on the twenty-fifth day of the ninth month). Assuming further a solar calendar of 364 days, he concludes that the 1335 days of v. 12 point toward the dedication of the temple in 164. The 1290 days of v. 11 would end on the fifteenth day of the eighth month, a plausible date for news of the death of Antiochus to reach Jerusalem.

The best of these explanations, however, is that of Gese (1991: 399-421). He sees 12.5-10, 13 as an independent apocalypse written sometime in 164, but later than 10.1–12.4 (414). It had a twofold message.

On the one hand, the 'end' would come in three and a half years; on the other hand, it would usher in eschatological events (Gese 1991: 415). He sees vv. 11-12 as a single addition, whose purpose it was to better explicate the meaning of three and a half years 417).

Gese shows that the three and a half years are calculated on the basis of a solar calendar, beginning on 7 December (the fifteenth of Chislev) 167, slightly before the winter solstice, and running to the summer solstice on 21 June 163, a period of roughly 1290 days (actually 1293). The 1290 days, however, are not the real concern of vv. 11-12. That concern is what would transpire 45 days later on 5 August (the twenty-fourth of Ab). It was the day (or perhaps, I would suggest, the anniversary of the day) Judeans returned to the open observance of Torah. By that date the author of the addition expected not only the temple cleansing already carried out by the Maccabees, but the restitution of the status of Zion by those who had defiled it, the Seleucids.

What, then, is one to make of all of this discussion in interpreting vv. 5-12? It seems likely that the number 2300 nights and days, understood as 1150 whole days, or three years and two months, fell close enough to the cleansing of the temple by Judas Maccabee for the Danielic community to accept the restoration of the temple as having been fulfilled. After all, who would worry if the temple were restored two months early? Even so, that victory was accomplished by military means and accompanied by an ongoing Greek presence in the land. Such conditions were not those anticipated in the rest of the book; there had to be more to come. Hence, the community would have raised the question again: how long would it be until the 'end' the community had been expecting? Daniel 12.5-12 was written to answer that question, and its date of composition fell somewhere between 7 December 164 (when the temple was cleansed) and 21 June 163 (day 1290). That means, though, that vv. 11-12 are not an addition to vv. 5-10, but their original conclusion which supply the answer sought in the whole passage.

Further, Gese is correct to say that vv. 11-12 attempt to understand the phrase 'time, times, and a half' and that they do so by means of a solar calendar. His interpretation of what those numbers point too, however, needs further examination. For one thing, it is not absolutely clear that the return to Torah observance was in 163; Goldstein (1983: 117) sets it in 165. It would make more sense to choose that date if Torah observance had already begun again, and people would recognize the significance of its anniversary. If that is true, then one may ask what exactly the author expected to happen on the 1290th and 1335th days?

That question is easier to answer for v. 12 than for v. 11. Since v. 13, the conclusion of the original vision, speaks of the resurrection of Daniel, v. 12 quite likely refers to the resurrection of the righteous mentioned in v. 2. As for v. 11, one should remember that the book of Daniel, from ch. 2 on, has been looking forward to the collapse of the foreign world empires and their replacement by God's kingdom. Further, one needs to recall that 12.1-2 had predicted a final period of tribulation before that collapse. The death of Antiochus occurred late in 164, about the same time as the rededication of the temple. The news was known in Babylon in December of 164 and would have been known fairly soon in Jerusalem as well (Collins 1993a: 390). News of that event and—if known—the uncertainty surrounding his successor (his nine-year-old son eventually was named king) might have suggested to the author of v. 11 that the last gasp of the Greek Empire and the collapse of the world kingdoms were really at hand. Further, the ongoing attacks by the soldiers garrisoned in the citadel at Jerusalem (Josephus, *Ant.* 12.9.3 §362; 1 Macc. 6.18) and by surrounding nations (1 Macc. 5.1) might have appeared to corroborate the prediction of further tribulations. Thus, v. 11 probably looked forward to the collapse of the world empires and v. 12 to the resurrection and the inauguration of God's kingdom at the earliest appropriate times (Redditt 1998b: 377-79).

The structure of the epilogue may be analyzed as follows. It begins with the report of the setting in vv. 5-6, with v. 4b perhaps inserted to tie it to 10.1–12.4a. One of the new characters raises the question: 'How long will it be until the end?' The answer in v. 7 is 'a time, times, and a half'. Verses 8 and 9 turn their attention back to Daniel, who complains that he does not understand the answer just given. He is commanded to leave and keep the words secret. Before he can go, however, vv. 11-12 offer a new estimate of the time: outcomes are projected for 1290 and 1335 days. Verse 13 concludes the book with the promise that Daniel too would participate in the resurrection.

Verses 5-6. These verses report the setting for this vision, and it is the same as the setting for 10.1–12.4. In addition to Daniel and Gabriel, **two others** (i.e., two men) appeared on the bank of **this stream**, identified as the Tigris in 10.4. They stood downstream from Gabriel, and asked him how long it would be until **the end of these wonders**.

The word *pl'* denoted things that were extraordinary or difficult. Such 'wonders' were stupendous or awe-inspiring, but here they were the terrible deeds of Antiochus that would lead up to the end, not the mighty acts of God.

Verses 7-8. Gabriel raised both hands toward heaven, took an oath, and repeated the phrase (from 7.25): 'a time, times, and half a time'. Daniel did not understand, and inserted himself into the conversation with the question **My Lord, what shall be the outcome of these things**. The probable situation for this question was described above: Judas had cleansed the temple and a report of the death of Antiochus IV had reached Jerusalem. Did those events signal the collapse of the world empires? Was the time of Jerusalem's punishment over? The question perhaps expressed hope the last kingdom was falling and fear that it was not.

Verses 9-10. These verses give evidence that vv. 5-12 were composed for their place in the book and were not an independent apocalypse as suggested by Gese. The evidence is the concentrated reuse in vv. 9-10 of specific words and phrases from the vision in 10.1–12.4, 13. Since no one suggests that vv. 9-10 were inserted into an existing document, the evidence from these verses is evidence for vv. 5-12 as a whole.

Verse 9. The command in v. 9 for Daniel to go his way anticipates the same command in v. 13. The words **secret and sealed** are used in 12.4 and 9 to designate the contents of a vision, with this difference: in v. 4 the word/book to be kept sealed is the book of names mentioned in v. 1, whereas in v. 9 the words to be kept secret and sealed are the words 'a time, two times, and a half'.

Verse 10. This verse repeats the thought of 11.35 that some believers would be **purified, cleansed, and refined**. In both places, the phrase means that believers would die. (See comments on 11.35.) The wicked would continue to act wickedly and not understand the meaning of the words. Hence, they would fail to act appropriately in the last days. **The wise**, by contrast, would **understand**. Indirectly the author addresses his readers, who would see themselves among the wise. Ironically Daniel, who had asked the question as a surrogate for the community, had not understood either, but Gabriel would explain things to him, thus allowing the readers to overhear and have their own question answered.

Verses 11-12. These verses have been dealt with at such length above, it will suffice here to summarize what they said. They are not a later addition to vv. 5-10, but carry the heart of the revelation of the epilogue. The author thought that indeed the end was near, but that the cleansing of the temple and the death of Antiochus that had just occurred were not the end. Rather, the end would be the imminent final fall of the world empires and the rule of the righteous (including many of those who had died) in God's new kingdom.

THE CONCLUSION TO 10.1–12.4A AND
TO THE BOOK OF DANIEL (13).

Verse 13 closes the book of Daniel on a high note, with a promise to Daniel that he too would participate in the resurrection at the end of time announced in 12.2-3. Thus, this verse forms the conclusion to the original narrative of 10.1-20 + 12.1-4a. It also offers a perfect conclusion for the book as a whole.

Gabriel told Daniel to **rest**. The verb *nwḥ* means more than simply taking one's ease. 2 Samuel 7.1 reads: 'Now when the king was settled in his house, and the Lord had given him rest from all his enemies around him...' (NRSV). The idea was that the struggle was behind David; God had defeated the enemies. In other places the verb even referred to death. Something of those ideas obtains in Dan. 12.13 as well. On the one hand, the vision was complete; Daniel's work was finished. He had seen all the way to the end of the time. On the other hand, his life was nearing its end too, but Daniel would rise in the resurrection predicted in 12.2 to live with the 'wise' of 12.3. Daniel could 'rest', assured of his place in God's future, and so could the other dead the community of the book of Daniel worried about.

THE THEOLOGY OF DANIEL 12.5-13

A point made about the theology of Daniel 7 is appropriate here too. It is the apocalypticist's burden to build the hope of his readers by forecasting an imminent upheaval, when God sets things right. In doing so, the apocalypticist needs to answer his readers' question: 'How long will things continue to go badly for the faithful?' He may be tempted to set a general period or even a specific date for the impending time of the end. Doing so, however, is risky business. If the projected date passes with no rectification of things, his audience may lose hope (in him, at least) and dismiss his message.

That is precisely the dilemma of the author of 12.5-12 (13). Antiochus IV had died, and the new beginning was supposed to follow. To
be sure, the temple had been cleansed and the worship of God had
begun afresh, but things really had not changed much so far as the

That is precisely the dilemma of the author of 12.5-12 (13). Antiochus IV had died, and the new beginning was supposed to follow. To
be sure, the temple had been cleansed and the worship of God had
begun afresh, but things really had not changed much so far as the
Danielic community was concerned. Hence, the author offered a more
precise timetable than before, but he was less precise about what lay in
the future. It is possible to ferret out the 'end' he hoped for (as done
above), but he did not make that end explicit.

What he did do, however, was to retain the hope of a new day. It was
a hope that included the demise of anti-godly empires, allegiance to the
coming kingdom of God on earth instead, and the participation of the
righteous dead through the resurrection. The legacy he left to biblical
faith lives on thousands of years later.

INDEX OF SUBJECTS

INDEX OF PASSAGES CITED

OLD TESTAMENT